A Golden Tyme Indeid

200 YEARS OF GOLF HISTORY AT ROYAL MONTROSE

A Golden Tyme Indeid

200 YEARS OF GOLF HISTORY AT ROYAL MONTROSE

By Harry Faulkner and Richard Phinney

First published in 2010 by
The Royal Montrose Golf Club
Traill Drive
Montrose
DD10 8SW
www.royalmontrosegolf.com

Catalogue record available from the British Library

ISBN: 978-0-9564561-0-6

Designed, printed and bound in Great Britain by 4word Ltd, Bristol

Contents

Carnoustie
Country

Great golf, great places to stay

Carnoustie Country congratulates the Royal Montrose Golf Club on its 200th anniversary

Follow in the footsteps of champions... play 32 courses including four on the world's most challenging links

The Dream Ticket
Play four of the world's top links courses £130 (winter) £260 (summer)

Carnoustie Country Golf Pass
3 courses from £73

The Classic Tournament 10-13 May 2010
Five night package £559

Stay & Play
From £50 per night

For more exciting golf deals check out

www.carnoustiecountry.com

Foreword

Our maister war teached to handle the bow for archerie, the glub for goff. . . . A happy and golden tyme indeid.

> James Melville, writing about his time as a Montrose schoolboy in about 1562

In setting out to write the history of four golf clubs, the first of which – Montrose Golf Club – was founded 200 years ago and whose bicentenary is to be celebrated in 2010, my colleagues and I were keen to set golf events in Montrose in the wider context, that of the proud history of golf in Scotland. In doing so, we have become very aware of the significant contribution that the original Montrose Golf Club – later the Royal Albert Club – has made to the history of the game.

The history of the four golf clubs that are part of this story has never before been researched in such detail. That is not to claim that we know all there is to know about their history. We very much hope that, in the years to come, others are encouraged to do more research into the contribution these clubs have made to the history of golf.

My heartfelt thanks are due to the following:

The Council of Royal Montrose Golf Club who recognised that a comprehensive history would be an essential part of the club's bicentenary celebrations;

William Coull, who first broke this particular trail in 1993 to write his excellent *Golf in Montrose,* and especially to his daughter Lynn for her painstaking trawl through the back issues of the local newspapers on our behalf;

Our sponsors, Rig Sol and Scotmid;

Angus Council, for their encouragement and support and whose 'Carnoustie Country' advertisements we are pleased to include;

Denis Rice and Jane Stock for assistance with editing and proofreading;

Club members who read early drafts or made useful suggestions for improvement;

Members and friends of the club who lent photographs and newspaper cuttings, many of which appear in this publication;

The staff of Montrose Library and Montrose Museum;

4word, our very professional printers;

Club members, Tony Smith and Morag Boyd, who researched and drafted chapters on the Victoria Golf Club and ladies' golf;

Scott Whitley, who read and offered valuable comments on early drafts;

And finally, and most certainly not least, my co-author and fellow-club member, Richard Phinney, whose constructive suggestions, creative contributions, writing talents and extensive knowledge of golf history have been invaluable in this undertaking.

Harry Faulkner OBE
Bicentenary Convenor
February 2010

Introduction

The Royal Burgh of Montrose has made a contribution to Scotland's history that belies its modest size. Montrose's citizens single-handedly won a famous military victory against an English fleet as early as 1548, and they would be a key source of support for the Jacobite rebellions in 1715 (the Old Pretender spent his final night in Montrose before fleeing to France) and in 1745. Montrose was home to several giants of the Protestant Reformation, and also to the extraordinary Marquis of Montrose, whose exploits on both sides of the Scottish Civil War remain controversial. Later, the town was an important fishing port, a centre for smuggling, and a prosperous financial and manufacturing hub. And in the first half of the twentieth century, it was a key locus of the cultural movement known as the Scottish Renaissance.

This book, however, concerns another contribution that Montrose has made, to that most Scottish of leisure pursuits, the game of golf. For centuries Montrose was at the very heart of the sport's evolution, and this volume has been published to mark the Bicentennial of the town's oldest golf club, Royal Montrose. It is only the second club in the world, after the Royal and Ancient of St Andrews, to have played over the same golfing ground for two centuries (although the layout has understandably changed from time to time).

In 1845, it became the third golf club to receive Royal Patronage, after persuasion by the future Prime Minister William Gladstone. The newly christened Royal Albert Golf Club (as it would be called for the next 141 years) ran many of golf's first important tournaments, including the famous 25-hole Open tournament of 1866. At over 8000 yards, that course remains the longest ever used for an important professional golf event.

As you will discover, the club's fascinating and historically important story is enlivened by princes, prime minsters and poets, and by its legendary professional, Bob Dow, who would help launch the careers of golfing pioneers that would profoundly influence the development of golf as far away as Australia and America. As befitting a town with a strong cultural tradition, the Royal Albert was also home to a quartet of extraordinary writers, whose landmark books, described in Chapter 8, changed forever the course of golf literature.

Members of the Royal Albert helped launch one of the world's first Ladies' Clubs in 1889, and almost a century later the club gained its own ladies' section when it merged with the North Links Ladies Golf Club and the Victoria Golf Club. The name of the enlarged club was then changed from the Royal Albert to Royal Montrose.

The book is structured chronologically, with accounts of the club's evolution interspersed with chapters relating to themes that cross over more than one era. We believe there will be plenty of surprises even for readers with a deep understanding of both the history of Montrose, and the game of golf. For until recently Montose's fundamental contribution to the sport's evolution had been shrouded in mystery.

That began to change in 1993, with the publication *Golf in Montrose* by William Coull, which was updated in 2004 by his daughters Lynn and Doreen. We hope this book builds on those outstanding efforts (it could not have been written without them), as we place their findings in a wider context, and dig even more deeply into the contribution made by one of the world's most historically notable golf clubs.

From our reckoning (see Chapter 2), Royal Montrose can be considered the eighth or even seventh oldest golf club in the world. But more important than such a ranking is the the unique role the club played in the first decades of the nineteenth century, when the sport was making the crucial transition from a haphazard pastime into the well organised, and well publicized sport we know today. The club's rules, tournaments and pioneering support of junior and ladies' golf were just some of the contributions that left their mark. And as its often defeated rivals in St Andrews and Edinburgh could attest, Montrose's golfers were second to none!

During this critical period (as you will read in Chapter 16) the club took full responsibility for 'the green', what was at the time the longest, and perhaps best golf course in the world, funding the improvements and various redesigns required as the town expanded. In doing this, they preserved for posterity the fine courses we enjoy today. They also made them available free of charge to generations of local golfers, most of whom were not members of the 'Royal'. The golf challenge would be further enhanced by some of history's greatest architects, including Old Tom Morris, Willie Park Jr and Harry Colt.

As Chapter 15 makes clear, the women golfers of Montrose have a special place in this history. They burst onto the golfing scene with astounding enthusiasm in the late nineteenth century, hosting one of Britain's most popular tournaments. Since then they have been champions both on and off the course, playing an instrumental role in preserving and expanding the links, while racking up many competitive achievements.

While we cannot hope to do full justice, in the following pages, to the extraordinary legacy that our fore-bearers have left us, we do feel it appropriate that our title should paraphrase the first person on record to write about playing golf. He was, of course, a Montrose man, James Melville. From a golfer's perspective, the last 450 years in Montrose have, for the most part, been 'a happy and golden tyme indeid'.

CHAPTER 1

Golf in Montrose before 1810

Playing of the golf is a favourite and wholesome amusement.

From the entry on Montrose in the *First Statistical Account of Scotland, 1795*

A depiction of Montrose in the early 17th century.

No one knows exactly how and where golf evolved in Scotland but the earliest records refer to Montrose as much as anywhere else. It is in connection with Montrose that we first hear mention of a golf lesson, a golf caddy and even a golfing honeymoon, and it may well be in Montrose that golf first appears in verse.

We know with certainty that, for at least 450 years, students in Montrose have played golf during breaks from their books. James Melville, a giant of the Scottish Reformation, did just that in or before 1562 as his diary tells. Son of a preacher in Maryton, a mile from Montrose, Melville would later become a key figure in the struggle to keep the Church of Scotland free from royal interference and become Moderator of the General Assembly.

But first he would gain a place in golf history.

Melville's initial few years of schooling were with the Rev. William Gray in Logie, just outside Montrose. Though he received an exceedingly well-rounded education – Latin and Greek classics – there was ample time for recreation as well. In his writing, Melville reflects on his idyllic childhood in the environs of Montrose:

> The air was guid and the fields reasonable fear. There were a good number of gentle and honest mens berns of the cowntrey about, well trained in both letters, godliness, and exerciese in honest games.

One of those 'honest games' was golf:

> Our maister war teached to handle the bow for archerie, the glub for goff, the batons for fencing; also to rin, to loope, to swoum, to warsell [wrestle]. . . . A happy and golden tyme indeid.

This is the first record we have of anyone, anywhere, writing about his experience playing golf. And it makes William Gray the first named golf teacher.

After attending the Montrose Grammar School, Melville went on to university in St Andrews where, he tells us, he was allowed enough money 'for archerie and goff. I haid bow, arrose, glub and bals, but nocht a purfs for Catchpull [an early form of tennis]'.

Melville mentions only a single 'glub' and it is partly on his say-so that historians believe that just one club was what all golfers used at the time. While those without resources could possibly have used a single curved bough of hawthorn, bow makers were already fashioning two-part golf clubs in which the head could be replaced. Melville's golf balls may also have been wooden though balls of leather stuffed tightly with feathers would soon be introduced, possibly from Holland.

Up until the seventeenth century, a short form of golf was played in town streets and even church courtyards – there are several references to churchmen railing against the practice, especially on Sundays. The use of linksland for golf (as opposed to more confined areas) is a key development in the sport's history and those playing in Montrose, with its super abundant links, were very much in the vanguard.

As early as 1628 Montrose was famous as a place for links golf. In a letter of that year, Sir Robert Gourdon writes of the links in Dornoch:

> *The fairest and lairgest links (or grein fields) of any part of Scotland. Fitt for archery and golfing . . . . they do far surpasse the fields off Montrois or Saint Andrews.*

Though a backhanded compliment to be sure, this is an indication that Montrose and St Andrews were already thought to be pre-eminent places to play golf at the time, an assessment that endured for at least another two centuries.

The lure of Montrose's links was captured in verse in 1632 by Aberdeen's Arthur Johnstone, considered one of the greatest Scottish poets of the era:

> *A large Field by the Sea is stretched forth,*
> *Begirt with waters both at South and North*
> *Some youths train Horses here, some use the Bow,*
> *And some their Strength in rolling great Stones do show,*
> *Some wrestle, some at Pennie-stones do play,*
> *The rolling Balls with Clubs do some drive away.*

This is a Victorian translation, as Johnstone wrote all his poems in Latin. Whether the last line refers to golf or shinty is tantalisingly unclear. However, given golf's close association to Montrose – and the fact that shinty was first and foremost a Highlands game – this may be the earliest poetic reference to golf on record.

One of the youthful golfers that Johnstone might have seen on the links was the first Marquis of Montrose. Born James Graham in 1612 on the Montrose High Street, he became one of Scotland's most controversial figures.

His eventful career as a soldier, statesman and politician ended in 1650 when he was hanged, drawn and quartered as a 'traitor' on Edinburgh's Grassmarket; eleven years later his head and limbs were gathered up and he was given a state funeral in the same city.

From family accounts, we know that Graham's father played golf in Montrose and the future Marquis made several purchases of golf clubs and balls while still a teenager. In 1628, the accounts show that he became the first golfer on record to hire a caddie to carry his clubs. He was only 16 and it cost him four shillings. One year later, Graham's wedding in Montrose to Magdalene Carnegie was a grand affair. The groom took advantage of the occasion to play golf with his invited guests. On the day before the ceremony, his 'pursemaster' made the following entry into the accounts:

> *Item, the nynthe day in Montrois, my Lord playing at the golf with the Laird of Lusse, for two golf balls . . . . 24sh.*

What passed for a honeymoon must have been spent on the links too, for only days after the wedding we find the groom ordering new golf balls and six new clubs (they broke easily in those days). That would seem to make new-bride Magdalene the first 'golf widow'.

Graham's golfing days were brought to a halt by a civil war in which he switched sides, winning a string of famous victories against the Covenanters, his former allies. Now the Marquis of Montrose, he ended up losing his final battle to the Earl of Sutherland – a former golfing companion. In a golf match, he might have just lost a wager but losing that particular contest had much more severe consequences – it cost him his life.

It is perhaps a mere coincidence that James Melville, the other recorded 'early' golfer on Montrose links, also ended his life prematurely, being imprisoned in Berwick by King Charles I for opposing his reintroduction of bishops into Scotland.

In the second half of the seventeenth century, golf seems to have declined in many parts of Scotland. The Kirk began to frown on any pleasure pursuits on the Sabbath (the only day of rest for many people). And there was, to say the least, considerable upheaval. Scotland endured the plague, civil wars, an economic depression, religious conflicts, a controversial union with England in 1707 and a couple of failed rebellions (in both of which, Montrose was rather at the centre of things, the majority of townspeople choosing to support the Jacobites, the losing side).

The statue of the Marquis of Montrose which stands outside the site of Montrose Castle where he is reputed to have been born, and a portrait of the young Marquis.

The persistence of golf's special place in Montrose is borne out in the *First Statistical Account of Scotland*, published in 1795 and written by local church ministers. A rich source of information about all aspects of the town, the *Statistical Account* reports, for example, that the population of the parish of Montrose was 5194, with another thousand living in the hinterland, and that it contained exactly 53 ships, 130 horses and 70 acres of turnips. The town imported 299 tonnes of whale blubber each year (for lighting presumably) and exported large quantities of barley, beer and salmon. It is also reported that there were forty licensed beggars, who were given a badge and allowed to beg on the first day of every month. The town's recreational pursuits are noted:

> *Playing of the golf is a favourite and wholesome amusement.*
> *There is excellent ground for this purpose and also for walking;*
> *as a large part of the links is level and dry in all seasons.*

That same excellent golfing ground had already survived one serious threat from the Town Council. In 1785, four prominent residents initiated a civil suit against the Montrose Burgh Council, demanding that they stop a tenant farmer ploughing up and fencing in parts of the links:

> *Thomas Carnegy of Craigo, Robert Scott of Logie, Robert*
> *Stephen of Letham and Major Alexander Turnbull of Ardo, all*
> *burgesses residing in Montrose for themselves and in the name*
> *of other burgesses and inhabitants of the said burgh hereby*
> *sheweth that the links of Montrose which extend an English*
> *mile northwards from the river South Esk towards the river*
> *North Esk have for over one hundred years past, as the*
> *petitioners are informed, been enjoyed by the inhabitants of the*
> *said burgh and set apart for their playing of golf, bowls, foot*
> *ball, riding and walking and also as pasture for their cows and*
> *horses.*

That golf is the first sport listed likely reflects its relative importance to the complainants. The legal papers indicate that the dispute had been simmering for some time:

> *The petitioners are nearly shut out of the links altogether. The*
> *petitioners have often remonstrated to the magistrates and*
> *town council against the encroachments which their tenants*
> *were daily making upon the links but they have paid little or no*
> *regard to these applications and . . . your petitioners are under*
> *the disagreeable necessity of applying to your lordships that*
> *you may put a stop not only to the encroachments made . . .*
> *but also to any attempt that may be made in time coming in*
> *further plowing up or enclosing the said links.*

The threat of litigation appears to have intimidated the Council into accepting all of the demands, and the links were preserved for recreational use.

What sort of men were these four 'petitioners' to whom today's golfers in Montrose owe such a debt? That they could vote, a privilege enjoyed by only about 100 men in all of Angus, places them in the very highest echelons of society. In 1788, in preparation for elections, the Whig Party prepared a secret file on every one of them. Robert Stephen of Letham, who also had 400 acres of land in Lunan, is described as 'very rich' and Thomas Carnegy 'in good circumstances'. Robert Scott of Logie owned an estate at Newtonshill and the High Street house where the Marquis of Montrose was born. Major Turnbull was less wealthy and required 'some office or other promotion', according to the Whig report.

The men needed to be well off since the sport they enjoyed had become expensive. Maintaining a standard set of four or five clubs, which broke frequently, would cost more than most people earned in a year. And a year's supply of 'feathery' balls, easily ruined in wet weather, might cost almost as much. Some golf historians now think that there must have been two kinds of golf coexisting in Scotland in the eighteenth century. 'Long golf' – as some surviving letters refer to it – would have been played with sophisticated clubs while a shorter, less refined version of the game was played on the links by more ordinary people with roughly hewn clubs, maybe even a shinty stick, and much cheaper golf balls.

No doubt 'long golf' thrived in Montrose partly because there was an unusually large number of residents for whom cost was no object. The *Statistical Account* of 1795 reports that Montrose was

> *a Town more distinguished by the residence of persons of opulence and fashion than commerce and industry.*

The wealth of Montrose, and its avid social scene, was remarked on by just about everyone who visited. Daniel Defoe, the author of *Robinson Crusoe*, noted that the road between Dundee and Montrose was 'bespangled . . . with gentlemen's houses, thick as they can be supposed to stand with pleasure and conveniency'.

Cambridge University historian Bob Harris has marvelled that in the early part of the nineteenth century 'Montrose boasted eight hairdressers, 6 wine merchants, 3 jewellers and silversmiths, 8 milliners and dressmakers, two silk mercers, a snuff box maker, a bird stuffer, a mineralist and lapidary and the only coach maker in Angus'. Harris comments that Montrose had more female servants per capita than any other community in Scotland!

In sharp contrast to St Andrews which was in decline, Montrose was entering a boom period. Farms around the town were prospering and the industrial revolution was creating new wealth. Civic improvement projects included Scotland's first 'lunatic asylum' and its first

Representation of Montrose around the end of the 18th century. The Old Kirk does not at this time have its new spire and the buildings in front of it probably housed the Grammar School, founded in the 15th century. Courtesy of Angus Council.

purpose-built museum. The High Street was widened, bridges were built that greatly eased travel to other parts of Scotland, and graduates of the new Montrose Academy, set up in 1815, would become famous throughout the Empire (as many graduates of the ancient Grammar School already were).

For the better off there was ample time for fun and games. The local lairds, who moved into the town for the winter months, competed with Montrose's merchants and professionals in the opulence of their social gatherings. A new town hall (now known as the Ball House) was constructed in 1763 on the High Street, principally as a place to hold balls and other entertainments, and a gentleman's club was formed in 1760 to help in organising them. By 1795, there was an 'assembly' every three weeks according to the *Statistical Account*:

> *It is conducted with the greatest decorum with none but proper company admitted. Actors occasionally perform there, and undoubtedly meet with too much encouragement though their mode of living is such that they generally depart in poverty and leave debts behind.*

There was also horse racing:

> *During the race week, the town houses of the inn dwellers were*
> *taxed to the utmost and the houses of the gentry equally thronged.*

The Montrose Races – held on the links – attracted gentry from all over
Scotland, and it was after one such meeting that one of the most out-
landish and famous golf matches of the era took place. It was between
Lord Kennedy of Aberdeen and James Cruickshank of Langley Park (just
outside Montrose), and the stakes were massive – £500 a hole, or about
£35,000 in today's money. To add extra intrigue it took place after dark!
The following eye-witness account of this golfing challenge appeared in
newspapers as far away as the *New York Times* – only the second reference to golf ever to appear in that publication:

> *It was about ten or half-past ten p.m., and quite dark. No lights*
> *were allowed, except one lantern placed on the hole, and*
> *another carried by the attendants of the player, in order that*
> *they might ascertain to whom the ball struck belonged. We all*
> *moved down to the golf-course to see this curious match. Boys*
> *were placed along the course who were quite accustomed to the*

*The view that James
Cruickshank,
participant in the
famous night match,
had of Montrose
from his Langley
Park estate.
Courtesy of Angus
Council.*

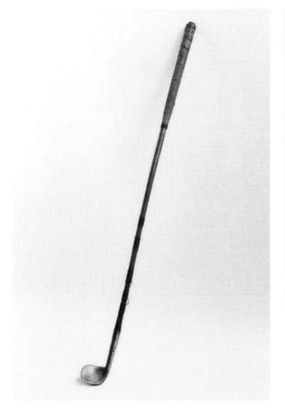

*Early 19th century golf club and golf ball.
Courtesy of the British Golf Museum.*

*game, to listen to the flight of the balls, and to run to the spot
where a ball struck and rested on the ground. . . . But the most
remarkable part of the match was that they made out their
holes with much about the same number of strokes as they
usually did when playing in daylight. I think, on an average,
that they took about five or six strokes in daylight, and in the
dark six or seven. They were, however, in the constant habit of
playing over the Montrose course.*

Golf games must have been exceedingly easy to arrange in Montrose,
with its frequent social gatherings, gentry and rich merchants living in
town as close neighbours in the winter months and the links only a
short walk away. That may explain why golfers in Montrose didn't feel
compelled to form a separate golf club quite as early as they did in
Fife, Edinburgh or Musselburgh.

Change began as the population continued to expand – Montrose
tripled in size between 1750 and 1850 – and pressure on the links
mounted. For avid golfers, protecting the golfing areas continued to be of
keen concern.

One of the most avid golfers of all was Captain James Bertram,
who took over the Turks Head Inn on George Street after he left the

British militia. The Turks Head, which was later named the Turf Inn, was already well known – Robbie Burns slept there in 1789 when visiting Montrose – and Bertram expanded the stables on the location where St George's (renamed St Andrew's) Church was later built. This helped make the Inn a favourite halting place of the numerous chaises and drags of the country gentry, many of whom were, no doubt, golfers.

On the first day of January 1810, Bertram and a few friends met and decided to start a golf club. They could not have imagined it would become only the second club, after the Royal and Ancient Club, to play golf on the same stretch of linksland – continuously – for two full centuries.

And that part of our story is next.

CHAPTER 2

A Club is Born

*With a view to form a Society for the protection, and a fund,
for the support of the Excellent Golf Course . . . the subscribers
hereby agree to associate themselves together in the name of the
Montrose Golf Club.*

From an early entry in the club minutes

Surprisingly little is known about the founding of the Montrose Golf
Club in 1810. There are no records of meetings called at or around the
time of the formation of the club (or of the Golfing Society of Montrose
as it was sometimes called). The *Montrose Review*, the first newspaper to
be established in the town, only began reporting national and occasional
local events in 1811. So how certain can we be of the actual date of the
club's formation?

   The strongest evidence is to be found in the first available club records.
A splendid minute book was brought into service around 1813. The first
entries, dated 21 March 1813, are copies of an exchange of correspondence between the club and the Town Council, so by that date the club
was obviously in existence.

   This minute book, which would continue in use for most of that
century, also has a handsome inscription on the front cover:

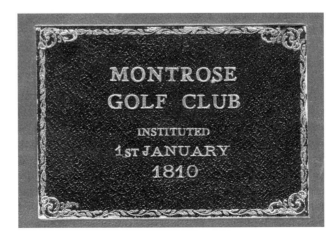

Clearly this was understood by the early members to be the date of their club's formation and it is also quoted on a number of occasions in later minutes. So the evidence to support 1 January 1810 is quite persuasive.

The more interesting question may be why the club was set up at that time. Looking back it might not seem like an auspicious moment. The country was embroiled in a major war with France and its allies, and in 1810 it was not going at all well. Though victory in the great naval battle at Trafalgar five years earlier had at least removed the immediate threat of a French invasion, a French victory was still the most likely outcome of a war that had already cost many thousands of lives, including, no doubt, many from Montrose. Trade was also severely circumscribed and, as Montrose had long relied on its position as a key trading port with Northern Europe, the personal wealth of many merchants in the area would also have declined.

However, this Napoleonic War was not like the global conflicts of the twentieth century when almost all civilian activities were curtailed to support the war effort. Much of the population would not have been greatly affected by the war with France. With the limited communications of the time, news of battles arrived days or weeks later so the war was not always at the forefront of people's minds. Many naval and army officers only served for periods of time while others' service was in local militias that gave them full rein to live normal lives.

So forming a golf club in the middle of a major war is not so incomprehensible. But the question still remains. Why did golfers in Montrose, who had been content to play golf on the Montrose links for their own amusement for centuries, seek to organise themselves into a club or golfing society in 1810?

The evidence suggests that the main reason was to protect that very golf ground which had been in use for at least 250 years. We have seen in the previous chapter that a similar concern roused a group of local golfers to organise themselves in 1785, and the members of the new Montrose Golf Club clearly saw themselves as following in the footsteps of this earlier generation – indeed, the first minute devotes the initial three pages to set out in full detail the actions taken in 1785 to see off the threat to their beloved links.

Now some twenty-five years later a similar threat seems to have arisen, again from a Montrose Town Council which was wholly unelected and not answerable to the local citizenry for its actions. Eager to raise revenue by renting more parts of the links to 'tacksmen', the Councillors were riding roughshod over the wishes of the local people who, for centuries, had used the links for many forms of recreation, not least golf.

One of the first entries in the club minute book, dated 29 March 1813, records that a letter had been sent to Provost Patrick Craigie

> *denying the right of the Council to enclose or interfere with the golf course and calling on them to say what their intentions were so that the club might adopt measures for protecting their privileges.*

This thinly veiled threat of legal action succeeded, just as it did in 1785. The Provost's reply is recorded in full. He accepted the club's demands: 'It is not at present the intention of the magistrates and Council to interfere with the golf courses.' The club would have noted the grudging acceptance reflected in the phrase, 'at present'.

Who were the founder members of Montrose Golf Club? At this first recorded meeting of the club in 1813, held in John Hill's house, the minutes lists those present:

> *Patrick Mason, who was Chairman, James Bertram, James Calvert, Hugh Thomson, David Mills, and Messrs Beattie, Ogilvy, Mudie and others.*

We can reasonably assume that this group included many of the founding members of the club in 1810, and it is to these golfers that we owe a debt of gratitude not only for starting up our club but also for seeing off potential threats to the links. And as the club grew and developed, it continued to take on the task of maintaining and improving the links not just for club members but also for all those other inhabitants of the town who continued to play golf on the links free of charge.

These club founders included a military man of modest rank (Mason), an innkeeper (Bertram, who had also been a captain in the militia), and a school teacher (Calvert). A bookseller, William Morris, would later be named the club's first Treasurer.

Noticeable by their absence are the landed gentry who largely initiated the legal suit in 1785 and whose matches on the links of Montrose were widely reported in Scotland and beyond. They would form their own golf club in 1822, just as they held their own balls and assemblies. It was called the Keithock Club, and its members played over the links of Montrose, met at the Star Inn and included the owners of the nearby estates. One member was James Cruickshank of Langley Park, just east of the House of Dun, who was Lord Kennedy's opponent in the famous night match at Montrose. But by severely restricting its membership, the Keithock Club seems to have guaranteed its own demise and it faded away in the mid-nineteenth century.

It is the Montrose Golf Club that would go from strength to strength.

The club our golfing ancestors set up in 1810 is one of the oldest recorded golf clubs in the world. While it has been called the ninth oldest club by some golf historians, there is a good case for it being labelled the eighth oldest if we use as the criterion clubs that have been in continuous existence since their foundation.

The seven golf clubs formed before the Montrose Golf Club in 1810 are:

1608   The Royal Blackheath Golf Club, London (1766 is
        regarded by some as the true date of this club's foundation)
1735   The Royal Burgess Club, Musselburgh Links
1744   The Honourable Company of Edinburgh Golfers,
        Musselburgh Links

1754   The Royal and Ancient Golf Club, St Andrews
1761   Bruntsfield Golf Club, Musselburgh Links
1774   Royal Musselburgh Golf Club, Musselburgh Links
1780   Society of Golfers at Aberdeen (re-constituted as Aberdeen
          Golf Club in 1815)

Four other golf clubs claim a foundation before 1810 – Fraserburgh (1777), Crail (1786), Glasgow(1787) and Burntisland (1797) – but golf historians generally agree that there is insufficient evidence that these clubs were in continuous existence since their foundation.

Glasgow Golf Club went out of existence for two periods, 1794–1809 and 1835–1870, with no competitions and no course to play on. At Crail, the club effectively dissolved in 1813, when it had only eight members, and it was not revived until the end of the nineteenth century. At Burntisland, there is good evidence of an early golf club but no proven connection with the subsequent golf club, and that is much the case with Fraserburgh. Aberdeen Golfing Society (one of the seven earlier clubs) was also dormant for a period until it was reconstituted in 1815.

In fact, as golfers in Montrose were forming their club, organised golf in the rest of Scotland was beginning to face grave challenges.

By 1810, the original club in Aberdeen had faded into obscurity. All the clubs at Leith were struggling, and the Honourable Company of Edinburgh Golfers was beginning a rapid decline into near bankruptcy. Even the Royal and Ancient found itself in financial difficulties.

The respected golf historian David Hamilton traces these troubles to the dislocations caused by the industrial revolution, which put pressure on the lands traditionally used for golf, and also changed the nature of leisure time. He goes so far as to conclude:

> There was a serious crisis in golf as in some sports in Scotland, starting about 1800. As a result of this decline, golf almost died out in the following decades.

But there was one place where golf was as vibrant as ever, and that was in Montrose. Thanks to the vigilance of the Montrose Golf Club, golf ground remained plentiful and became an attraction even for the working classes, who had little time for golf in other centres. Rather than declining, Montrose added no fewer than six golf clubs in the first half of the nineteenth century. They included three golf clubs set up by working men in the town – the Weavers, the Flaxdressers and the Mechanics – and one set up by the students at the Montrose Academy, which may well have conducted the world's first junior golf tournaments. By 1850 Montrose had more golf clubs than any other town.

Only the original golf club formed on the first of January in the year 1810 has survived to the present day. And it is to the fascinating story of the evolution of the Montrose Golf Club that we now turn.

CHAPTER 3

The Early Years: Montrose Golf Club, 1810–1845

That the members of the club be distinguished by a green short coat with black velvet collar, ornamented by a thistle of silver lace.

Minutes of the Montrose Golf Club, 1818

The earliest years of the club's development, until the granting of royal patronage in 1845, are of considerable historical interest.

At a time when golf was in the doldrums in much of Scotland the Montrose Golf Club was quickly coming of age. During these years it would run its first competitions, establish its own rules, make a social splash in the town and support what may be the world's first junior golf club. And perhaps most importantly, it would begin its role as custodian of what may well have been the best and most expansive golf course in the world.

Early Club Organisation

A picture of how the early club organised its affairs, recruited new members and funded itself emerges gradually, if not always with the greatest of clarity, from the first minute book.

The first set of club bye-laws are dated 1820, yet the list of club Captains prominently displayed in today's clubhouse begins with James Bertram in 1817.

It does seem that he was the first Captain of the club. In the first available club minute of the meeting in John Hill's house on 29 March 1813, there is no reference to a Captain being in post. Patrick Mason acted as Chairman at that meeting and Messrs Ogilvy and Mudie (who were thanked for sending the letter to the Council threatening legal action) are not given any official title, so it seems likely that the club managed its early affairs through informal meetings without benefit of a Captain.

Nor does it appear that this, the first recorded meeting of the club, was the club's first meeting: Patrick Mason, who wrote and signed the minute, reported that the letter to the Council had been sent 'in compliance with the direction of the club' – presumably given at an earlier meeting.

At the next recorded meeting held on 11 July 1817, the club appears to have decided to follow the example of other clubs (with whom members may have had occasional contact) and appoint a Captain and other office bearers, and to begin to formalise the loose arrangements that had been in place since the club was founded in 1810:

> *With a view to form a society for the protection and a fund for the support of the excellent golf course lately made out in Montrose Links, the subscribers hereby agree to appoint themselves together in the name of Montrose Golf Club.*
>
> *1st Each member to pay ten shillings and sixpence of entry money.*
>
> *2nd The concerns of the club to be conducted by a captain and two Councillors who with a Treasurer are to be elected at an Annual general meeting of the members to be held on the last Wednesday of June yearly.*
>
> *3rd Until the first General Meeting, Capt Bertram to be Captain, Messrs Mason and Caird Councillors & Mr Morris, Bookseller, to be Secretary and Treasurer, to the latter of whom the entry money shall be paid at subscribing this paper.*
>
> *4th The annual subscription to be fixed at the Annual general meeting not to exceed what is necessary for the immediate purposes of the club.*

Over the next year, twenty-six golfers appended their signature to this subscription and presumably paid their ten shillings and six pence entrance money, an amount equivalent to an average man's weekly wage.

There was a flurry of general meetings of the club in 1818. James Calvert was appointed as Captain in succession to James Bertram. It is not clear if he was elected, or the club was anticipating the 1820 bye-laws of the club, which decreed that the winner of the newly-purchased Gold Medal was to act as Captain. That medal was first played for on 24 June and was won by the same James Calvert.

The club adopted seventeen bye-laws at their general meeting on 21 June 1820. Now, all ex-Captains – each a good golfer presumably who had won the Gold Medal – were to be Councillors ex-officio, along with the two Councillors elected by the members. To complicate the issue further, these bye-laws, after much changing of minds at meetings about this issue, laid down that the Gold Medal was to be played for twice a year, which explains why there are two Captains of the club listed for the years 1821, 1822, 1823 and 1824.

There were to be two general meetings a year. Members were to be informed of the date of these by circular letter. At a meeting in March

1825, the perhaps hard-pressed Secretary tried to persuade the club that advertising the date for the Medal and the subsequent general meetings in the *Review* might suffice. He was given short shrift by the Council, which decided that 'instead of advertising, proper circular letters shall be printed for the purpose and issued to all members'.

The 'Green Jacket'

The first bye-laws relating to club dress were set out at a meeting in 1818, when it was agreed:

> *That the members of the club be distinguished by a green short coat with black velvet collar, ornamented by a thistle of silver lace.*

The meeting also ruled that after playing for the Gold Medal, the members would be expected to dine together in the uniform. Only two years later the club altered this dress code rather significantly:

> *The uniform of the club shall be, in future, a scarlet single breasted coat with a black velvet collar and plain buttons.*

This revised club dress was similar, if not identical, to what members of other golf clubs were wearing, an indication that some local golfers were in contact with members of other clubs. In *Scotland's Game*, historian David Hamilton attributes the fashion for such uniforms to the military nature of the period. With Britain often at war or preparing for war, 'the clubs copied the habits of the regiments in seeking a uniform and this gave an esprit de corps among the club members'.

These early members must have looked an impressive sight when they met together. Their distinctive garb would certainly have been noticed in the town, no doubt as was intended. According to Hamilton, 'uniforms were an ostentatious show of power and rank'. This uniform was to remain largely unchanged up to the twentieth century when the practice of wearing uniforms ceased.

The First Club Rules

In these early days, the Captain did not chair general meetings of the club, held either on a day set aside for this purpose or preceding the playing of the Medal. The members, it seems, chose a Chairman on the day who, in the minutes, is frequently referred to by the Latin term, *Praeses*. This practice continued up to 1830 when it was ruled that the Captain automatically should take the chair.

That was one of the new rules adopted that year, a significant point in the club history, moving as the club did from a loose set of bye-laws to a set of club rules shared with every member.

Follows copy of the
Rules of
The Montrose Golf Club,
(instituted 1810),
revised and consolidated,
and approved of by a general meeting
held on 26th April, 1830:
with the
Rules of the Game of Golf
established by the Club.

First. — Rules of the Club
1. This Society, in conformity with its original
institution in 1810, shall continue to be called
the Montrose Golf Club, having for its object,
the prosecution and encouragement of the ancient
and national Game of Golf.

These 1830 rules are in two parts. One part sets out rules for playing the game on the links – more of that in a later chapter. The other sets out twenty-one club rules, written in beautiful script.

Like all club constitutions, much discussion no doubt underpinned the drafting of these rules. Meant to stand the test of time, invariably they didn't!

Under these rules, in the Captain's absence, the Medal holder (note the continued honour paid to the best golfer in the club) was to take his place. He together with the Captain, two Councillors and the Secretary/ Treasurer, would manage the club affairs. The first club Captain elected under these new rules was Charles Barclay. The quorum for meetings was raised from five to seven. To the club's uniform rules laid down in 1820 were added 'gilt buttons and white trousers which may be adopted

Excerpt from the 1830 club rules in the minute book.

by the members at their own option'. Rules to deal with improper conduct were created for the first time: members could 'be expelled by the votes (by ballot) of three fourths of the members present'.

And finally, the rules were to be printed! Each member was to 'provide himself with a copy for which he shall pay such a sum as may be fixed on a general meeting'.

Membership

Starting with the twenty-six golfers who paid their entrance fee in 1817, the club then accepted new members at almost every meeting. Prospective members were proposed by club members either at the meetings that preceded the playing of the Gold Medal or at the general meetings of the club. Initially, the club wasn't choosy and the meetings accepted all such nominations; the club would be keen to grow in size and new members would improve its finances. The first recorded new member was William Jamieson, a future Town Provost, admitted in November 1818.

Less than a year later the rules were revised with the stipulation that 'no gentleman shall be admitted as a member unless recommended by three or more resident members of the club'.

At the same meeting the first of what we would call annual subscriptions were agreed: 'The sum of four shillings be paid to the Treasurer by each member . . . for the purposes of keeping the golf course in repair.' (A fuller description of early greenkeeping can be found in Chapter 16.)

If this sum was not paid by the due date the consequences were severe:

> *Those failing to pay their proportions shall not be allowed to compete for the Medal nor shall they be afterwards considered members of the club.*

After this first levy had been paid in full, members could pay a shilling quarterly, an early form of an instalment plan. In 1820, the amount was reduced to two shillings a year for a period of time. There is no evidence that these new rules relating to subscriptions, agreed in a flush of enthusiasm for regulating the affairs of their new club, were fully adhered to in the coming years. Non-payment of fees, then as now, was a constant irritant.

The bye-laws adopted in 1820 had tried to refine the procedure for admitting new members:

> *Any gentleman desirous of entering Montrose Golf Club shall signify his intention to the Captain who shall desire the secretary to give notice of the same by circular letters for a general meeting to be held as soon thereafter as possible when the gentleman is then to be voted and if there is a majority of votes to be admitted accordingly.*

These were quite cumbersome procedures and may not always have been followed even by established club members. On 7 May 1822, James Bertram, very much a club stalwart, proposed that 'Lieut Wyness be admitted a member of the club at the next meeting which takes place tomorrow after the competition for the medal'. He was duly admitted the next day and Bertram, who had just won the Medal that day, then proposed that a Captain Gibson be admitted as a member at the next meeting.

Lieutenant Wyness and Captain Gibson were among the first of many officers of the army and navy to be admitted as members of the club. Most were officers in the local militia based in Garrison Street or posted to other garrisons in the area, and the club seems to have agreed to grant automatic membership to those who were golfers. The first of a number of Rectors of the local academy to become members of the club – Andrew Johnston – was admitted in 1822, and the first Provost of the town to be admitted as member while holding that post – George Paton – joined in 1828.

In 1821 the club agreed 'to procure suitable diplomas' for members, a procedure followed by some other clubs in Scotland. These diplomas were given out for a number of years but, unfortunately, no example survives.

At every meeting of the club during the 1820s, varying numbers of new members were admitted. In addition to army officers, recruitment at this time was largely of local men from the merchant and professional classes, as the minute of the 16 December 1828 illustrates. Admitted as new members on that date were:

> *Mr James Taylor, bookseller, Mr James Scott, merchant, Mr James Hill, merchant, Mr David Scott, Writer, and Mr James Nicoll, bookseller.*

The club was growing quite rapidly, perhaps too rapidly in the eyes of some who may have grown concerned about the suitability of some new members being accepted without due scrutiny. At a meeting in April 1829, Patrick Mason gave notice that at the next meeting:

> *He would move that the bye laws of the club, as far as related to the admission of members, should be altered so that new members be admitted by ballot. And that at the same meeting at which they are proposed, that their names be communicated to the Captain and Councillors previous to their calling a meeting and that their names should be notified in circular letters for that purpose.*

A month later, the proposal to ballot new members was voted in and three new members were admitted. Somewhat revealingly, the names of two gentleman nominated at the previous meeting were withdrawn. William Morris, who had proposed two prospective members at the

April meeting – a Mr Shand of the Montrose Hotel and Charles Bass of the Theatre – declared that he would withdraw his motion for admitting these two gentlemen 'for the present'.

The club rules agreed in the following year confirmed these arrangements for balloting for new members: a prospective member needed the support of three-quarters of the members present.

The first honorary member of the club was a 'Mr James Lyall, Writer, Edinburgh' in 1820. There is no reference to honorary members in any of the early bye-laws and rules; it is probable that the club offered this honour to men in important positions. James Lyall was a solicitor, referred to as 'Writer' at these times. The procedure for nominating honorary members was to be regularised in the 1830 rules for the first time.

A meeting in 1839 cancelled the membership of thirteen members who had failed to pay their dues. If this was intended to encourage other slow-payers, it seems to have been rather unsuccessful. As in present times, not all members were practising golfers and, at the meeting about a year later, the idea was floated that if non-golfers paid three shillings – three-quarters of what was due – they could continue as members. Nothing seems to have come of this idea, to have a category of what we might call 'social members'. It may be reassuring to club officials down the years who have considered such an idea that the concept is not new!

By June 1844, membership had grown to fifty-five. These included:

- thirty-six local members;
- eleven 'members at a distance', whose residences ranged from St Andrews to Edinburgh, and places such as Buttergask, Bonnyton and Usan that we might consider to be quite 'local'; and
- a further eight gentlemen who were honorary members.

Finances

Until a separate Treasurer was appointed in 1848, the financial affairs of the club in these early years were handled by the Secretary. The club does not appear to have had bank accounts, so the members paid their dues to the Secretary, who held these funds as cash and he, it seems, paid all expenses from this source. He then presented a summary of income and expenditure and reported on the cash balance carried over to the next year or, if there was a deficit, the amount that was due to him personally. As we might expect, this approach eventually caused a problem.

In April 1831, James Wills, who had been Secretary and Treasurer for ten years, became seriously ill, resigned, and died shortly thereafter. A three-member 'audit' team appointed by the club found that Secretary Wills owed the club £8 from the accounts. This debt was apparently acknowledged verbally by Wills when he was still alive but he had died before he had a chance to deal with the issue. A year later the club was still hoping to retrieve the arrears from the estate by 'prosecution or otherwise.' As the matter was not mentioned again in the minutes, it seems likely that the club was unsuccessful.

In spite of this episode, the club continued to entrust the club funds in cash to the Secretary, though for a time the practice of auditing the accounts seems to have continued. It seems that a Secretary quite frequently had to draw on his own personal funds to meet a club overspend. In 1842, this deficit amounted to over £5. Club Secretaries and Treasurers of today might be pleased to escape that particular liability.

The 'Grand Match' – Montrose vs The Honourable Company

A common practice in all of the early golf clubs in Scotland was the playing of private matches often involving wagers, and the issuing of challenges made whenever golfers met socially. These challenges were often recorded in the minutes or a separate bet book.

One of the earliest-known matches in Montrose involved a well-publicised visit from the Honourable Company of Edinburgh Golfers; it might be called a first inter-club match for the fledgling Montrose club.

It took place over two days in September 1829. A note in the *Scotsman*, which got its information from the *Montrose Review*, alerted readers to an upcoming match between two Leith golfers and a team from Montrose, consisting of James Bertram – one of the founders of the Montrose Golf Club – and James Cruickshank of Langley Park, a member of the Keithock Club:

> *Important Golf Match.*—The match, Major Cruikshank and Captain Bertram against Mr John Wood and Mr James Hay of Leith, is to take place here on the 10th and 11th September, for L100 a side, the best of two day's play; two rounds of the course (28 holes). St Andrew's rules to be played each day. From the celebrity of the players, a keen contest is expected. Betting equal.

Hay and Wood were members of the Honourable Company of Edinburgh Golfers, arguably the sport's oldest golf club which in 1829 still played at the Leith links. John Wood won the club's Gold Medal the following year and was also good enough to win the St Andrews Medal more than once; interestingly, he was made an honorary member of the Montrose Club in 1829, the year of this match.

In researching this book, it was discovered that this match even made its way into the Bets Book of Royal Blackheath Golf Club where the following entry of 5 September 1829 is found:

Mr Robertson noticing that a great match at Golf to be played on the links at Montrose during the ensuing week, Cruickshank and Bertram versus Hay and Wood, backs the latter party, and Mr Lindsay takes the former. Lost by Mr Robertson.

Robertson lost his wager, as the crack Edinburgh players were no match for the Montrose golfers, losing by a total of 23 to 15. The *Scotsman* reported on the play, commenting on the numbers attending and recording the results of the play over two days, 28 holes each day:

GRAND GOLF MATCH.

Montrose, 11th September 1829.

The great golf match (for L.100 a side), between Major Cruikshank and Captain Bertram, on the one side, and Messrs Hay and Wood, from the Edinburgh Golf Club on the other, was decided here to-day in favour of the two former gentlemen. The match, which excited great interest in the town and neighbourhood, and on which bets to a considerable amount depended, began yesterday morning about half past eleven o'clock, and better playing was never witnessed on our course. The Edinburgh gentlemen are capital players, and excel at playing long balls, but in nearing the hole and putting the Montrose gentlemen have the decided advantage, as was shewn at the conclusion of yesterday's sport, when they were eleven holes a-head of their opponents. In the course of the day many admirable strokes were played on both sides, and one by Major Cruikshank excited the admiration of all who saw it, he having played his ball out of a pretty deep pool of water at a very considerable distance from one of the holes to within a few feet of it.

The sport commenced to-day about the same hour as yesterday, and the game was contested with great keenness and spirit. The Edinburgh gentlemen were more successful on this day's play, and gained three holes upon their rivals, so that the game upon which the bets depended, and which occupied the two day's sport, was decided in favour of the Montrose gentlemen, they being on the whole eight holes a-head of the gentlemen from Edinburgh. Better or more scientific golf playing was never witnessed on our course; and Captain Bertram, who has long been unrivalled at the game, never played better in his life, and he declares he has seldom met with more powerful opponents than Messrs Hay and Wood, whose drives were indeed astonishing.

The game excited a lively interest, and on both days, the weather being fine, a great concourse of spectators, both on horseback and on foot, were on the ground.

At the commencement of the match betting was equal, but the result of the first day's play rendered the odds much against the Edinburgh gentlemen. The terms of the match were—the best of the two days' play; two rounds (28 holes) each day—St Andrew's rules. The issue was as follows:—

FIRST DAY.		SECOND DAY.	
Montrose,	19 holes.	Montrose,	4 holes.
Edinburgh,	8	Edinburgh,	7
Halved,	1	Halved,	10
	— 28.	Not played,	7
			— 28.

The Scotsman's *report of the 'Grand Match' between Montrose and Edinburgh in 1829.*

The result seems to have surprised golfers further south (including, presumably, Mr Robertson of the Blackheath club). A week later the *Review* was fuming about reports of the match in Dundee, Edinburgh and 'other journals' which it felt were the 'subject of very gross and seemingly interested misrepresentation'. Apparently some writers had attributed the result not to the superior play of the Montrose pair but to the fact that Hay and Wood were less familiar with the course. The *Review* dismissed this theory out of hand, declaring: 'They lost the match through their ignorance of putting.'

That Challenge matches were still very much part of the golfing life of the Montrose Golf Club is confirmed in a club minute in January 1843 when, for reasons not made clear, a number of private matches, arranged either at the general meeting or possibly beforehand, were appended for the first time. These provide a fascinating insight into the golfing experience of some members in this period:

Matches to be played

1. *Mr J Calvert and Mr Alex Cowie against Captain McNeill and Robert Trail on Wednesday 24th at 1.00pm*

2. *Mr James Calvert against Mr John Jamie. To be played within one month. Mr Jamie to fix the day.*

3. *Captain Leighton &Mr Patrick Mason. The time not fixed.*

4. *Mr Patrick Mason and Mr Pat Mason Junior against Mr James Calvert Junior and Mr William Beattie. To be played within a month.*

5. *Captain McNeill and Mr Cowie against Mr James Calvert and Patrick Mason Jr. To be played within a month.*

6. *Captain McNeill and Mr Patrick Mason. To be played within one month.*
   Two gallons of Porter a side.

7. *Captain McNeill and Mr Cowie against Mr James Calvert and Mr D. Scott. To be played within one month.*

Note that four of these challenge matches were foursomes and the remainder singles. The matches may have been agreed far in advance so that other club members and, possibly, members of the public could accompany the matches and cheer on the participants, probably with some side bets placed on the outcome.

The Original Gold Medal

We know little about the members' early golfing activities around the time the club was founded. We can only surmise that they met as a club on the links, most likely on a Wednesday, to play a game and it was probably some form of match-play.

However, in a meeting on 7 May 1818, there was a very significant step forward when it was agreed

> *that a gold medal not exceeding ten guineas in value be immediately ordered and the medal engraved with the appropriate insignia.*

In taking this step, the club was probably influenced by the practice at St Andrews and other clubs. This Gold Medal was the club's first prize of any kind and, for almost all of the following 192 years, club members have continued to compete for it. It is now known as the Original Gold Medal and, in recent times, has been competed for by all of the season's Medal winners towards the end of the golfing season. A list of all the winners of this prestigious Medal since 1818 can be found in Appendix 2.

The Original Gold Medal.

The 1818 meeting also set out in some detail the arrangements for playing for the Medal and, in so doing, they set a pattern that, with some minor adjustments, was followed for over one hundred years:

> *That the medal be played for on the last Wednesday of June, on which day the members agree to dine together in the uniform of the club.*

That after the last Wednesday of June 1818, the medal shall be played for twice a year, on the first Wednesday of April and the first Wednesday of October, on which days the members agree to dine together.

That the person who gains the medal shall not be allowed to compete for the medal till the expiration of two years after the time he receives it.

Within six weeks of the decision to purchase the medal, it was in the possession of the club and was first competed for on 24 June 1818. Meeting beforehand, the committee appointed at the May meeting made the arrangements:

The club should dine at Mr Hunter's on Wednesday first at 4 o'clock and Mr Stewart Jolly to take the chair.

The meeting then proceeded to settle the manner of playing for the medal and agreed that members should play in parties of three and the person who shall play the round in the fewest strokes shall receive the medal. Each of the parties to be attended by a clerk and the number of strokes to be ascertained as soon as the whole finish play.

The members shall start at Mr Paterson's holes, play round the course to the hole at the foot of the Bleaching Green and out again to the Brander, after which return to the hole at the foot of the bleaching green making in all 17 holes. The hour of play to be noon.

The meeting directed the Secretary to insert an advertisement in the *Montrose Review*, the first of many such notices:

> NOTICE.
>
> THE MEMBERS of the MONTROSE GOLF CLUB are to play for the GOLD MEDAL, on Wednesday first, the 24th current, at noon, and to DINE in the Star inn, the same day, at four o'clock. Such members as intend to play, will give in their names to the Secretary, on or before Monday; and will receive their tickets, for dinner, at the bar of the Star-inn, on that day.
>
> W. MORRIS, Secretary.
>
> *Montrose, June 18, 1818.*

The minutes later record the results of this first-ever competition in the club's history (note the sub-three-hour round!):

A long spoon c 1830 and a 'gutta'. Courtesy of the British Golf Museum.

This day at 12 o'clock the following members started to compete for the Gold Medal. Messrs Calvert, Mason, Leighton, Webster, Wills, Richard, Caird, Bertram Jnr and Morris. The match was finished at three o'clock and the medal was gained by Mr Calvert who played the 17 holes at 103 Strokes.

The runner-up was Patrick Mason with 112 strokes, and the highest score was 149 strokes, by William Morris. Bertram Junior, who may have been the first junior golfer to play in a club competition (his father, an expert golfer, must have regretted being unavailable to play himself), scored 132.

The minutes note that each group was 'to be attended by a clerk and the number of strokes to be ascertained as soon as the whole finish play'. Whether these clerks were fellow club members or clerks on attachment from members' places of work we do not know, though the former would at least be able to adjudicate on the rules of play.

The Gold Medal was what we would call today a scratch stroke-play competition. Though informal handicaps were common in individual challenge matches, there was as yet no handicapping system for larger competitions. To ensure that other members had a chance to gain the medal, the club debarred the Medal Winner from winning it again for a period of time, although the original ruling regarding the length of that period was to be subject to various amendments.

From 1820 onwards, the Gold Medal winner was further honoured by automatically becoming Club Captain until the Medal was competed for again. When the club decided to elect its future Captains at general meetings after 1830, the Medal winner's special position in the club continued to be recognised by being automatically appointed a club Councillor until that practice ended in 1860.

The Gold Medal on exhibit in the club today, still adorned with its original clasp, would be worn with pride by each of the winners on the chest of his green (later red) club uniform jacket at the dinner that followed play. He would also keep the medal until it was played for again, and from 1820 he had to sign a declaration to guarantee its safe return. On 23 April that year, Patrick Mason put his signature to the following declaration recorded in the minute book:

The Gold Medal of the Montrose Golf Club, having been played for this day, was gained by me and the same has been accordingly put in my possession and I therefore oblige myself and my heirs etc. that the same shall be restored to the club on the day that the medal shall be played for again.

For over one hundred years, the winners of this and the other two medals the club later played for – the Albert and the Keithock – continued to be entrusted to the winners although, in 1861, it was decided that no winner who lived in England would be allowed to take the medal out of the country, leaving it instead in possession of the Captain. It is a tribute to these early golfers that two of these medals are still in the possession of the club. Only the Albert Medal was to be lost (though possibly only temporarily, as we shall later report).

These first arrangements for the competition didn't specify what would happen if two or more golfers returned the same score. This happened for the first time in 1821 when three golfers – Messrs Leighton, Clark and Webster – all recorded 107 strokes and a two-hole play-off took place, with Leighton prevailing. There were to be no more tied scores until 1850 and on that, and all subsequent occasions, a 17-hole play-off was instituted which took place immediately, but they still always arrived in good time for dinner at the chosen venue after playing thirty-four holes!

We don't know why or exactly when the golfers in Montrose settled on the idea that a round of golf consisted of 17 holes, but it stayed that way until the 1860s. Though a round at St Andrews had consisted of 18 holes since the eighteenth century, this did not become accepted practice elsewhere in Scotland until much later. Each round at the first Open Championship at Prestwick in 1860, for example, was played over 12 holes.

Sweepstakes and handicapping

In May 1839, the date for the Medal was changed from the second Wednesday in May to the second Wednesday in June. The reason stated in the minutes for this change is a reminder to us that golfers then as now were pretty competitive:

> The meeting considering that the time for competing for the medal is rather too early in the year in so far as it prevents the players from practising previous to the date of competition.

Another resolution from the minutes of a meeting later in the same year confirms that in some members the competitive instincts were being further honed:

> That a sweepstake for a few golf balls should be played for monthly in order to encourage the game and be an inducement to the whole members to practice and compete.

It was agreed to submit this idea to the Captain and a committee 'for the purpose of classifying the players and making the necessary arrangements'. There is no further mention of these monthly sweeps in these early minutes nor of any attempts to 'classify' the players – to agree a rudimentary handicapping system – but that may well be because monthly sweeps did became a routine part of club life. The episode suggests there was a growing demand for some form of handicapping, to allow lesser golfers a chance to win some glory.

Handicapping had long been used in challenge matches, including contests played in Montrose and reported in the national press, as a way of levelling the sides and increasing wagering.

The jargon used at the time in Montrose would surely have been the same as that described by St Andrews writer H. B. Farnie in 1857:

> *Third-one* – a shot every three holes
> *Half-one* – a shot at alternate holes
> *One more* – a stroke a hole
> *Two more* – two strokes a hole

By the nineteenth century, a 'half-one' was the most commonly-assigned odds in matches between more and less accomplished players.

Club Dinners

A pattern was set early and continued more or less unchanged for the next fifty years. Whenever members met for a general meeting, an important part of the business was not just to fix the day for playing for the Medal but to make arrangements for dining thereafter. The first newspaper advertisement in 1818 informed members that they will receive their ticket at the bar of the Star Inn.

On the day of play, members usually met in a local coffee shop or inn where they conducted brief business and presumably fortified themselves with a good lunch and alcoholic drink before reporting to the green at the appointed time. After play, all of the players, other club members and invited guests assembled for dinner. The following entry from the minute of May 1819 is typical:

> *It was unanimously agreed that the medal be played for on the last Wednesday in June, the manner of playing to be the same as last year, the dinner to be furnished by Mr Wm Bertram at 3s 6d each not including liquor, and to be on the ground at four o clock.*

The minute from a month later records that 'a party of 30 sat down to dine in the Turf'. William Bertram and brother James would seem to be joint-owners of the Turf Coffee Room, one of the early meeting places for the club.

The attendance of the Medal winner at these dinners was compulsory; he was presented with the prize by the previous winner. On only one occasion in these early years, in 1824, was the former Medal winner not present; according to the minutes, Capt. Caird was unable to attend and asked the Chairman to do the honours: 'Capt Bertram was then invested with the medal with due solemnity and an appropriate speech by Mr Mason'.

An important early meeting place for the club was the Star Hotel just off the High Street. The arch was erected much later, in 1891, and removed in 1959. Courtesy of the Montrose Society.

The club used various hostelries as their meeting places in these early days. In June 1820, after playing for the Medal at noon, 'the club then sat down to dinner at Mr Hunter's at 4 o'clock and concluded the day in hilarity and cordiality'. Hunter's later became the Star Inn.

In April 1821, which was also the King's birthday and the cause for further celebration, the club sat down to dinner at Mr Hunter's, 'Mr Jamieson in the chair along with a number of visitors amounting altogether to 36 in number and spent the evening with a great deal of humour and conviviality'.

From the outset, these gatherings were almost certainly one of the highlights of the social calendar for the men of the town. A Chairman was always chosen for the evening – Stewart Jolly took on this role at the first dinner in The Star in June 1818. The Chairman would most probably be responsible for proposing the various toasts and would lead the entertainment.

In 1823 there is the first reference to the appointment of a 'Croupier'. This role fell to a club member in the early days but, in later years, it was usually filled by the Medal holder and this was confirmed as standard practice in 1841:

> *On the motion of Mr James Calvert it was unanimously resolved that the usual rule of giving the medal holder the privilege of acting as Croupier at the Annual Dinner should be continued as a rule of the club and that he should act himself in the capacity as Croupier or appoint another in his stead.*

What the Croupier did at these gatherings is rather unclear. In a 1913 dictionary definition, a croupier was 'one who, at a public dinner party, sits at the lower end of the table as assistant chairman'. Among other duties, the Croupier may have recorded the various wagers that were made about forthcoming golf matches; he may even have set the odds on occasion, given that he was a good golfer himself and well able to assess the relative abilities of other golfers.

The club did not have a clubhouse at this time – not until 1866 – a situation that was not untypical of golf clubs of the time in Scotland. The Montrose Club met variously in the Turf Coffee Bar, Hunter's Inn and the Star Inn or in a member's house. In 1829 they decided to alternate between the Star Inn and the Montrose Hotel but that suggestion was soon abandoned – around the time the Montrose Hotel's owner's bid for membership ended – and from that date, the club had virtually all its meetings and dinners at the Star Inn, which is the only one of the establishments mentioned in these early minutes that still exists today, and in the same location.

Hints about the entertainment on offer at these dinners come from various reports as recorded in the minutes:

> *Mr Henderson, Spirit and wine merchant was a visitor. The evening was spent in great harmony and humour with many patriotic toasts and songs from the chair and members. [1827]*

> *The club afterwards dined in the Star Inn when 25 gentlemen sat down and the chair taken at five o'clock by Provost Paton assisted by Baillie Crawford and Mr Mason as croupiers, and the evening was spent in much enjoyment and harmony, the club having been enlivened by a select band of music that played fine English and Scottish Tunes and Airs. [1829]*

> *The club sat down to an excellent dinner and spent the evening in a harmonious manner, many good speeches being delivered and songs sung on the occasion. [1836]*

Further insight into the forms of entertainment at these early club dinners can be gained from two poems taken from Alexander Low's *Mixture of Poetry and Prose*, published in 1841. Alexander Low was a local man, though not apparently a club member and thus likely to have been an invited guest at a club dinner.

Two of his poems were read or sung at a club dinner. 'A Golfer's Song', was written as a song to be sung at the club dinner, no doubt with considerable gusto, to the Robert Burns tune of 'A Man's a Man for A' That':

A representation of the town in the 1830's. The Old Kirk by now has its new spire and the Star Hotel, probably the second or third building on the left, is still located on the same site. Courtesy of Angus Council.

A GOLFER'S SONG – *Made for the Montrose Golfing Society.*

Let misers hug their sordid wealth
And bad men break the law, yet;
We'll to the healthful links a while
And drive the golfing ba' yet.

For a' that, and a' that.
The medal fair, and a' that,
The club, the ba', the queen, the hole.
And muckle mair nor a' that.

And when the game is play'd all o'er
We'll to the inn awa' get,
The dinner waits us – 'tis the hour,
Let's round the table a' sit.

For a' that, and a' that.
We' cheerful look, and a' that,
The social glass we'll let that pass.
And muckle mair nor a' that.

When song, and toast, and speech are o'er.
For friends and foes, and a' that,
We'll to our cheerful hames repair
And tell our loves of a' that,

For a' that, and a' that,
Ye bachelors ne'er saw that;
Wi' loving wife that cheers our life
And children dear, and a' that.

A second poem, likely written in 1841, was composed for the same or, possibly, another golfing dinner. The poet prefaces the poem by noting who was present: 'the Rev. Mr. Hill of Logie, Captain Bertram, Captain M'-Neill, Messrs. Calvert, Burnes, Mason, Robertson, and many others.'

The galaxy above.
Any poet would move,
And I being present much more;
Such manners complete.
To see was a treat,
I never saw better before.

Each one play'd their part.
At the golfing art –
Brave Bertram the medal did gain;
Gallant Mason stood firm,
Such play was a charm,
It's like you might look for in vain.

Learn'd Calvert was there.
Of majestic air;
And so was Peninsular M'Neill; *
A gentleman sweet,
Whose manner's a treat
Good soldier, keen golfer as weel.

Ingenious Burnes,
Of lively address –
Mr. Robertson in Buttergask,
Of golfing the pride,
That won't be denied.
It's history to us did unmask.

Many others were there.
Who blythely did share.
Reason's feast and the flow of the
  soul.
Each well tim'd remark
sent forth a bright spark
More cheering by far than the
  bowl.

* Captain McNeill bravely fought
in the Peninsular War.

'Peninsular McNeill', who seems to have had a distinguished war record and was also known as a good golfer, was probably an honoured guest at the dinner; he is not recorded as joining the club up to this point, though his name later appears among the Medal winners in the 1840s.

The Golf Club 'Balls'

'A Golfer's Song' quoted above makes a passing reference to 'Wi' loving wife that cheers our life/And children dear, and a' that'.

In fact, no mention at all is made in the club records until 1825 of 'the ladies' – the wives, sweethearts or female family members of the gentlemen golfers of the Montrose Golf Club – those who, in later times, might be known as 'golfing widows'. Ladies would certainly not have been invited to the all-male gatherings in the Star Inn nor were any of them likely to have played the game on the links at this time.

Perhaps some of these early male golfers were on the receiving end of complaints about the amount of time they were devoting to the golf club. For whatever reason, the club made plans to involve the ladies in one of their future social activities:

Mr Mason brought forward his motion regarding the propriety of having a Ball and recommended to the different members of the club (who were willing to promote the same) to endeavour to obtain a sufficient number of subscribers for carrying the purpose into effect.

Though there is no record of a Ball actually being held in 1825, the idea seems to have taken root. In December 1828, when Patrick Mason again suggested a Ball, the club moved quickly to appoint a sizeable committee to carry forward the proposal. That committee reported within two weeks, and its recommendations were approved. Provost Paton – who seems to have greatly enjoyed the social side of the golf club that he had so recently joined – was to work with selected members to carry forward the Ball as proposed:

The committee have every reason to believe there will be thirty subscribing members and therefore 15 or 20 visitors will be sufficient to make up a number for a respectable ball. Members may nominate any ladies as each may wish to be invited by the Director and committee.

This Ball was indeed held on 8 January 1829 and seems to have been such a success that when, a year later, a proposal is made to have another, this idea is taken forward speedily and a special meeting of the club was held to approve the arrangements. This particular Ball was to be held in February 1830 and the *Review* carried this report:

On Friday evening, a ball, under the patronage of the Montrose Golf Club took place in the Guild Hall, which brought together a numerous and respectable assemblage of the ladies and gentlemen of the town: Provost Barclay, director. The dancing was kept up until an early hour next morning. This is the second ball given by the club and, from the universal satisfaction as well as the pleasure they have afforded, we have little doubt but they will be at least an annual occurrence.

The *Review's* optimism about future functions seems to have been misplaced; there are no further mentions of Balls being organised for the ladies.

The Play's Not the Thing!

In 1826, the club initially lent its support to a play in the town to be produced by a Charles Bass, proprietor of the theatre at No. 36 Bridge Street that is now a private residence. It is a curious affair in many ways. Bass wrote to the Secretary in May, 'requesting that the club would honour with their patronage a play in the theatre'. It seems a majority of members agreed to Bass's proposal, and he accordingly announced in his playbill that the play was to be under the patronage of the Captain and members of the club.

This seems to have upset the club: the members changed their minds about the play and unanimously agreed that those who had given Bass the nod had acted 'contrary to the regulations of the club'.

This episode reveals two things. First, that the club's reputation in the town had grown such that its patronage of a public event was something to be prized. Second, that the club so valued its reputation that when Bass overstepped the mark in mistaking expressions of support for official patronage, the club quickly sought an excuse to back out of the arrangement.

In 1829, Charles Bass's name was one of two put forward by Mr William Morris, and then withdrawn for consideration as club members, just as the club had introduced a ballot system for approving (or not) applications. It seems quite possible that the club was not prepared to forgive Bass's audacity, and therefore put in train procedures to block his membership.

The Montrose Academy Golf Club

In the first chapter, we have seen how James Melville is the first 'junior' golfer on record, and the first to receive golf instruction. Three centuries later, the Montrose golfers would also have a historic role in the development of junior golf.

In 1832, the club formally thanked David Duncan of Montrose, who had won the St Andrews Gold Medal the previous year, for 'the patronage he has given to golfing in general and especially to the golfers of Montrose and to the scholars attending the Academy to whom he has given a medal to be played for annually'.

A print of the 'new' Academy built in 1815 adjacent to the golf course that lay to the North and East, and the home of the worlds' first Juvenile Golf Club.

The Academy Golf Club (sometimes called the Juvenile Golf Club) was established at Montrose Academy in 1832, presumably in order to compete for the medal Duncan had donated.

In the early days, the Montrose Golf Club seems to have run these competitions, which may well be the first properly-run junior tournaments in golf. Before the 1841 competition, a meeting of the club was informed that

> *the boys would feel gratified were the present meeting to fix a day of competition for the medal. The meeting fixed Saturday 12th June for the competition and recommended that the Office Bearers should take an interest in the proceedings.*

A report in the *Montrose Review* confirms that the competition went ahead as planned:

> *Admirers of this healthful game have had good sport this week. On Saturday afternoon, the medal of the Juvenile Golf Club was played for and carried off by Master Ewart Watson, Union Place. On Wednesday, a keen competition took place for the Gold Medal of the Montrose Golf Club.*

Again in 1844, there is a report of the two medal competitions being played for in the same week. On this occasion, 'the silver medal presented to the young gentlemen attending the Academy was played for and, after a keen competition, gained by Master John Burnett, son of Captain Burnett RN'.

The Academy would receive at least three more medals (including one for girls) from members of the Royal Albert, and would compete for them right up to the outbreak of the First World War and beyond.

The Montrose Triumverate

If Montrose seems to have been a well-led club for its first 35 years, credit must go to its three most prominent members – Patrick Mason, James Bertram and James Calvert. Almost certainly, all three were founder members of the club in 1810. They remained as members for the rest of their lives and, coincidentally, each had a son with the same name who also became a member.

Patrick Mason
At the first recorded meeting of the club in 1813, Patrick Mason took the chair. Over the next thirty-five years no one did more to preserve and develop the golf course. He also found time to enhance the social side of the club and later in life helped navigate it through the process of securing royal status.

Mason was Captain of the club on five occasions and winner of the Gold Medal four times, so he was no mean golfer. But it is his work behind the scenes that did so much for the golfers of Montrose.

Perhaps his most important achievements were during the early years, when the still tiny club successfully took on the Town Council to preserve recreational space for the town's citizens. His work on behalf of the club was so noteworthy that after just a few years of the club's existence, it was recognised by his fellow members. In October 1821, James Calvert moved that

> *this meeting taking into consideration the important services*
> *rendered by Mr Mason to the interests of the club and in*
> *particular for having devised and effected the present extended*
> *golf course, and for having manfully and successfully resisted*
> *every encroachment upon the rights and privileges of the golf*
> *club by the hand of power, resolve that some small mark or*
> *tribute of esteem be presented to him for his valuable services.*

From this excerpt, we can also justifiably call Mason the first recorded course designer at Montrose. The committee appointed to deliberate on a tribute recommended the purchase of a silver snuffbox from club funds to be suitably engraved.

Mason's work for the club was certainly not over. During his long period of membership, he hardly ever misses a meeting, more than adequate testimony to his concern for the welfare of the club. It was he, for example, who instigated the Balls for the ladies in the 1820s and 1830s. But it is to the golf course that he seems to have devoted most of his energies. From the earliest days, he takes on responsibility for 'the green' and he may also properly be referred to as the first 'Greens Convenor' in Montrose (though that term was not in general use for another 100 years or more).

Perhaps to better protect the golf links, Mason got himself a place on the Town Council and for a time served as Dean of Guild, an influential position with particular responsibility for the golf courses.

Two decades on, Patrick Mason is still a hugely influential figure in the club. In the period 1843–45, in his role as Captain, he takes the leading role in efforts to gain royal patronage for the club, writing both a loyal address to Prince Albert and a letter to William Gladstone. An entry in the club's minute book lists Mason's residence as Balbegno Castle, just outside Fettercairn, so Mason was, for a time at least, a near neighbour of the Gladstones who played a key part in securing royal patronage.

In March 1848, Mason was again appointed Captain and chaired the meeting, during which a committee of three members was appointed 'for the purpose of keeping the course in proper order and giving instructions to the man in charge of the links'. It was fitting that Patrick should be present at that meeting which arranged for the work he had done for over thirty years to be carried on. It is a poignant moment because, by the next meeting a month later, he had died.

A special meeting was called in April 1848 'to take such steps as the death of Mr Mason may have rendered necessary'. Arrangements were made for James Calvert, who was senior Councillor, to take over as Captain until the next general meeting. A letter was also sent to Mason's family to express the club's deep regret 'at the lamented and sudden demise of their respected chairman'. The letter went on:

> *He had been a very keen member and a most vigorous and persevering advocate of the privileges of the club. . . . He was found to the last day of his life maintaining with undiminished vigour the rights of the citizens of Montrose to the free use and enjoyment of their golfing course.*

James Bertram

By all accounts the finest golfer in Montrose in the early nineteenth century, Bertram was the first Captain of the club, and no doubt a principal force behind its formation.

Indeed, it is likely that the idea for the club would have been hatched at a meeting of golfers at the Turf Inn on George Street, which James operated with his brother William. This was one of the leading hotels in Montrose at the time, and a place where the gentry first stopped on a visit to the town to stable their horses and have a reviving refreshment.

One of those gentry – James Cruickshank of Langley Park – would team up with Bertram to record Montrose's first famous golf victory against the Honourable Company of Edinburgh Golfers in 1829.

James Bertram held the post of Captain on a further six occasions, those in the 1820s by virtue of being the winner of the Gold Medal. He won the Gold Medal seven times between 1819 and 1840 so he was clearly a formidable golfer for most of his life. On his last triumph in 1840, the *Review* declared that 'he was considered one of the most adept golfers not just on the links at Montrose but on any course'.

Club records have him playing in virtually every competition for the medal and he was ever-present at club dinners and meetings. In the early days, he was also extremely active in introducing new members to the club and helping it to grow.

Bertram had been an officer in the local militia and was known as Captain Bertram in the club records. He was a member of the golf club for nearly forty years. The club does not record his death but his last attendance at a club meeting was in 1847 so it is probable that the club lost two of its stalwarts at around the same time.

James Calvert

James Calvert was the first winner of the Gold Medal and therefore has a particular place of honour in the club's history. He won the Medal again in 1825.

Calvert was Captain three times and played an active role in the club's management, participating in almost all competitions. The 'learned Calvert' mentioned in Alexander Low's poem was a schoolmaster, commonly referred to at the time as a 'dominie'. In 1815 he was Rector of the Grammar School that co-existed with the newly-established Academy.

In his *History of Montrose* (1860) David Mitchell gives a full account of his own education at the Grammar School in the 1810s:

> *Mr Calvert was the one that we stood most in awe of, for he was a powerful man, and it was no joke to incur his displeasure. He would have given a 'dozen of Palmies' at any time ; and we would have been shaking in our shoes if we had not our lessons – it was in fact some times a reign of terror.*

Laying on the tawse – a short leather belt – heavily to the palms of the hands of recalcitrant boys would have been well within the capabilities of a golfer accustomed to hacking a ball out of the whins on the Montrose links. Some of the boys at the Grammar School were boarders in Mr Calvert's house, and Mitchell recalls that 'On Sabbath evening Mr C. took us all out a walk in the links, down from his own house along the golf course, and when we got home we retired to the school-room.'

In spite of his reputation as stern disciplinarian, Calvert must have been highly respected as his former students presented him with a tea service in 1834 to mark his retirement from teaching, and they arranged for his portrait to be painted by a local painter, James Irvine. He died at 63 High Street on 23 December 1856.

We can only speculate on how many Montrose boys took up golf on Calvert's urging, but he certainly passed on a love of the game to his son, James Calvert Jr, who became one of the best amateur golfers in Scotland in the mid-nineteenth century. He won the Gold Medal at Montrose on seven occasions between 1834 and 1847, and won two Medals at St Andrews, and at least one at Monifieth.

Calvert Jr became Montrose Town Provost in 1850, but both his golfing and political career were unfortunately curtailed by bankruptcy. He emigrated to Melbourne where he died in 1878. As such a keen golfer, he doubtless took his clubs with him and may have been one of the earliest golfers in that city.

CHAPTER 4

The Montrose Rules

Stones, bones &c. are not to be removed in order to play a Ball, except on the putting green, and that only within six Club-lengths of the hole.

Rule 4 of the Montrose Golf Club, 1830

The first set of written rules for playing golf in Montrose were set down in the club's minutes in 1830. They are an important contribution to the evolution of the rules of golf that millions of players follow today.

Because there was not yet a single rule-making body, early Scottish clubs established their own codes, based on what had long been practised in their locality, but also influenced by any written rules that other clubs had come up with.

In 1825, for example, the Montrose Golf Club had received an extensive communication from the Thistle Golf Club that played its golf on Leith links near Edinburgh. With their letter, the Thistle sent three copies of their rules and a copy of their 'Historical Account' of the origins and early history of the game of golf. The Montrose club were clearly delighted to receive these and replied in the most glowing terms, indicating that both the Historical Account and Rules would be retained by the club for perusal by members over the forthcoming years.

In formalising their own rules, the golfers at Montrose borrowed a little from the Thistle, and also from Aberdeen, St Andrews and the Honourable Company of Edinburgh Golfers. But they also put their own twist on things. The Montrose Rules, for example, are the first to explicitly ban the stymie (when a ball is blocked by an opponent's ball) in stroke-play competition.

In general, the Montrose Rules can be described as uncompromising. Unlike most other clubs, they offer no relief for loose impediments or plugged balls on what we would call the fairway. Given there was little maintenance at the time, this may well reflect on the excellent quality of the ground for golfing that was so often mentioned by visitors.

The seventeen rules set out on the following pages offer us a fascinating glimpse into the conditions for golf in Montrose at the time. The notes in italics are meant to provide the contemporary reader with some helpful context.

The Montrose Rules of 1830

1   The Ball must be teed not nearer the hole than two Club-lengths, nor further from it than four; and the tee must be on the ground.

There were no separate teeing areas – the ball was teed up on a pile of sand, often taken from the hole just played to.

2   The Ball farthest from the hole, after being struck from the tee, must be first played.

3   The Ball struck from the tee must not be changed before the hole is played out; and if at a loss to distinguish one Ball from another neither of them is to be lifted till both parties agree.

4   Break-clubs such as stones, bones &c. are not to be removed in order to play a Ball, except on the putting green, and that only within six Club-lengths of the hole.

A 'break club' was something that could break a golf club. At this time, St Andrews, Aberdeen, Musselburgh and the Honourable Company of Edinburgh Golfers, all allowed such impediments to be removed anywhere on the course as long as the ball was 'on grass' Most also make special mention of improving the lie of a ball if 'it sticks fast in the ground'. That Montrose golfers felt it unnecessary to make such concessions may well reflect on the fine natural quality of the links.

5   When it is impossible to play the Ball, the player shall be entitled to lift and drop it at such a distance as he thinks proper, behind the hazard and lose one stroke, but where he cannot get behind the hazard, without going off the green, he shall be entitled to drop his Ball on the green, in a line with the place where it lay.

An early unplayable lie rule.

6   Should a Ball get into any hole on the putting green that comes within the denomination of made-holes it shall not be considered a hazard; but in such case, the player is entitled to lift the Ball and drop it behind the hole, and play without losing a stroke.

7   If a Ball on the green is half covered with water or filth, the player is at liberty to take it out, drop it behind the hazard, and play with an iron or putter without losing a stroke, and where the Ball is completely covered with fog, furze, or grass, so much thereof may be set aside as that the player shall have a view of his Ball before he plays.

'On the green' here means on grass on any part of the course. Filth would include sheep or cattle dung. Stipulating that an iron must be used was a significant penalty since iron clubs at the time were used for extracting balls from bunkers, ruts, tracks and other bad lies, and not for distance. St Andrews and other clubs allowed the golfer to tee up the ball and

Montrose seems to be the only club to allow a putter to be used. Again, these suggest that playing conditions at Montrose were less rough than at other courses.

8   When two Balls only are playing, the Ball, betwixt the other and the hole on the putting green, is not to be lifted; but when more than two Balls are playing, or when the match is to be decided by the number of strokes, as in playing for medals or prizes, if one Ball lie on the putting green, betwixt another and the hole, the Ball nearest the hole shall be lifted till the other is played.

Montrose is the first club in the world to specifically ban the 'stymie' in stroke-play competitions – a rule that only became universal in the twentieth century. However, Montrose was also unusual in not allowing any relief whatsoever in match-play – most other clubs allowed lifts if the balls were within six inches of each other.

9   If a ball be stopped by accident, it shall notwithstanding be reckoned as a stroke; but the hole shall be declared lost to the party who may, by himself or his cady, stop or interrupt the Ball of his opponent.

Another example of how the rules are geared to match-play, which was the dominant form of golf at the time.

10   If a ball is lost, the player shall drop another behind the place where it was lost and lose one stroke.

Montrose still resisted the stroke-and-distance penalty of St Andrews – this penalty is closer to today's unplayable lie.

11   Every attempt to strike shall be considered a stroke, whether or not the Club break, touch the ground or pass the Ball.

One of the very first definitions of a 'whiff' which was still not considered a stroke in St Andrews unless the club broke during the swing.

12   At putting, the direction of the hole is not to be marked, but the Ball is to be played honestly for the hole; – all loose impediments, however, may be removed, if within six Club-lengths of the hole.

The word 'honestly' is meant to deter players from deliberately playing away from the hole in order to stymie their opponent or to knock their ball away, croquet style.

13   When several parties are playing over the ground, no stroke shall be played from the tee till each of the advanced party has played his second stroke; and should the party following advance on the latter, they must call out before playing their Ball.

At the time, 'fore!' was generally yelled before a shot, not afterwards, which also helped alert other people using the links that golfers were approaching.

14   In all cases where a Ball is to be dropped, the party dropping shall front the
     hole to which he is playing, and drop the Ball over his head.

     *Since 1984, the golfer has dropped the ball in front of them, at arm's
     length.*

15   Parties are at liberty to ask advice for directions from their partners, or
     cadies, in playing, but not from onlookers, whose observations on the play
     are not to be listened to; and while the one party is prohibited from
     walking before the other, it is understood, that no spectator shall interfere
     in the most distant manner with the game while playing.

     *This is adapted from the Thistle Club Rule Book the Montrose golfers had
     received in 1825.*

16   Disputes, relative to the reckoning of any hole, must be settled before the
     parties strike off for the next hole.

17   All disputes respecting the play shall be referred to the Captain and his
     Council, whose determination shall be binding on the parties.

✻   ✻   ✻

The Club Council agreed that these rules should be printed, and that
'each member is to be provided with a copy and that the pricing of each
copy shall be sixpence which is to be paid at the next annual general
meeting'.

   The club would issue revised rules in 1851 and 1888, but by this time
there was a growing consensus that the rules of golf should be standard-
ised. Accordingly, Montrose decided to adopt the most recent edition of
the rules of the Royal and Ancient Golf Club of St Andrews. There was
one exception however:

     *When a ball lies on clothes or within a club-length of a washing
     tub, the clothes may be drawn from under the ball, and the tub
     may be removed.*

In 1851, the Secretary crossed out the above St Andrews rule; it apparently had no relevance to the more pristine golfing ground of Montrose!

CHAPTER 5

The Royal Patrons

The Prince has graciously acceded to it.

The Rt. Hon. William Gladstone in a letter
to the Montrose Golf Club

The history and fortunes of the Montrose Golf Club changed on 11 April 1845 when it learned that Prince Albert, Consort to the young Queen Victoria, had granted the club his royal patronage.

That it was a signal honour cannot be doubted. Victoria and Albert had become in the eyes of the British public the 'golden couple' who had restored to a high level the monarchy's standing from the low levels it had experienced under their immediate predecessors. In modern day parlance, everyone would have wanted 'a piece of them'.

It was a great boost for a golf club in a small Scottish town, albeit one at the height of its prosperity, to receive this honour from a very popular prince who had not previously granted it to any golf club (nor had he shown any enthusiasm for the game).

It meant that the Montrose Golf Club became only the third golf club in history to be honoured with royal patronage and thereby given the right to call itself 'Royal'.

The Perth Golfing Society was the first, so honoured by William IV in 1833, and he conferred a similar honour on the St Andrews Club in 1834 so that it became the Royal and Ancient Golf Club. Montrose was the next club to be so honoured. (There are now sixty-one 'Royal' golf clubs spread around the world.)

It didn't happen by accident. Certain club officials seemed to have decided to seek this status for the club from the early 1840s. Two members of Royal Perth were made honorary members of Montrose about this time and it may well be that they encouraged the club to seek this honour (as we will later see, Montrose golfers considered their course to be vastly superior to the one in Perth).

Seeking royal patronage became a stated objective for the club in 1843 when members heartily endorsed the following proposal:

The club considering that it would be very gratifying if they could procure the royal authority so as to enable them to rank in the

*same status as the club at Perth and other golfing societies,
resolved to present a dutiful and loyal address to Prince Albert on
the birth of the Prince and remit to the Captain and Councillors to
prepare and transmit the proper address and to use other
measures necessary for attaining the object in view.*

We don't have a copy of the 'loyal address' but we do know that it didn't
sway the Royal Household to grant royal patronage at that time. It was
necessary for the club to resort to the 'other measures' mentioned in the
minutes, and this involved an approach to the Gladstone family.

The Gladstones had moved from England to live at Fasque Estate just
outside the village of Fettercairn, some ten miles from Montrose (their
descendants continued to live there until 2007). John Gladstone, the
eldest son, inherited the estate on the death of his father.

His younger brother, William, whose period at Oxford University
had marked him as a man of considerable talent, suffered considerable
pangs of conscience in rejecting a career in the church and choosing,
instead, a career in politics. He became a Member of Parliament in 1832.
Few though could have foreseen at this early stage of his career that
the same William Ewart Gladstone would become leader of the new
Liberal Party in the 1860s, be Prime Minister of Britain on four separate
occasions, and play a pivotal part in the history of the Montrose Golf
Club.

In 1845 Gladstone was, at only 36 years of age, President of the Board
of Trade in the Conservative government headed by Prime Minister
Robert Peel (another revered politician in Montrose, as witnessed by the
statue which still stands in the centre of town).

Club members turned to John Gladstone, though he was neither a
golfer nor a club member, and, through him, transmitted the following
letter to his brother William. It was sent on 4 April 1845, no doubt
benefiting from the new postal service introduced in 1839 to ensure swift
delivery to London, and included the following appeal:

> *Sir, the members of Montrose Golf Club being desirous of having
> their club honoured by the patronage of Royalty, take the liberty
> of addressing you whose family is extensively connected with this
> neighbourhood, to ask if you will allow an application for that
> purpose to His Royal Highness, Prince Albert, to be sent through
> you.*
>
> *The honour to which the club aspires is to obtain the gracious
> consent of his Royal Highness that it shall in future be styled
> 'The Montrose Royal Albert Golf Club'.*
>
> *The club has existed under its present designation for many years
> and is composed of most of the respectable inhabitants of this
> town. You are probably aware we possess a golf ground
> unequalled by any in Scotland.*

The golf clubs of St Andrews and Perth have both been honoured by being allowed the title of 'Royal'. The Montrose Club does not pretend to rank so high as the former but they consider themselves on an equality with the latter and they therefore hope their claim may be treated with equal consideration as their's was.

If you will be so kind as to consent as to receive our application and present it, and if His Royal highness shall be so gracious as to confer this honour of patronising our club, it will be additional satisfaction to us that this honour shall be obtained to us through one toward whom in common with the public at large, the members entertain the deepest feelings of respect.

Where the loyal address of 1843 failed, this appeal to William Gladstone to use his political connections in London succeeded. In an astonishingly quick time, Gladstone persuaded the Prince's household to agree to the request. He wrote back to the club immediately with the welcome news and his letter was read out by the Captain at a special meeting of the club called for 15 April 1845:

The young William Ewart Gladstone and Prince Albert.

Sir, I have the pleasure to inform you that through Mr Anson, I have brought under the notice of His Royal Highness, the Prince Albert, the wish of the Montrose Golf Club communicated to me in your letter of the 4th and that the Prince has graciously acceded to it without putting you to the trouble of any more formal communication, so that the club is at liberty to assume its amended designation forthwith.

As the minutes record, the grateful club immediately decided to change its name in honour of their new patron:

> *They unanimously resolved to avail themselves of the gracious permission of HR Highness and that the club be hereafter styled Montrose Royal Albert Golf Club. The Captain was further directed to transmit to Mr Gladstone the thanks of the club for the interest he had taken for promoting the object in view and . . . unanimously resolved to request Mr Gladstone to allow his name to be placed in the list of honorary members.*

The club was clearly delighted to announce its new royal status and, presumably with the Town Council's blessing, arranged to have a celebratory dinner in the Guild Hall.

Montrosians however have always had an independent streak; not everyone was pleased that they now had a royal club in their midst. The redoubtable 'J.' who wrote a letter to the *Montrose Review* in 1845, appears not to hold any golfers in high regard, especially those who now belonged to a royal club:

THE GOLF NUISANCE.

DEAR MR. EDITOR,—I hope you will not deny me the privilege you allow your readers of the other sex, of publicly protesting against what I consider a great grievance. There has been much talk lately about the *amenity* of the Commonty or Links: I wish some steps were taken to infuse that quality into those who amuse themselves with golf. I think it very unjust that our much-lauded Links should be monopolized by a few golf clubs and balls; yet such is the case; for I and many other ladies are frequently obliged to curtail our walk because of the risk we encounter from the continual whizzing past of these nasty projectiles; and we have the prospect of soon debarring ourselves entirely from that pleasure, in consequence of the increasing rage for that selfish amusement. I have little doubt we will soon have the 'Prince of Wales Golf Club'—the 'Princess Alice Golf Club'—as well as the Royal Albert Club; and then *we* shall be *clubbed* most effectually out of *our* harmless recreation,—as effectually as the community is at present clubbed out of its amenity or good manners.

Do, good Mr. Editor, try to convince those whose intellect dwells in their arms and hands, that *they* do not compose *the community*—that the Links is not designed for *their* exclusive use—and that, although golfing is the most childish of amusements, it does *not* exempt those who practise it from paying the ordinary marks of respect to my sex,—and you will oblige your constant reader,   JULIA.

P.S.—Dire was the list of evils some imaginative men anticipated on the introduction of a railway train to their golfing preserves; but they forgot that the steam-engine—less poetical, it may be, but decidedly more courteous, than the golf-players—always takes care to sound an alarm when it sees a person of either sex before it—a practice they (the golf-players) would do well to imitate, before they lodge one of their balls in face of an unfortunate pedestrian.   J.

Montrose, July 2, 1845.

A letter to the Review from a 'confirmed' non-golfer.

At some point, Prince Albert agreed to become an honorary member of the club and in 1848 the committee decided that he should receive a Loyal Address from the club. The club was aware that the Royal Family were to holiday in their newly-acquired Highland retreat at Balmoral, and such an Address would also celebrate the royal couple's visit to Scotland.

The Address is very flowery in tone, verging on the sycophantic, but no doubt genuinely reflecting the delight of many in Scotland that the Royal Family were choosing to make Balmoral Castle their holiday home. It thanks the Prince for the great honour he has bestowed on them by allowing the club to use his name in their designation and also 'for the countenance you have thus extended to an ancient and notational sport in which many of the kings of Scotland had been known to participate with enthusiastic pleasure'.

Club Captain James Calvert, who appears to have been the principal author of the Address, had written to ask if he could present it in person at Balmoral Castle. The response from the Prince's secretary was clear: 'HRH Prince Albert does not wish to receive any person during his stay at Balmoral.' The club was told it should forward the Address to him in the usual way, which they did, receiving a brief note of thanks from their Patron.

Edward VII

Following the untimely death of their first Royal Patron in 1863, the club requested that the Prince of Wales become Patron in place of his much-lamented father and he gave his acceptance. He continued as Patron until his death in 1910. After he assumed the throne as Edward VII in 1901, a reply to a communication from the club indicated that 'His Majesty had been graciously pleased to continue to the club the patronage which he had extended as Prince of Wales.'

King George V

In July 1910, the club received a communication from the palace that the new monarch, King George V, was 'graciously pleased to become Patron of the Royal Albert Golf Club, Montrose'.

Prince Philip

When Queen Elizabeth II came to the throne in 1952, the club discovered to its considerable discomfiture that its royal patronage was in question. The club had neglected to make an official application for the royal patronage to be continued during the brief reign of Edward VIII in 1936.

With the accession of George VI later in the year, the club urgently consulted with the Royal and Ancient Golf Club about this lapse, only to be informed by them that the question of royal patronage of clubs was being considered and no official application was therefore required. This advice seems to have been erroneous because, when the Royal Household was approached in 1952 to request the Queen's patronage, the Royal Household queried if royal patronage had in fact been officially conferred in the past. Once the club had written to clarify the position, Her Majesty indicated that Prince Philip was pleased to be the club's Patron, doubtless to much relief all round!

Prince Andrew

Royal patronage of the new club was re-confirmed in 1986 when Prince Philip graciously consented to continue the patronage that he had formerly bestowed on the Royal Albert Club and he also gave his approval to the change of name. In 1996, he indicated that he was withdrawing his patronage, and the club wrote to Prince Andrew, the Duke of York, who readily agreed to become Royal Patron in succession to his father. The club is delighted that this royal patronage continues to the present day and note with pleasure that the Duke of York is the first of our Royal Patrons over the past 165 years to regularly play the game, a pleasure shared by some of the early monarchs of Scotland and England which led golf at one point to be called 'the royal game'.

HRH Prince Andrew, Duke of York, our Royal Patron.
Courtesy of HRH Household.

CHAPTER 6

The Golden Years: Montrose Royal Albert Golf Club, 1845–1910

The Earl of Dalhousie accompanied Messrs Brand and Cunningham on horseback and took a great interest in the play.

London newspaper account of a match
on the links of Montrose, 1872

After thirty-five years in existence, this golf club had made its mark in the local community and, with its royal recognition, far beyond. The next sixty-five years until its centenary are in some respects its 'golden years'. The club draws in more members, many from the great landed families in the area, hosts a series of historic tournaments, engages one of the great figures in Scottish golf as its professional and greenkeeper, and is generally recognised by its contemporaries as one of the foremost golf clubs in the land. It also makes a variety of contributions to the health of a wide variety of other local clubs that would make Montrose Scotland's most active golf community.

Membership grows steadily, but not dramatically, during the second half of the nineteenth century, growing from 55 members in 1844 to 120 in 1888. By then there were five honorary members, still including the Rt. Hon. William Gladstone, by this point a four-times Prime Minister.

Those were healthy numbers in a town with at least half a dozen golf clubs. But a more significant change came in the backgrounds of new members. The club still attracted the main business and professional men of the town but, for the first time, we see large numbers being recruited from the landed and titled families in the area. It is likely that in earlier times many of these would have joined the Keithock Club.

A not untypical minute of October 1865 lists a proposed group of new members:

The Right Honourable John Inglis of Glencorse, Lord Justice Clerk
Harry Maxwell Inglis of Logan Bank, Principal Clerk of Session

George Thomson of Burnhouse
James Hay, Merchant of Leith
Frederick Pitman, Writer to the Signet
John Inverarity of Rosemount

A scrutiny of the lists of Captains in the second half of the century reveals many famous names, including the Earl of Southesk, Lord Kennedy, Lord Arbuthnott, and W.H. Kennedy-Erskine (a grandson of King William IV). The Earl of Dalhousie was elected an honorary member in 1861. In addition to its new royal status, the acquisition of a clubhouse would certainly have been an attraction.

With this new exclusivity comes the first reference (in 1870) to the use of the black ball in the balloting procedure for new members:

> *No ballot shall be valid unless five members are present; one black ball in five shall exclude, two black balls in ten and so in proportion to the number of those who ballot.*

We don't know how the vote was actually conducted in these early years, but in 1878 a ballot box was acquired. The balls used were all white, but any ball placed in the right hand side of the box was counted as a 'black' ball. Once a member had taken a ball and inserted his hand, no one could know where he placed his ball – in the right or left side – so a proposed member could be rejected entirely on anonymous objections.

Members in this period were being introduced from some distant places. They included, for example, Patrick Gibson of the Peruvian Consulate in Liverpool. Officers of the armed forces still continued to be admitted under special terms, usually without paying an entrance fee.

Perhaps feeling in need of spiritual guidance in their golfing affairs, the club in 1861 elected an Honorary Chaplain for the first time, the Rev. Seller. He was one in a long line of clergy who had been members since the club's foundation. In less than a year, he was replaced in this role by Rev. Woodward, who is still recorded as the Honorary Chaplain in 1888. Indeed, at a club meeting in April 1893, no fewer than five ministers are recorded as being in attendance – a statistic unlikely to be surpassed in the future!

The ballot box used at the Royal Albert from 1878 to 1968, which is still displayed in the clubhouse.

Wining and Dining

Up to 1870, club minutes consistently record that, after playing for a medal, the club continued the tradition established in the early period of dining in a local hostelry. The venue continued to be the Star Hotel on most occasions but twice in 1848, for reasons unknown, the club dined in the Royal Hotel before returning to their usual haunt for their regular meetings and dinners.

More insight into the nature of these social gatherings can be seen in the minute of April 1856:

> *After the competition, members sat down to dinner in the Star Hotel, Captain Jamie in the chair, Adam Burness acting as Croupier, and the evening spent in a happy and an agreeable manner and the company separated about eleven o'clock. After the usual loyal toasts had been given . . . a few matches were made by some members to come off on an early day.*

Doubtless many of these matches made 'in drink' were accompanied by wagers!

Club patronage was still valued by those organising public entertainments in the town, and the club at this time seemed keen to support community events. In April 1848, there was 'an application from Mr Cook of the circus for the patronage of the club on some future night, whereupon the club unanimously agreed to the request and appointed Tuesday first for that purpose'.

Two years later, a meeting was called to respond to 'an application having been made by Mr Pollock, the present lessee of the theatre in the Thistle Hall, to the Captain requesting that the club would honour with their patronage a play in the theatre'. The suggestion seems to have delighted club members who unanimously agreed to the request and 'gave their countenance to use their influence in obtaining for the lessee a Bumper House'.

With the acquisition of a first clubhouse at Southfield in 1865, club meetings were now invariably held there but, up to 1870 at least, the club still met for dinner after Medal competitions in the Star Hotel. After that date, no mention of club dinners is recorded. Perhaps the practice died out, though the club rules printed in 1888 continued to state that, on the days of competition for the three Medals, 'members will dine together in such place as may have been fixed upon at the General meeting'. They may have dined in the clubhouse, at least after the move to larger premises in 1890.

The Southfield clubhouse did provide a place for members to lunch before playing for the Medals, and refreshments were certainly served there all year round. A rule passed in 1870 decreed that no refreshments be supplied after 9 p.m. in the summer months and after 6 p.m. in the winter.

In July 1887, the Master of Arbuthnott proposed 'that the lunch on medal days be free to those playing for the medal, liquor excepted, but members bringing friends must pay for their friend's lunch'. There is no record of this interesting idea being agreed but it does confirm that the tradition of members meeting for lunch with ample liquor consumed prior to playing for the Medal was continuing in these times.

As for the ladies after 1845, there is no mention at all of social events being organised to involve the ladies, so we can reasonably assume the men were content with their all-male gatherings.

There was some golf played, too, of course. The historic tournaments organised by the club during this period are discussed in another chapter, but the club also added several competitions for its own members, many of which are still on the fixture list today.

The Albert Medal

In 1845 over £6 was raised by subscription to buy a silver medal for a new competition. Events, however, overtook this idea; when the club gained its royal patronage later that year, it promptly decided to purchase a medal instead to honour their Royal Patron. An aspiring member, James Fitzimmon Scott of Commieston, made a substantial subscription towards the purchase of the same (and was promptly admitted as a member without having to pay the usual entrance fee).

The competition for the Albert Gold Medal immediately became the second most important golf event in Montrose, and the *Review* reported on the very first contest on 1 November 1845:

> The club, having procured a richly executed and very beautiful
> gold medal, Wednesday was appointed for the first competition
> for the golden reward; when, after a keen contest, it was carried
> off by Mr John Jamie of Richards & Co Linen works. In the
> afternoon, the club – its Captain Patrick Mason in the chair and
> Alex Cowie Esq Croupier – dined sumptuously in the Star inn.

The *Standard's* report on the play for the Albert Medal in 1846 evokes the exciting atmosphere surrounding these competitions:

> On Wednesday we saw one of our old national Scottish sports
> come off in a style far superior to anything we have ever wit-
> nessed. The sport to which we refer is golf. The gentlemen who
> engaged in this sport were all animation, and the spectators took
> a deep interest in it, and a few novices were almost petrified when
> they saw the ball, with an apparently irresistible force, pass
> through the air. The competitors in this exercise exerted every
> nerve to gain the prize (Prince Albert Medal) which, after a keen
> and manly contest, was awarded to James Calvert, Esq., he taking
> the seventeen holes in ninety-three strokes. In a word, golfing is
> the most natural, and has the most chastening, absorbing, and
> purifying effect, and its reminiscences are by far the most delight-
> ful of any that flicker in the mind, as we look with regret on the
> pleasures that are past.
>   After the competition, the members of the club dined in the
> Star-Inn – Mr Mason, Captain, in the chair, and Mr Calvert,

*croupier. The Chairman was supported on the right by our worthy
Provost, and on the left by David Greenhill, Esq., Charleton, and
the whole proceedings were conducted in that pleasing spirit and
interchange of courtesy which always characterises the Golf Club.*

The club also sought advice, possibly for the first time, from the Royal
and Ancient Golf Club in St Andrews on whether a previous Medal winner could compete again for the same Medal the following year. This is
an interesting recognition of the growing status of the R&A as the
supreme arbiter on the game. The Royal Albert accepted the advice
received from St Andrews and allowed Medal winners to play for and to
win the same Medal, but decreed that the same person could not win
both Medals in the same year.

Three years later when James Lindsay won the Gold Medal, he
declined the prize (as he had already won the Albert Medal) and those in
joint second place – Robert Trail and Robert Cowie – were forced to play
another full round of 17 holes to decide the winner. Unfortunately, for
the first recorded time in the club's history, James Calvert Jr, the previous
year's winner, had forgotten to bring the medal along to the dinner so
Robert Trail had to wait for another occasion to be invested.

In July 1905, the club agreed to engrave winners' names on the medals
and, as a consequence of this decision, the original Albert Medal went
missing – the only one of the club's first medals and trophies to suffer this
fate. What seems to have transpired was that the medal was won by
R.C.H. Millar in 1905 and taken back by Club Secretary Joseph Galloway,
so that Millar's name could be engraved on it. Millar won it again in 1906
and claimed he had returned it to the Secretary but Galloway denied he
had ever received it. Both gentlemen set out their positions in detailed letters to the Council in 1908 but the mystery of the disappearing medal had
some further twists that are taken up in a later chapter.

The Keithock Medal

The continued rise in the fortunes of the club seems to have meant the
demise of the Keithock Club, which had been home to the sort of
Montrose-area gentry who were now quite happy to join the Royal
Albert. In October 1869, the Royal Albert minutes report that:

*Mr A. Duncan, the only member of the Keithock Golf Club,
proposed that all members of the club be constituted members of
the Keithock Club and that the Keithock medal be played for on
the last Thursday of July annually.*

In readily accepting this offer, the club thus acquired its third Gold
Medal for play but in rather sad circumstances, in that it marked the
demise of 'the other club' – the Keithock – with which it had shared
the links for the past forty-seven years. The first Royal Albert winner of

Keithock Medal.

the Keithock Medal, still competed for annually in the club, was George
Keith of Usan with a score of 98 strokes for the 18 holes.

Early handicap competitions

Though the idea had been discussed by the Club Council as early as
1839, the first record of a handicap system being used in a stroke-play
contest occurs in 1851, when a handicap sweepstake was played alongside the Gold Medal. Over the next eleven years, the results of these
sweepstake competitions are recorded in the minutes by the admirably
efficient Secretary, William Alexander.

When Alexander himself won the sweepstake in 1860, the press report
noted that he had 'saved six strokes on the number named by the committee, while all the other competitors were above'.

We can get a better idea of what this meant by looking at the relevant
extract from the minutes of 1852 (shown opposite).

It shows that nine players paid 2s 6d each to enter the sweepstake and
the winner therefore gained £1 2s 6d. Notice the use of the word 'gainer'
entered opposite the winning score – this is the term consistently used in
this period to denote the winner.

In this early handicapping system, it seems that the committee set each
player a target score based on his perceived abilities and awarded the
sweepstake to the person who bettered it by the greatest margin. On this
occasion, only one player gained a single shot, the other eight players fell
short of their target by a total of 79 strokes. Handicap Secretaries
through the ages might consider this result to be evidence of a fair handicapping system; golfers then as now might disagree!

№	Name	Strokes allowed	Strokes Played	Gain	Loss	
№ 1	Mr Robert Cowie	106	105	1	0	Lame
2	Mr Robert Armit	106	108	"	2	
3	Mr Alexander Cowie	106	112	"	6	
4	Mr James Cruickshank	114	121	"	7	
5	Mr Robert Trail	106	113	"	7	
6	Mr John James	98	107	"	9	
7	Mr Samuel Thomson	106	118	"	12	
8	Mr Hay	106	122	"	16	
9	Mr James C. Lindsay	102	121	"	19	

Handicap. 9 Players @ 2/6 each L1. 2. 6

Results of a handicap sweepstake in 1852, from club minutes.

In April 1857, Samuel Thomson of Broughty Ferry won the Gold Medal with a score of 99 over the 17 holes and also won the sweepstake because he gained three strokes on his 102 'strokes allowed'. The report of the dinner that followed play that day lists a series of matches that 'were agreed to be played':

> *Match No 1*
> Mr Samuel Thomson, agreed to play Mr William Mitchell for a bottle [of] wine, the former giving the latter 13 strokes on the round of 17 holes.
>
> Messrs Mackie and Smith back Mr Mitchell against Mr Cruickshank backing Mr Thomson, on the match, for a bottle of wine, to be played on Saturday this 2nd of May at twelve o'clock noon.
>
> Result of the Match   Mr Thomson   118 stokes
>   Mr Mitchell   <u>127</u> strokes
>   Difference   9
>   Mr Mitchell gains by 4 strokes
>   Allowance given 13 strokes

<u>Match No 2</u>
Mr Alexander Cowie agreed to play Captain McNeil, giving the Captain half a stroke a hole, the strokes to be taken with alternate holes for a bottle [of] wine, match to be played within a Month. Mr Jamie backs Mr Cowie against the captain backing himself for a bottle wine.

The match was played on the 30th May when the result was as follows.

Mr Cowie	*112 strokes*
Captain McNeil	<u>*113 strokes*</u>
difference	*1 stroke*
allowance	*8 strokes on the round by agreement, the Captain gaining by 7 strokes.*

<u>Match No 3</u>
Mr Jamie bets Mr Robert Cowie that for the first fifteen rounds he (RC) goes round the course, he will not come in under 100 strokes, for five shillings.

Result. Mr Robert Cowie played 17 rounds up to the 30th May when he came in with 99 strokes, consequently losing the match.

Mr Foote bets a bottle of wine against Provost Mackie that Mr Jamie will beat Mr Cowie, if Jamie wins Foote loses.

<u>Match No 4</u>
Provost Mackie bets Mr Gray on equal terms for a bottle [of] wine over the short course of 13 hole, within a month.

<u>Match No 5</u>
Mr Mitchell plays Mr Robert Cowie for a bottle of wine with one stroke in favour of Mr Mitchell, within a month.

<u>Match No 6</u>
Provost Mackie plays Mr Mitchell on equal terms for a bottle of wine around the short course of 13 holes.

Such match arrangements were possibly a common part of every club dinner in this period but were not usually recorded. They show not only the challenge and the side stake but also the number of holes to be played – note the use of a short course of thirteen holes for some matches – and varying kinds of handicapping used to determine the outcome of the matches. Above all, they also offer us a good insight into the camaraderie and enjoyment members gained from membership of their golf club.

Match number three is fascinating. John Jamie, who was Captain at the time, threw down a most unusual challenge to his good friend,

Robert Cowie: he wagered five shillings that in his next fifteen rounds, Robert would not break 100. Note the remarkable fact that, between 29 April and 30 May, Robert played seventeen rounds – an indication of how frequently some golfers played at this time – and only on the seventeenth occasion did he break 100. Although he lost the challenge and the five shillings, he certainly wins our respect for pure determination!

The first handicap match-play competition was played in 1889 on the suggestion of two members, Alex Foote and Robert Millar, who provided a handsome trophy for the winner.

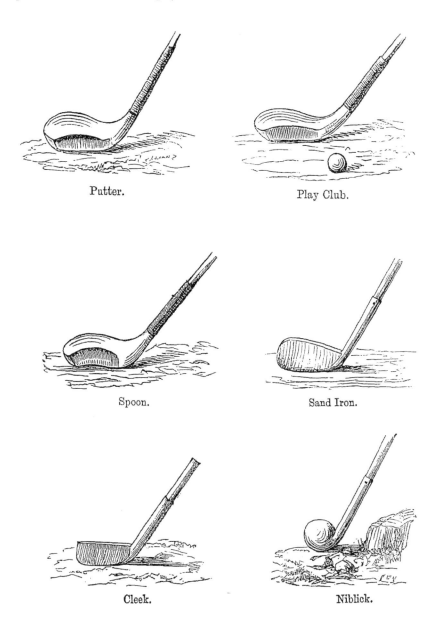

The type of golf clubs that would have been used in Montrose in the mid-nineteenth century, as depicted in a men's magazine from that time.

Putter.

Play Club.

Spoon.

Sand Iron.

Cleek.

Niblick.

The 1890 medal. The engraving on the reverse is of the newly-opened Stonebridge clubhouse.

By 1889 handicaps were being expressed by a number as they are today, though the player with the greater handicap would start that number of holes up in the match rather than being awarded strokes on particular holes.

No sooner was there a handicap match-play trophy introduced than a Medal for handicap stroke-play was available, presented to the club in 1890 by another two members, the Reverends Duncan and St Clair. This was played for alongside the Albert Medal and the first winner of this Handicap Medal was a Mr A. Smith who returned a net score of 87 playing off a handicap of 6. They certainly did not dally around the course, because after play for the medal concluded that day, the first round of the Foote-Millar was played, eight first-round matches in total. This 1890 Medal, as it became known, is another that is still competed for today and is the fifth oldest of our trophies and medals.

In some ways the most exotic trophy played for is the Rangoon Trophy, donated in 1897

The Rangoon Trophy.

by R.H. Adamson of Rangoon. Who Mr Adamson was, why he was in Burma and why he wanted to donate a trophy to the club, are not now known. But his trophy is still played for, more than a century later, according to the original rules: 'It was agreed it should be played for annually in June and that it should be a bogey competition.'

Adding an Eighteenth Hole

In October 1863, after 52 years of playing for the Medals over seventeen holes, this rather terse statement appears with reference to arrangements for playing for the forthcoming Albert Medal: 'The meeting resolved that on the occasion of the competition the holes shall be restricted to 18.'

A similar entry appears in relation to the Gold Medal competition in May 1864. In making this change, the club was coming into line with established practice at St Andrews and elsewhere, and 18 holes it has been ever since – with one very notable exception, the remarkable 25-hole golf tournament in 1866, discussed elsewhere.

Scoring in Medal competitions around this time becomes noticeably lower, whether due to a better standard of player, improved equipment, a better-prepared or shorter golf course – we can only speculate. Whereas winning scores had rarely been as low as 90, we find in July 1884 the first recorded score under 80 in a club Medal – a magnificent 77 by Patrick Chalmers, whose achievement should not go unrecorded.

Club history was again made a year later when the club decided to play Medals on a Thursday. Wednesday had been the chosen day from the club's inception, but the minutes note that 'being a half holiday, the links are most inconveniently crowded on the afternoon of that day'. This refers to the fact that shops in Montrose were closed on Wednesday afternoons (many still are). One of the surviving clubs of the town, the Caledonian, actually started life as the Half-Holiday Club, attracting shopkeepers who couldn't play golf on Saturday because of work demands.

The Forfarshire Challenge Cup

In 1869 the Royal Albert decided to set up the first inter-club match with the recently-formed Dalhousie Club in Carnoustie (though whether the 1829 challenge match with the two golfers from the Honourable Company was the club's first inter-club match is a moot point).

The impetus for this new match came from the Hon. Charles Carnegie MP, who gave a trophy – known as the Forfarshire Challenge Cup – for the match, to be played once each year in July, alternating the venue between Montrose and Carnoustie. The growth of the railway system made matches with golf clubs elsewhere much more feasible, and several other clubs in Montrose – including the Union, Mercantile and the Victoria – had already played clubs in other nearby towns.

There was no doubt a class element at play here, as the Dalhousie Club aimed to attract a similar stratum of society as the Royal Albert. Charles Carnegie purchased a handsome book which is still in the possession of the club, in which he set out the rules for this challenge and recorded the scores in each of the years it was played. He was also a member of the Dalhousie Club and became that club's third Captain in 1870, the year the match began. He was Captain of the Royal Albert around the same time.

The first match was staged in Montrose on 27 July 1870, on the day preceding play for the newly-acquired Keithock Medal. It was a stroke-play event rather than the match-play format that characterises inter-club matches today. Seventeen Royal Albert members played and eleven from the Dalhousie Club made the journey northwards from Carnoustie, the large numbers a clear illustration of the enthusiasm generated by this new event, and all doubtless enjoyed the social aspect also. A Dalhousie member, Mr W.C. Thomson, carried off the new trophy on behalf of his club with a score of 86 strokes.

Enthusiasm waned somewhat in later years – only two Royal Albert members travelled to Carnoustie in 1871 and 1873 – but participation improved in the years up to 1883 which was the last year that the match appears to have been played.

The 1872 match at Montrose was quite fully reported in the *Scotsman*. The tribulations of Mr Brand at the notorious 'Gully' hole are confirmation of the terrors of that hole, and the image of the Earl imperiously watching proceedings from horseback is one that is readily conjured up. The report also suggests that golfers from Panmure Club in

The Forfarshire Cup.

Golfers playing on Carnoustie links, opposite the Dalhousie clubhouse in about 1890.

> MONTROSE.—GOLF COMPETITION.—On Wednesday, the silver cup presented by the Hon Charles Carnegie, M.P., for competition among the members of the Royal Albert (Montrose), the Dalhousie (Carnoustie), and the Panmure (Monifieth) Golf Clubs was played for on Montrose Links. Seven couple appeared on the ground, and the weather was very favourable. The play, on the whole, was scarcely up to the mark, and when all had come in it was found that the cup had been won by Mr G. Gibson (of the Dalhousie Club) with a score of 94. The next lowest scorers were Messrs Brand and Cunningham, also of the Dalhousie Club, who tied at 96. Mr Brand played an excellent round until he came to the "gully" hole, where he "heeled" his ball into the bents and lost it, and getting still further into grief he took 11 to the hole. The Hon C. Carnegie was among the competitors, and the Earl of Dalhousie accompanied Messrs Brand and Cunningham on horseback, and took a great interest in the play.

Monifieth were also involved (but since the newspaper reported that the winner was a Mr G. Gibson when, in fact, it was a Mr G. Gilroy who won the trophy that year, the newspaper may have been confused about that also; there is no mention of Panmure Club golfers in Charles Carnegie's record book).

The last winner, in 1883, was a Mr Cunningham of the Dalhousie Club. The rules dictated that the trophy stayed with that club until it was competed for again; as this particular match was not to be revived again until 1967, it had a long stay in Carnoustie.

Lending a Hand: The Royal Albert's links with other local clubs

While the Royal Albert became a more exclusive club in this period, it nevertheless contributed greatly to the development of golf in the town. Unlike many clubs in other parts of Britain with a similarly upper class make up, it never sought to purchase its own land to create a private golf course.

Instead, it continued to maintain the public links out of its own purse and thereby enabled many other golf clubs to come into being. Before 1845, the Keithock Club seems to have been the only other club in the area, but after royal patronage was gained there was a veritable explosion in the number of clubs that came into existence in Montrose.

Many of the clubs were just as defined by occupation or social standing as the Royal Albert. The Union Club – the result of merger of the Weavers and Flaxdressers Clubs – obviously emerged from the mills in the town. The Star Golf Club seems to have been aimed at merchants and shopkeepers who couldn't play golf on Saturdays, and the Victoria existed on a social scale somewhere between the Star and the Royal Albert. There were also short-lived clubs based around churches, individual mills, holiday visitors and even the Sunnyside Lunatic Asylum. And of course a Ladies Club came on the scene in 1891.

The Royal Albert was the obvious model for new clubs to copy, whether it be the adoption of its rules (as the Victoria and Caledonian both did initially), or the use of Bob Dow for lessons or to lay out their course on Medal Day.

The club made many other concrete gestures of support to the other clubs that sprang up in Montrose.

The most successful of the early clubs was the Mechanics Club – it became part of the Mercantile Club towards the end of the century – and the Royal Albert seems to have encouraged this club at every turn. As the name suggests, it was a club primarily for the mechanics who maintained the equipment in the several mills in the town, some of which would be owned or managed by the Royal Albert members.

It was founded in 1846 and, on a Friday of that year, the *Review* reported that the members were to play on the Saturday for 'the silver medal presented by several members of the Royal Albert golf club to the Mechanics Golf club. . . . The competition is expected to excite a great deal of interest and keen competition as there are about forty members belonging to the club, and several of them are good players'.

A month later there was more to report: 'A match of golf among the working classes came off on Saturday, for a set of clubs and a dozen golf balls – the gift to the working classes of Messrs Calvert, Davie, Pithie and Thomson.' Names of Royal Albert members again figure prominently in this list of donors (and what suitable prizes these were for those embarking upon the national game). The reporter waxed enthusiastically about the play that day:

> *Upwards of forty competitors on the ground; the concourse of spectators was pro-di-gi-ous. . . . It is a pleasing sight to see so many of our working population assemble, after the labours of the week, upon the green sward to engage in the national game – Scotch, if you will, from tip to toe. . . . If one link – one circumstance – binds in the thread of common interest the lowly and the humble, long may this game excite a fellow feeling amongst its lovers.*

This was not a 'one-off' gift of golf equipment to the Mechanics Golf. In 1850, there is another report that 'the next competition for two clubs and nine balls, presented by Mr Traill and other gentlemen of the Royal Albert will take place on the 8th of June'.

The *Review* later that same year reported:

> *A numerous and spirited competition by the members of the Mechanics club took place on Saturday, for prizes awarded periodically by certain members of the Montrose Royal Albert Club. Upwards of 30 good players started and the honours were awarded not according to the number of strokes but to the comparative success of the players to a standard previously fixed on.*

Notice that this newly-formed Mechanics Golf Club had evolved some rudimentary handicap system, one almost certainly based on the practice of the Royal Albert, that agreed a score for each player based on their abilities and awarded prizes to those who bettered it by the greatest margin.

In other press reports of similar competitions in this period, prizes on offer included golf clubs, balls, books, a ring, and 'a model of a ship'. In 1871 the Mechanics Club members competed for eleven prizes in total:

> *The first prize was a snuff box, second and third prizes were gingerbread loaves, and the remainder consisted of cash and golf balls.*

For the record, the winners of the gingerbread loaves were Thomas Forbes and James Strachan!

The Montrose Ladies Club, founded in 1889, also received considerable assistance from the Royal Albert, which genuinely seems to have welcomed all of these new clubs and was clearly happy to see more golfers on the links that it still maintained and on which, until near the end of the century, allowed play free of charge. Royal Albert members' subscriptions also funded the employment of Robert Dow, whose services as a golf teacher were available to most of this generation of new golfers.

In another important development, in 1889, two Royal Albert members, Captain Boothby and Morton Campbell, presented a Challenge Shield for annual competition between golfers in all the clubs in Montrose.

It was to be known as the Boothby Challenge Shield and, outwith the war years, has been competed for every year since, being the trophy awarded to the Links Champion – arguably the best golfer in the town in a particular year.

The original set of rules laid down that it should be open to members of all clubs in Montrose and any new clubs formed in the future, and that it should be a singles tournament decided by match-play. The first winner was Alexander (Sandy) Keillor, a very fine golfer of the period who was a Mercantile Club member. After honing their skills for this competition, many players embarked on highly successful careers as club professionals in England, America, Australia and Canada.

While it is still keenly competed for today, and the responsibility for the arrangements now fall to Montrose Golf Links Ltd, it is hard to appreciate how popular the competition for this Challenge Shield was among Montrose golfers. Local newspapers carried weekly reports of the various matches played – the *Review* in 1910 records that a crowd exceeding 3000 watched the final that year.

It is a sign of how far other clubs had come that Royal Albert members – though frequent entrants – were not good enough to seriously challenge for the trophy until well after the First World War. Yet up to the 1970s, it was the Royal Albert that continued to organise the competition and supply the prizes.

But any account of the club's contribution to golf in Montrose must culminate in the remarkable generosity of William Jameson Paton.

Jameson Paton was a member of the Royal Albert for over 30 years. He may be best remembered as the owner of Paton's Mill, at one time providing employment for over a thousand workers in the town. He supported golf in Montrose in a number of ways, personally overseeing some course improvements, providing medals for the Academy, lending the Royal Albert money when they were in tight spots and serving as its Captain three times. But nothing really compares to his remarkable gift to the Mercantile Golf Club – not a trophy, or a Medal, or a loan, but an *entire clubhouse*.

Built for the sum of £800, the clubhouse was opened in 1904 with all the town's worthies attending. The building, Jameson Paton said, was to be handed over 'with no restrictions or conditions whatsoever'.

Many of its members were his employees, and after more or less absorbing the Mechanics and Union clubs, the 'Merky' had some 240 members and no suitable facilities. According to a local newspaper report, at the opening ceremony for the new clubhouse, Jameson Paton stated:

> *He wanted to show his esteem for the working classes in Montrose. . . to promote and foster the enjoyable game of golf*

The Boothby Challenge Shield. Note the inset of a typical golfing scene from 1890 with the caddies still carrying their golfer's clubs under their arms.

among them. . . . [Spending time at the club would be] a far more sensible way of spending their leisure time than by frequenting public houses, sitting in stuffy rooms, meeting objectionable company and partaking of refreshments that were neither agreeable to the palate or conducive to health.

Modern day golfers, possibly even some of those early golfers themselves, might not see golf club membership as totally excluding all these 'undesirable' activities!

The Mercantile Clubhouse gifted by Royal Albert member, Jameson Paton. The boys in front were caddies. Courtesy of William Coull.

Golf House, Montrose.

Professional Bob Dow, with Royal Albert members Jameson Paton, Kennedy Erskine and Morton Campbell posing outside the Stone Bridge clubhouse. Courtesy of the Montrose Society.

The Royal Albert All Rounder: Harry Renny Tailyour

Colonel Harry Renny Tailyour, who became a Royal Albert member in 1889, enjoys the unique distinction of being the only Scot to have represented Scotland in football and rugby, winning a solitary cap in each, both against England.

He was a member of one of the leading families in Montrose, residing at Dubton House just outside the town. He was an accomplished athlete, a cricketing all-rounder who played for Kent and the MCC, a footballer and rugby player.

The rugby international against England was held in 1872, and the football international was held at the Oval cricket ground a year later – the first official international between the rivals (he also played in the first unofficial international in 1871). Although Scotland were beaten 2–4, Henry Renny Tailyour had the enviable distinction of scoring Scotland's first-ever goal against 'the auld enemy', an achievement of which Scotland's football team supporters may not be aware, but one which might give them good cause to chant his name.

Renny Tailyour remained a member of the golf club until his death in 1920, though, for most of the last two decades of his life, he was resident in Dublin, occupying the prestigious (and, some might say, enviable) position of Managing Director of the Guinness Company.

Club Organisation: The Rise and Fall of William Alexander

In 1847, the club separated the posts of Secretary and Treasurer for the first time when Robert Cowie replaced Thomas Barclay as Secretary and John Jamie was appointed Treasurer. A payment of one guinea was made a year later to Thomas Barclay's clerks, 'as a small remuneration for the trouble they have had in performing the duties of the club'. This is a confirmation that at least some club Secretaries in these times directed their lowly-paid clerks to take on some mundane tasks of club administration.

Robert Cowie was Secretary for a year only before pleading to be relieved due to pressure of work (he was a doctor). The club then agreed to something quite unique to fill the vacant Secretary's post. John Jamie proposed

> *Mr William Alexander as an ordinary member of the club with the view of his acting as permanent secretary and in consideration of the services already tendered to the club and offered by him for the future, the meeting direct his entry and annual fees to be dispensed with.*

What prior services William Alexander had performed for the club are unclear (perhaps he was one of Thomas Barclay's clerks), but the club now had a Secretary who had been 'fast tracked' into club membership and was also being paid a form of honorarium. The club was becoming more professional and, due in part to William Alexander's efficiency, there is a noticeable rise in the quality of the club's administration from this point. John Jamie was not prepared to continue as Treasurer after 1858 and, for the next five years until 1863, the club returned to the earlier practice of having a joint Secretary/Treasurer in the person of William Alexander.

He has a further claim to fame. Though certainly not the best golfer in the club, he was an ever-present competitor at medal competitions and, as the following extract reveals, his sole triumph was marked by a determination to play the game in all conditions that modern-day golfers might do well to emulate. He himself provides an account of the competition for the Albert Medal on 24 October 1855:

> *The day was so inauspicious for golfing that the members*
> *from Dundee and the other towns were prevented from making*
> *their appearance. . . . The Montrose members, some by*
> *indisposition and others from the inclemency of the weather,*
> *declined to take any part in the day's play, the result of which was*
> *that the Secretary of the club was the only party who could be*
> *prevailed upon to start and therefore had to walk the course,*
> *coming in at 105 strokes, for the usual number of 17 holes.*

Those who know what a very stormy day on the Montrose Links can be like in late October can salute his achievement.

For the club historian, Alexander is an attractive figure for he, among all of the club's early Secretaries, wrote the clearest and most informative minutes, almost as if he knew they might be preserved for posterity.

He was the first Secretary to record every score in the medal competitions and, on each occasion, he even worked out the average score, making him one of the earliest golf statisticians. So it is with sadness that we must report that Alexander's time with the club seems to have ended less than amicably. Perhaps his extended tenure in these posts caused him to believe that he was indispensable and to resent any criticism. In reading between the lines of his final minute of a meeting in June 1863, there are clear indications of serious dissent and questions raised, hinting at possible mis-management of the club accounts. In the minute of the next meeting, the first for many years not written in his distinctive hand, there is a curt entry:

> *The meeting, understanding that the Secretary had resigned his*
> *office, appointed WS Strachan to the office of Interim Secretary.*

Club Rules

In 1888 the club reprinted an up-to-date version of its (now twenty-eight) rules, including complete lists of Medal winners and current members (a copy is held in the club records). The management of the club was still vested in the Captain, three Medal holders, two Councillors, a Secretary and Treasurer. Captain and Councillors could serve for a total of two years but had to be re-elected annually at the general meeting.

The Secretary soon discovered that printing the rules in booklet form did not limit further changes. Within two years, there were various amendments and new rules added, including one prohibiting dogs from being brought into the clubhouse 'under a penalty of 2/6 which the steward is hereby authorised to levy'.

In 1896, club rules were changed to allow for the appointment of five Councillors instead of two. In a further sign that club business was taking up more time, it was agreed that meetings were now to be held on the day preceding the Medal competitions (though this did not always happen).

The front cover of the 1888 Rule Book.

Finances

Funding the club was to be very much dominated by the clubhouse sagas, described more fully in another chapter, but in the early part of this period it was not yet the major issue it was later to be.

In 1845, the annual subscription 'for members who play the game' was fixed at three shillings, while 'gentlemen members who do not play the game' were charged two shillings, an indication the club did seem to have a number of social members. The entrance fee (raised to fifteen shillings in 1866) was much higher than the annual subscription, which shows how important recruitment of new members was to the financial health of the club.

The first surviving set of club accounts is dated April 1853 and appears to have been compiled for the annual general meeting by the Treasurer, John Jamie. They show that the club now had a bank account with the Montrose Savings Bank and reveal both the balances and the total expended, presumably on the course and on club management, for the years 1852 and 1853. By today's standards, these amounts are very modest.

A cash-book showing income and expenditure in more detail was brought in use from 1861. The largest sums appear to have been spent on printing circulars, payment for advertisements in the local newspapers for the Medal competitions and 'various expenses' at dinners in the Star Hotel, offering quite a clear picture of their priorities at this time.

But the golfing needs of the club – and the wider community – were far from forgotten.

In 1861 there are three payments to 'fore cadies', one of two shillings and two of one shilling, plus 'an allowance for two boys', presumably to assist the greenkeeper, Thomas Grundison, who was paid a half-yearly salary of £1 10s. He was replaced by Bob Dow in 1863, who received the same level of payment as his predecessor. This is the first mention of Bob who would go on to play such a pivotal role in the development of golf in Montrose as the club's first professional and club keeper.

Other golf course expenditure items in 1861 included '6 pence for making holes'. In 1863 the club records spending '3/9 replacing flags, Mr Hastie', and in 1864 it paid five shillings to a Mr Japp for 'flags and rods'. In 1864, a James Gordon was paid ten shillings for 'cutting whins' which, taking relative costs into account, must have entailed a substantial whin-clearance programme.

John Hastie did not only provide flags, it seems. He was also the landlord of the Star Inn and the club made two payments to him for 'refreshments'.

There are also expenses for the competition on 27 April 1864 for the Gold Medal that cast some light on how play was organised. There was five shillings to 'Mr Greig for use of the tent at the competition' and seven shillings to 'Robert Dow for expenses of tent'. This is the only reference to the hire of a tent, and we may assume Robert Dow was dispensing the drinks. The club clearly desired a hospitality base beside the course for their major golfing events and, given this, we may better understand why they took steps to acquire a clubhouse a year later.

By 1880, the club reported a balance of over £41 and it was agreed that the remaining debt of £50 be paid off immediately. By 1887, the club had a balance of £136.

In December 1888, just as the club were about to explore the idea of a new clubhouse, the Treasurer, Jamieson Paton, presented a summary of the balance sheet, set out on page 72, which is the only example available to us from that period.

It is interesting to note the entry of £5 for rent of the clubhouse – this was payment of rent from the Star Inn Golf Club (one of the many new clubs that Robert Dow took a keen interest in) to have use of the clubhouse before and after their competitions. The bar in the clubhouse also appears to be operating at a substantial profit, indicating that members were making use of the facility throughout the year.

Non-payment of fees was a recurring issue, and in 1893 it was so considerable that two members were appointed to work with the Treasurer in obtaining payment of arrears. In 1896, the club decided to post the names of those in arrears in the clubhouse.

In 1870, there is the first mention in the minutes of an issue that was to continue to trouble the club for the next thirty years – that of visitors and the fees they paid. Initially, the club laid down some rules for guests of members who wished to use the clubhouse facilities; if the stay was to be longer than two days, the guest would have to pay 2/6 for a week.

As the nineteenth century progressed and golf was being played by many more people, the number of golfing visitors to the town became a veritable flood. The Royal Albert had its share of these visitors using the clubhouse. On at least eight occasions over the next forty years, the club considered its charges for visitors, now seen as a good source of additional revenue. The issues which arose then are well known to clubs nowadays – how to balance the needs of members and visiting golfers, and how high to set charges so as not to discourage visitors from coming to Montrose.

The 1888 Club accounts, from the club minutes.

CHAPTER 7

The 25-Hole Open and Other Historic Tournaments

A golf competition open to all players, including professionals, shall take place on the Montrose Links, over twenty-five holes, being one round of the golfing course.

Advertisement in the *Scotsman*, 1866

During its golden age, the Royal Albert was among a handful of clubs that organised the very first golf tournaments. These laid the groundwork for the major championships that are so important to the popularity of the game today. Though possessing perhaps the largest and best golf facility in the world at the time, Montrose was somewhat removed from the tightly-knit golfing fraternities of St Andrews, Edinburgh, Musselburgh and Prestwick. So the Royal Albert's remarkable tournaments were a way of promoting both the stature of the club, and the excellence of golf in Montrose, to the rest of the country. However, the club's first involvement in a tournament was to be 'across the water' in St Andrews.

The Grand National Golf Club Tournament of 1857

In 1857, golf history was made and the Royal Albert was part of it. The club participated in the Grand National Golf Club Tournament in St Andrews, the first event of its kind, which helped to trigger the idea of another national tournament, the Open Championship, three years later.

Two amateurs represented each club, paying a £2 entry fee: Messrs Robert Cowie and D.C. Thomson represented the Royal Albert. Matches were over 30 holes – one round of the links, and a further six holes out and back.

The Royal Albert pair lost quite heavily to Royal Burgess in the first round and were eliminated from the tournament, which was eventually won by the only English entrant, the Royal Blackheath Golf Club, defeating the Royal and Ancient by seven holes.

Competitors in the 1857 tournament at St Andrews. Courtesy of William Coull.

The Claret jug carried off by Blackheath in 1857.

Although historic in retrospect, it seems to have aroused only modest interest in Montrose. Absolutely no mention is made of it in the Royal Albert minutes.

The 'Amateur Championship' of 1860 – The Rifle Tournament

The first national golf tournament outside St Andrews was organised by the Royal Albert in August 1860, predating by two months what is now considered the first Open Championship, at Prestwick.

At the time, the Montrose tournament may well have been the more important event.

It featured more prize money than at Prestwick, and a larger field, and it took place against the backdrop of one of the greatest sporting festivals of the nineteenth century – the Montrose Volunteer Gathering. The tournament also featured an important milestone in the evolution of golf competitions: the first dispute about 'amateur status' in the sport's history!

The Royal and Ancient had followed up the historic 1857 Grand National tournament with similar competitions in St Andrews in 1858 and 1859, but then seems to have lost interest in the idea. The Royal Albert filled the gap. The Montrose tournament was arguably the 'amateur championship' for 1860, and as such would have had a higher stature than the all-professional event at Prestwick.

The biggest challenge was getting good players to come, as many had never ventured as far north as Montrose. The solution was to make the tournament part of the great Montrose Volunteer Gathering when, the club minutes correctly predicted, 'a number of strangers, members of other golf clubs, will visit the town'. The golf tournament itself would be timed 'for the first free day and following days if necessary' of the rifle-shooting competition.

Overseen by Royal Albert member Major Renny Tailyour (the father of the sporting all-rounder of the same name), the Montrose Gathering was the culmination of a sudden surge in patriotism, fuelled by fear of the country's vulnerability to a French invasion. A campaign started in 1859 to form a volunteer citizen army to back up the regular troops had caught the national imagination, and more than 100,000 signed up, the genesis of today's Territorial Army.

Members had to provide their own rifles and purchase their own uniforms, and shooting competitions were organised to test and improve their skills, and boost morale. The first were held in 1860 – on the Wimbledon common in the spring, and on the links of Montrose in late August.

As many as 30,000 people flocked to Montrose from all over Scotland – there were special trains put on from Edinburgh and Glasgow – for the mammoth shooting competition and also for other sports, including cricket, golf and Highland Games. There were civic balls, banquets and military reviews and, as the *Montrose Review* reported, the streets were adorned with floral arches and coloured lights that 'were beautifully delineated in gas'.

The phenomenal success of the Montrose event was critical in demonstrating national support for the Volunteer Movement, and the town's vast areas of linksland played a vital role. It was remarked in the press that the event was so large it could hardly have been held anywhere else.

An added attraction was the presence of Montrose native Edward Ross, who had won the title of 'champion shot' of England at the Wimbledon meeting. He kicked off the Montrose event with an exhibition of his prowess, shooting at casks placed on boats over a mile away in the Basin. Things got rather out of hand when the spectators (many of whom naturally had brought their rifles along) decided to have a go as well!

The Royal Albert's golf tournament, which drew the gathering to a close, was a less boisterous affair, but it did indeed attract numerous entries from the leading golfing centres of St Andrews, Edinburgh and Perth.

Golf tournaments were still a novelty, and the *Montrose Standard* was prepared to assert that the tournament had 'been looked forward to with interest by lovers of the game in all parts of Scotland'.

The tournament was, paradoxically, both that year's biggest 'money tournament' (with £5 to the winner) and its most important 'amateur' competition. An entry fee of ten shillings (five shillings for the handicap category) would have kept less affluent amateur golfers at bay.

Since the tournament was not open to professionals, the allocation of prize money may be puzzling to modern readers. The Royal Albert had determined that the tournament was to be open to 'all gentlemen players, members of any established golf club' – a vague definition that they had borrowed from the St Andrews tournaments of the previous three years. There were still no hard and fast rules about what an amateur golfer was.

It certainly had nothing to do with whether or not a player accepted prize money, and was more related to his social status. A gentleman/amateur was someone who was at arm's length from the messy business of having to make a living from the sport. But how long those arms needed to be would vex golf's administrators for decades. And the debate starts with the Montrose tournament of 1860.

It all started calmly enough. In the main scratch event, ten golfers entered, and the five winners of the first round proceeded to the second round (unlike the 1857 tournament in St Andrews, entrants participated as individuals, not as teams). William Christie of Montrose won his second match as well, while Hugh Alexander of Fife received a bye. But controversy erupted after the remaining match, in which Royal Albert member Robert Clark – a fine golfer – was thumped by Ronald Ross of Edinburgh 6&4. As reported in the club minutes:

> *At this stage of the proceedings a dispute arose as to Mr Ross being eligible to play at the tournament having once belonged to a professional club, but having been allowed to play in the first set of Matches, the Umpires decided that the better way to act under the circumstances was to divide the prize among the three highest of the Competitors Messrs. Ross, Christie and Alexander.*

A depiction of the Wimbledon meeting at which Edward Ross shot. Note the considerable number of spectators, which would have been matched or exceeded at the Montrose Gathering.

Though not specified in the minutes, newspaper accounts make it clear that Royal Albert Captain Adam Burnes made the decision to halt proceedings, which amounts to the first disqualification in golf tournament history.

With Ross out of the way, Christie and Alexander then played an exhibition match. William Christie won by two holes, securing the bragging rights, at least, as the unofficial amateur champion of Scotland for 1860!

The grounds of Ronald Ross's disqualification are still not clear. The reference to 'a professional club' may indicate that Ross once belonged to one of the handful of clubs that had sprung up for those lower down the social ladder, and which admitted professionals, greenkeepers, clubmakers and others who earned at least a partial living from the game. The fact that Ross and Clark both lived in Edinburgh raises the possibility that Clark learned of the previous associations of his triumphant opponent during their match.

The two-day handicap competition for what was termed 'Class No. 2' was scarcely less extraordinary. An extract of the results of this Class, as set out in the club minutes, is reprinted on the following page.

As handicaps had not yet been established, they were decided by committee. If a player didn't like what he was given he could withdraw but he had to forfeit half of his entry fee.

After winning three matches each, Joseph Smith and John Renny met in a 17-hole final. That match ended all square, so they immediately played another 17 holes, and drew again. With darkness falling, they 'agreed to divide the prize between them rather than risk a third day's play, being anxious to get to Perth by the last train on that day'.

After 85 holes of golf over two days, they might be forgiven for falling asleep on that train!

So after two full days of competition, a clear winner was decided in neither the scratch nor handicap competitions of Montrose's first tournament. The *Review* said that while the tournament 'did not pass off so agreeably as was expected' it had succeeded in 'making known to a number of players from a distance the great advantages which the Montrose Links afford for golf practice'.

Any bad aftertaste from the sport's first case of disqualification was presumably washed away at a dinner that evening at the Star Hotel, at which the golfers were joined by other gentlemen who had taken part in the cricket match held as part of the Volunteer Gathering. Royal Albert Captain Adam Burnes presided over the dinner, which according to the *Standard* included a huge number of toasts, all drunk 'with great enthusiasm'. There is no mention as to whether the unfortunate Mr Ross joined in the festivities.

First Set of Matches of 17 holes for Class N 2

No 1	Mr John Renney	110	4 holes a head
2	Mr Laurence Thomson	112	
3	Mr John Thomas	108	3 holes a head
4	Mr James Moore	110	
5	Mr Alexander Mitchell	108	
6	Mr Gavin Spence	110	2 holes a head
7	Mr John Imrie	108	3 holes a head
8	Mr Adam Burnes	112	
9	Mr John P. C. Mason	110	2 holes a head
10	Mr William Mann	108	
11	Mr Chambers	108	
12	Mr Joseph Smith	108	4 holes a head
13	Mr Robert Paul	110	Equal
14	Mr W. S. Johnstone	112	

Results of the first round of the handicap section of the 1860 Royal Albert Golf Tournament. The three digit number represents 'strokes allowed', a rather arbitrary figure reflecting the number of strokes the player might be expected to take in an average round. Much more important is the <u>difference</u> between the players. A participant with strokes allowed of 112 would be considerably less accomplished than a player at 108 and would be given a 4 hole head start – a very large margin in a 17-hole match.

The 25-hole Open of 1866

In 1866, the Royal Albert hosted one of the most remarkable golf events ever staged – a 25-hole Open Competition featuring the world's best professionals, battling it out on what is still the longest golf course ever played in an important tournament. And to top it off, it generated a sensational and historic result – the very first victory by an amateur in a field of leading professionals.

The first reference to the tournament is found, of course, in the club's minute book:

> *A golf competition open to all players, including professionals, should take place on the Montrose Links, over twenty-five holes, being one round of the golfing course, when the golfer who shall hole the round in the fewest strokes shall receive a prize of £10. A prize of £5 and £3 shall also be awarded to the second and third competitors.*

William Doleman, winner of the 25-hole Open. Courtesy of Glasgow Golf Club.

That the Royal Albert now wanted to host a professional tournament is a tribute to the publicity that had begun to grow around the Open Championship, still played every year at Prestwick. The professionals – rather than simply serving the needs of the gentlemen amateurs they often caddied for – were becoming stars in their own right.

To ensure the world's best golfers would make the trip to Montrose, the Royal Albert offered cash prizes that exceeded what the professionals were playing for at the Open Championship. The club went further by insisting on a compulsory and rather expensive sweep competition. This played into the hands of the best players, of course, and some lesser talents dropped out, leaving an elite field of twelve golfers.

Since the Royal Albert had always played its Medal competitions over either 17 or 18 holes, we can only assume that the decision to use a 25-hole course for the 1866 professional tournament was a deliberate effort to show off the abundance of Montrose links, which offered more golf than anywhere else (Prestwick had only 12 holes). Though no layout seems to have survived, given what we know about the average length of holes at Montrose at the time and the scores that the professionals turned in, we can safely assume the course was over 8000 yards, making it still the longest ever used for a major professional tournament.

According to the *Review*, the tournament was 'one of the grandest golf contests that have taken place in Scotland for many years; indeed it is seldom that so much professional skill has been concentrated in one competition'.

Even accounting for home-town bias, the *Review*'s claim was most certainly true, as the field was arguably stronger than in any of the Open Championships held to that time. The starting line-up at Montrose included four past and future Open champions, who would win 11 titles between them.

When play began on the morning of Thursday 23 October, Jamie Anderson set the early target. But his 119 would soon be bettered by the fine play of St Andrews' Robert Kirk, who carded a 117. Surprisingly, the Open champion of the year before, Andrew Strath, could not better this total.

Then, a shock. Word rippled through the large crowds that 28-year-old William Doleman, no doubt benefiting from playing with the amiable Bob Dow of Montrose, had carded a 112, consisting of one 2, three 3's, nine 4's, seven 5's and five 6's.

Willie Park Sr with his Open championship belt, won just a month before he played in the 25-hole Open at Montrose.

William Doleman (Glasgow)	112
William Park (Musselburgh) Open winner 1860, 1863, 1866 and 1875	115
Robert Kirk (St Andrews) Two-time Open runner-up	117
James Anderson (St Andrews) Open winner 1877, 1878 and 1979	119
Andrew Strath (Prestwick) Open winner in 1865	119
Tom Morris (St Andrews) Open winner 1861, 1862, 1864 and 1867	121
John Allan (St Andrews)	122
Thomas Hood (Musselburgh)	127
Robert Dow (Montrose)	127
Robert Andrews (Perth)	128
William Dow (Musselburgh)	129
Stewart Petrie (Montrose)	132

Results of the 25-hole Tournament of 1866.

Rob Andrews, Perth's best golfer, and William Dow, a fine professional from Musselburgh, could not come within 15 strokes of Doleman's score, which left the honour of the professionals in the hands of the reigning Open champion Willie Park, and his arch nemesis, Tom Morris. This top pairing was followed by the largest crowds, but Morris was not on his best form, and Park, while proving the best of the professionals, could not match the miraculous performance of Doleman.

The *Scotsman* reported that 'several heavy bets were lost in consequence of the turn the play took' and that the unexpected victor 'drove a baker's van every day through the streets of Glasgow'. While this made good newspaper copy, Doleman's performance, while extraordinary, would prove not to be a fluke.

The very next year Doleman would again outplay the professionals, shooting a 55 on the 12-hole Prestwick layout, to become the first amateur to lead after any round at the Open Championship. Though he then faded, Doleman would be low amateur in the event on eight separate occasions.

One of four golfing brothers originally from Musselburgh, Doleman led an astonishingly varied life. Years before his triumph in Montrose he may well have been the first person to hit golf balls in Canada. As a 16-year old seaman visiting Quebec in 1854, he climbed the Heights of Abraham which Wolfe's Highlanders had stormed a century before and, to the astonishment of the locals, proceeded to practise golf shots with the clubs and balls that he had carried ashore!

On his 70th birthday, the Glasgow Golf Club, which he joined in 1874, honoured him for his contribution to golf with a written testimonial (and, more practically, a purse filled with sovereigns).

Despite suffering defeat to an amateur, the professionals seemed to have enjoyed their first competitive experience in Montrose. Some of the professionals stayed on in the town for a few days, playing matches with local golfers that would help them to make their journey to Montrose financially worthwhile. According to the *Review*, 'they were loud in their praise for the course and the Royal Albert Golf Club who had given them excellent treatment, compared with that received at other places'.

To celebrate this unique event, the club arranged, at quite short notice, a Ball in the Guild Hall on the Tuesday evening. Key roles in its organisation were taken by many of the leading families of the area represented in the club membership. The *Standard* reported that it was a great success:

> *Of late year, the notion has been growing up among the gentry in Scotland that the only enjoyment of this kind – for which, in days gone by, Montrose used to be famous – is only to be got in Edinburgh or London. They should now see that it is not so.*

The 'Amateur Championship of Golf' of 1874

In 1874 the Royal Albert Golf Club placed a notice in the national press to promote what it called 'The Amateur Championship of Golf'. There were still no widely acknowledged national competitions for amateurs, though by now other clubs had tried their hand at holding tournaments. So the Royal Albert's claim was as good as any.

The Montrose tournament was to be decided by match-play, with a £20 cup to the winner. There was also to be an open stroke-play tournament for a lesser prize.

Possibly to prevent the kind of embarrassment experienced in 1860, entries were now restricted to 'all Members of *invited* clubs' (emphasis added). There were to be no Ronald Ross's this time around.

As in 1860 and 1866, the aim seems to have been to promote the golf Montrose had to offer. According to the *Review*, the object was 'to induce gentlemen to visit the town, and get acquainted with the fine course'.

GOLF TOURNAMENT
OVER THE LINKS OF MONTROSE,
ON
TUESDAY, WEDNESDAY, AND THURSDAY,
the 6th, 7th, and 8th October 1874:

THE ROYAL ALBERT GOLF CLUB of MONTROSE offer Cups of £20 and £10, or Money if preferred, to the Winners of a Tournament over the Links of Montrose.

CUP No. 1 (£20 and the AMATEUR CHAMPIONSHIP of Golf) will be played for on TUESDAY and following days by holes.

CUP No. 2 (£10) will be played for on THURSDAY by strokes, and the players will be Handicapped.

The Competition will be open to all Members of invited Clubs, on payment of 10s. Entry Money for Cup No. 1, and 5s. Entry Money for Cup No. 2, for each player.

The Rules of the Competition, and all disputes, to be decided by the Captain and the Green Committee.

Gentlemen intending to compete for either Cup must send their names to the Captain not later than Saturday the 3d October.

Montrose, September 9, 1874.

Advertisement on the front page of the Scotsman in September 1874.

As in 1860, the golf tournament was in some ways a very expensive sweep. The prizes were paid for by a hefty ten shillings entry fee, a small thing to a gentleman of leisure but a very large amount indeed to members of the less fashionable golf clubs in Montrose, whose membership consisted of factory workers and shopkeepers. These 'artisan clubs' (as they were sometimes called) had gone from strength to strength, often with the active support of the Royal Albert. But their members were not expected to participate in the Amateur Championship of Golf of 1874.

In foul weather, sixteen gentlemen took part, including a sprinkling of entrants from St Andrews, Edinburgh, Carnoustie and Aberdeen.

The winner – Robert Clark – was the same man who had been controversially beaten in the 1860 tournament. That Clark was by now 49

Report on the 1874 'Amateur Championship of Golf' in the Montrose Standard.

GOLF TOURNAMENT AT MONTROSE.

On Tuesday a golf tournament began on the Links of Montrose, the competitions being open only to members of Clubs invited by the Montrose Royal Albert Golf Club, for cups of the value of £20 and £10 respectively. The first (which carries the championship of golf along with it) was played by holes, and the other by strokes, the players in the latter being handicapped. The only competition that commenced on Tuesday was that for the £20 cup. Unfortunately, the weather was most unpropitious, but, notwithstanding, sixteen gentlemen started, and played with much enthusiasm. The course was what is known as the North Course. After all the players had come in, it was found that the following were the successful competitors, who were then paired, and started as follows :—

Dr Argyle Robertson and Mr Charles Clark.
Mr Robert Clark and Mr Blyth.
Mr George Keith and Mr Drimmie.
Mr Colin M'Cuaig and Mr Anderson.

The gentlemen who were successful in this heat were Dr Argyle Robertson, Mr Robert Clark, Mr George Keith, and Mr Charles Anderson.

On Wednesday the competition for the amateur championship of golf and cup of the value of £20 was concluded in favour of Mr Robert Clark.

The gold medal of the Montrose Royal Albert Golf Club was also competed for, and gained by Mr More Gordon of Charleton with a score of 98.

The tournament terminated yesterday. A considerable number of gentlemen competed for the £10 cup which was played by strokes, the players being handicapped. The weather—barring a rather strong wind—was very favourable for the game, and the greens were in capital condition. Some ten couples started, and when the last competitors had come in, it was found on comparing the cards, that the cup had been won by Mr George Keith of Usan, who played the round at 93, and being handicapped 7 strokes, his score was entered at 86. The best rounds were those of Dr Argyle Robertson and Mr Robert Clark, who played scratch, and came in at 88 and 89 respectively. Mr Alexander Foote, Brechin, who was handicapped 11, played the round at 101 (90) ; Mr Montague Macdonald, handicapped 15, came in at 105 (90) ; and Mr James Irvine, handicapped 11, was 102 (91). Several interesting foursomes were played. It is to be hoped that one result of the tournament over the North Course—which demands as much science in playing as any course in Scotland —will make it better known to gentlemen amateurs at a distance.

years old is an indication that the tournament did not succeed in attracting the calibre of players its organisers sought. The *Review* certainly wasn't impressed with the event:

> *It may be said that on the whole, it has been a failure. The numbers that have been attending being fewer than was expected, which may be accounted for by the exclusive nature of the competition. Had a more liberal spirit actuated the members of the Albert, a more successful meeting might have taken place.*

The following year, the Glasgow Golf Club showed how things might have been done. Its genuinely all-comers amateur event attracted more than 40 entries, including two fine golfers from Montrose – the Cobb brothers – who presumably were not invited to the 'Amateur Championship of Golf' event in their own town!

From the distance of 136 years, the Royal Albert's 1874 tournament seems a missed opportunity to begin to break down the class barriers that would plague amateur golf for another half century. And what better place to do it than in Montrose, where vibrant working men's clubs had emerged before anywhere else?

But it has to be remembered that a sensitivity to class distinctions was deeply ingrained at the clubs with which members of the Royal Albert wished to associate, and it would remain a feature of the amateur golf scene for another half century. What is now considered the first official Amateur Championship – in Hoylake in 1885 – was also limited to 'invited clubs' (including the Royal Albert), and early Walker Cup teams were routinely selected from Cambridge and Oxford graduates despite the presence of better players from humbler backgrounds. For many years other golfers in Scotland contented themselves with playing in an unofficial amateur championship sponsored by an Edinburgh newspaper.

However, the Royal Albert seems to have learned a valuable lesson from its disappointing Amateur Championship of Golf. The next, and last, major tournament it would organise would be a much more inclusive and successful affair.

The Circular Course Tournaments of 1888

In 1888, the world's best professionals again descended on Montrose for a tournament to mark the opening of the new Circular Course, designed with the help of Old Tom Morris. On this occasion five Open champions were entered, and this time they weren't upstaged by an amateur.

Royal Albert had footed the bill for laying out the new course, and again took the lead role in organising the golf event, providing a guarantee of £50 in the event of the tournament making a loss. But this time it consulted with the other clubs in the town, and ensured that the week would include tournaments open to everyone.

The result was a wildly successful four-day golfing extravaganza that contained three distinct tournaments:

- a stroke-play event to crown the champion of Montrose;
- an amateur match-play contest for gentleman golfers of 'invited clubs'; and
- an all-comers stroke-play event open to both professionals and leading amateurs.

The Royal Albert also managed to squeeze in their Albert Medal, played in conjunction with the all-comers tournament, and the presence of so many leading professionals meant that there were plenty of side matches as well, no doubt for considerable stakes.

In many ways, this ultra-busy golf week was in the mould of the later Montrose Open tournaments of the twentieth century. It took place over the five days from Saturday 29 September to Wednesday 3 October (there was, of course, no play on Sunday).

The opening Saturday – the day the most people could be away from work – was sensibly devoted to the tournament to crown Montrose's champion golfer. A modest entry fee of six pence encouraged participation, as did a very handsome £40 prize fund for scratch and handicap prizes.

An advertisement in the Review *alerting golfers that the draw would be posted at the Piazza, the open area under the Ball House.*

GOLF TOURNAMENT.

THE DRAWING for Partners and Order of Playing will be posted up on the BILL BOARD at the PIAZZA To-Night, at 8.30.

ALEX. LYELL, Hon. Sec.

That such a competition was long overdue is evident from the extraordinary number of entrants. No fewer than 108 golfers took part – from all of Montrose's clubs – making it by far the largest field ever assembled in Montrose to that time. Indeed, the *Montrose Standard* noted that there were so many people involved in the tournament, there was no one left over to watch:

> *Several of the better known players were honoured by small attendances of spectators, but as the bulk of the golfing fraternity in town were personally engaged, either playing or marking, no crowd accompanied any single pair.*

The tournament was a showcase for the very high level of skill that Montrose's 'artisan golfers' had developed. Although H.G. Grant of the Royal Albert managed third place, the other leading golfers were from other clubs. The winner was the Mechanics Club's Alexander Keillor, who became one of Montrose's sporting heroes. Despite 'devoting more time to football than golf as of late' (according to the *Standard*) Keillor shot a very creditable 81 on the new course, only a couple of strokes higher than professional luminaries such as Willie Park Jr would record later in the week.

Keillor's net score of 79 also won the first handicap prize, and so he carried off a total of £13 in prize money, a pound more than the first place in the professional tournament! This caused some disgruntlement among other players who, the *Standard* reported, thought that 'in future no more than one prize should go to the same player'.

After the Sunday rest day, Monday and Tuesday were devoted to the opening rounds of the amateur match-play tournament. Here the Royal Albert reverted to form, and restricted entry to members of 'invited clubs'. Of the Montrose clubs, only the Victoria seems to have made the grade, though it is an open question whether golfers from other clubs could have taken three days off in the middle of the week to play in the event, or to pay the 10/6d entry fee – twenty times what had been charged for the Saturday competition for Montrose golfers.

Alexander Keillor: Scottish football international and champion golfer of Montrose in 1888. Courtesy of William Coull.

The event did, however, attract a healthy entry of thirty-four, including many of Scotland's finest amateur players. The semi-final on Wednesday morning featured a widely followed match between Patrick Chalmers – the Royal Albert's best player – and a Captain Burn from St Andrews. Chalmers went two up thanks to a pair of stymies (on one occasion Burn knocked Chalmers' ball into the hole) and he more or less clinched the match on a hole played where the 11th is today. The *Standard* gave a detailed account:

> Mr Chalmers drew his tee shot badly and landed amongst the stooks in a field on the farm at Southfield. He got fairly well out. The Captain's shot landed in a thick whin on the right. He played strongly out with his iron and got into another whin on the other side of the course. He followed up with a good iron shot onto the green, but the ball ran over and landed in a hole almost unplayable. He got it out with a niblick almost onto the putting green, and 'foosled' two successive putts and the hole went to his opponent.

In the final, Harry Everard of St Andrews (who would later write the definitive history of the R&A) defeated Chalmers by two holes, winning a handsome cup worth £30.

Although this gentlemen's final attracted its fair share of interest, it was overshadowed by the professional contest. The format was an early version of today's pro-am, with amateurs – mainly Royal Albert members playing in their Albert Medal competition and who had paid 2/6d to enter – paired with the professionals. Fifty-two players in total took part, including all of the leading golfers of the day.

According to a writer in the *Scotsman*, there was considerable anticipation:

> *Speculation was rife as to the probable result with Archie Simpson, after his recent victory over the champion, Willie Park, of Musselburgh, being looked upon by many as the most likely man. . . . There was a large attendance of spectators, and there were few couples who did not have their quota of followers.*

The early running was made by the charismatic Ben Sayers of North Berwick, a two-time runner-up in the Open championship who also became famous as a golf club maker and course designer. But his 76 was beaten by Andrew Kirkaldy of St Andrews. With Open champion Willie Park Jr having an off day, Kirkaldy seemed a certain winner, especially after his closest pursuer, Willie Fernie, took a 6 on the 17th hole.

Needing a birdie 3 just to tie Kirkaldy, Fernie then played what are probably the two greatest shots ever seen in Montrose. With a mammoth, but accurate drive he reached the green on the short par 4 and then, according to the *Scotsman*, holed 'a long stealing putt the full length of the green' for a sensational eagle 2.

With this incredible finish, Fernie nipped Kirkaldy by a single shot, and pocketed the £12 winner's prize. But as there were a number of ties in the lower positions, the fun was just getting started.

An 18-hole playoff was played for the three players tied for third, and also for the three players tied for sixth. In each case, the prize fund was topped up by Royal Albert members, presumably to make it worth the professionals' time. It was a popular move, as the *Standard* reported:

Troon's Willie Fernie, whose sensational eagle 2 on the final hole clinched the 1888 professional tournament in Montrose.

> *As might be expected from the mettle of the players, they were accompanied by a large crowd and, while it is only fair to say that although there was no official to keep order, the followers did nothing to disturb play.*

Carnoustie's Archie Simpson beat Willie Campbell and Ben Sayers for third, while sixth place went to Hugh Kirkcaldy, who handily defeated an out-of-form Willie Park Jr and Bob Mearns of Aberdeen.

The *Standard* concluded its extended report on the week-long tournament by heaping praise on the organisers:

> *The tournament has been certainly the most successful ever held in Montrose. Players from a distance have been almost unanimous in*

their praise of the new course, and the Hon. Secretaries and Greens Committee of the Royal Albert deserve the thanks of local golfers for the way in which the meeting has been conducted.

This would by no means be the last important tournament in Montrose. Another stellar field of professionals competed in 1905, with Harry Vardon defeating Sandy Herd 3&1 in the final. The town would also hold Scottish Amateur Championships in 1913 and 1919. But Willie Fernie's amazing victory in the 1888 tournament makes a fitting end to that period when the Royal Albert Golf Club took upon itself the main responsibility for 'the green'. That arrangement was to end in 1893 when the Town Council and the other clubs in the town decided to share the responsibility.

The full entry list and the scores for the 1888 all-comers tournament. The annotation of 'Prof' against certain names was not a mark of academic distinction but an abbreviation for professional. From the club minutes.

CHAPTER 8

The Montrose Masterpieces

Now, Muse, assist me while I strive to name
The varied skill and chances of the game.

George Fullerton Carnegie

As we have seen, Montrose's unique contribution to the history of golf literature begins with the diary of James Melville – the first autobiographical reference to golf on record. And in 1632, or thereabouts, we find a poem about Montrose by Arthur Johnstone that may well contain the first reference to the sport in verse.

Though important historically, these are mere fragments next to the cluster of classic works written in the nineteenth century by individuals who were, at one time or another, members of the Royal Albert Golf Club. These are all among the very first golf books written – and original editions are worth thousands of pounds when they come up for auction today. They include an epic golf poem, the first and most influential history of the sport, the first popular golf instructional book, one of the very first comic golf stories and, very likely, the first fictional account of ladies' golf.

Here then are what we might well call the Montrose Masterpieces.

Golfiana: or Niceties connected with the Game of Golf (1842)
By George Fullerton Carnegie

George Fullerton Carnegie was made an honorary member of the Royal Albert in 1845 after his book of poems, *Golfiana*, created a sensation in the golf world of the time by cleverly depicting many of its best-known members in verse. Though Carnegie was small in stature (and widely known as 'Little Carnegie') he was also larger than life, and one of the most colourful figures in the history of the sport.

While Carnegie often played in Montrose, his wealthy social clique was centred farther south, and *Golfiana* focuses primarily on St Andrews and North Berwick, and the golfers who played there. The opening stanza of its first poem gives a foretaste of the rest of the volume:

*St Andrews! they say thy glories are
  gone,
That thy streets are deserted, thy castles
  o'erthrown:
If thy glories be gone, they are only,
  methinks,
As it were, by enchantment, transferred
  to thy links.*

The poet was the grandson of Susan Carnegie, one of the Montrose's most famous worthies. But George was, by all accounts, her direct opposite. His father died when he was a small boy and he eventually inherited three large estates, including Charleton within two miles of the links at Montrose. When he came of age in 1820 he donated £20 to the Montrose Poor Fund at the urging of his grandmother who had already founded Scotland's first mental hospital in Montrose. But when Susan Carnegie passed away a year later, it seemed to free her grandson to embark on a life of extraordinary extravagance.

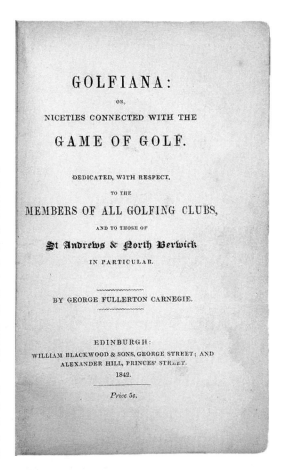

According to William Tulloch, the first biographer of Old Tom Morris, Carnegie became a popular member of a well-known Edinburgh fast set who 'kept racehorses, betted, played high and hunted a great deal'. As an example of what he calls their 'high jinks', Tulloch cites a famous anecdote in which Carnegie and friends – no doubt exceedingly drunk – threw a waiter out of the window of their hotel room and, when told the man was injured, are said to have replied: 'Put him on the bill!'

That seems an overly cruel story for a man whose poetry (he published three volumes of non-golf verses as well) is gentle and never mean-spirited. What it *does* contain are frequent references to gambling, as in the following lines from the mock-heroic poem, 'The Golfiad':

*We make our matches from the love of playing,
Without one loathsome feeling but the paying.
And that is lessened by the thought, we borrow
Only to-day what we shall win to-morrow.*

In Carnegie's case, there was clearly more borrowing than winning, for when he died in 1851 he had sold all three estates and squandered his fortune. While his downfall was described as an 'embarrassment' by the family biographers, his fellow golfers were more forgiving.

'Notwithstanding certain peculiarities, he was a thorough gentleman in manner' wrote a fellow writer from Montrose, Robert Clark, who added:

> *Carnegie had a passion for golf (though never much of a player except as a putter), which continued to the last, playing at St Andrews, Montrose, and Musselburgh. Though reduced to a comparatively small income, he enjoyed life to near the end, living much with his friends, Ross of Rossie, the late Lord Saltoun, and many others, by whom he was much appreciated.*

Near the end of his life Carnegie wrote a kind of epitaph to his golfing life, one that still holds a certain melancholy power:

> *And now farewell! I am the worse for wear –*
> *Grey is my jacket, growing grey my hair!*
> *And, though my play is pretty much the same,*
> *Mine is, at best, a despicable game.*
> *But still I like it – still delight to sing*
> *Clubs, players, caddies, balls, and everything.*
> *But all that's bright must fade! And we who play,*
> *Like those before us, soon must pass away;*
> *Yet it requires no prophet's skill to trace*
> *The royal game thro' each succeeding race;*
> *While on the tide of generations flows,*
> *It still shall bloom, a never-fading rose.*

George Fullerton Carnegie died in 1851 and was buried next to his grandmother at Charleton. Once Montrose's largest landowner, he died with only £161 to his name. He would no doubt be wryly amused to learn that a single first-edition copy of his golfing rhymes is today worth 100 times that.

Golf: A Royal and Ancient Game (1875)
By Robert Clark.

Like James Melville long before him, Robert Clark was schooled in Montrose (at the Academy) before being sent to Edinburgh as an apprentice compositor in the printing business as a 13-year-old. His father, also Robert Clark, was a Montrose solicitor and club member who won the Original Gold Medal in 1822. Starting with an initial investment of £200, the younger Clark would build one of the most prestigious printing houses in Scotland, producing fine and wildly popular editions of Kipling, Shaw, and Tennyson, and the Waverley novels of Sir Walter Scott.

Clark also found time to regularly travel back to Montrose for golf. He won the major prize in the so-called 'Amateur Championship of

 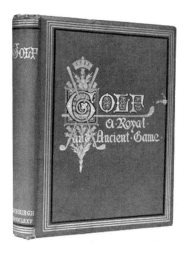

Robert Clark and a first edition cover.

Golf' organised by the club in 1874. He also won the Albert Medal three times, his last triumph coming in 1875, coincidentally the year he published a volume of his own, entitled *Golf: A Royal and Ancient Game*. It is the first serious history of the sport, bringing to light many original documents that hugely influenced our understanding of golf's evolution. It remains a classic and was reprinted as late as 1975.

We can only assume that Clark was thinking of Montrose – the 'happy golfing ground' of his youth – when he wrote the introduction to the 1893 edition of his famous work:

> *Scotland . . . may well be proud of her ancient game, by the spell of which king and cobbler alike are led captive; and although her hardy sons, in search of fame or fortune, carry their favourite game South, East, and West, – 'far as the breeze can bear, the billows foam,' still they never forget their native greens, and gladly return to the happy golfing-ground of their youth, where every hole seems eloquent with recollections of famous putts and glorious drives! Pastime passing excellent! We owe thee much.*

The Golfer's Handbook, including History of the Game, Hints to Beginners, the Feats of Champion Golfers, Lists of Leading Clubs and their Office-Bearers, &c. (1881)
By the Rev. Robert Forgan

Son of the famous St Andrews clubmaker of the same name, Robert Forgan Jr entered the church and was ordained at the St George's Free Church in Montrose in 1886. He was admitted as a member of the Royal Albert in 1887. He quickly demonstrated that he was a very able golfer, winning the Gold, Albert and Keithock Medals in succession, the only

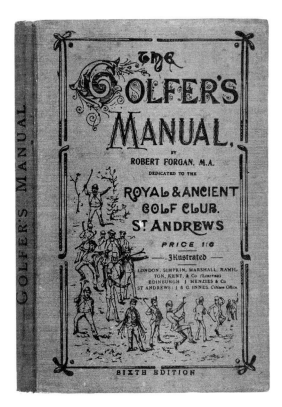

person to do so. His round of 82 in securing the Gold Medal was the lowest winning score to that time.

The Rev. Forgan, while briefly serving on the committee of the Royal Albert, was no doubt also working on revisions to his spectacularly successful *Golfer's Handbook*. Issued in no fewer than eight editions during the next quarter century, the book was the first commercially-successful golf book ever.

Initially written when Forgan was in his early twenties, it is part history, part instruction manual and part course guide and directory (of Montrose, Forgan writes that it has a 'links admirably suited for golf'). *The Golfer's Handbook*, which was later changed to *The Golfer's Manual*, made its debut at the beginning of the boom in golf in England, and reading the book today (the British Library has two editions) it is easy to understand its popularity. Written in a lively, opinionated style, its authoritative tone no doubt provided a sense of security to the tens of thousands of Englishmen (and Englishwomen) who were taking up this strange new game for the first time.

'Keep your eye steadfastly on your ball – this is the first and last secret of all true Golfing,' is a typical example of some of Forgan's timeless and pithy advice.

Given his family background, it is perhaps not surprising that Forgan is particularly strong-minded when it comes to advising on the kind of equipment to purchase. His advice also provides a vivid insight into the conditions that Montrose golfers faced during the latter part of the nineteenth century:

> *We should recommend all players to buy their balls fresh, and 'season' them for themselves. No ball should be used until it is at least 6 months old.*
>
> *Skill in handling the six or eight clubs that are really essential will be far more effectual than a superabundance of tools, with the absence of dexterity in their use.*
>
> *The Niblick [a lofted iron] . . . is specially employed to jerk the ball out of the steep face of a bunker, or to extricate it from rough stones or stiff whins or the deep track of a cart-wheel.*
>
> *The Driving Cleek [a one or two iron] . . . is further of great service in playing half strokes to the hole, and in putting out of bad lies or cups on the green.*

Golf club makers were keen to profit from the golf boom and Forgan is particularly scathing about some newfangled golf clubs that had just come onto the market promising great benefits. He has this to say about one briefly-popular club, called 'The President', that had an oval-shaped hole right through its face:

> The hole is, we believe, intended to allow the sand to pass through in playing in a bunker. But what particular advantage is hereby to be gained we cannot imagine, and have never heard stated. The President is, in fact, better at hacking the 'gutta' than at anything else.

Forgan left Montrose for Rothesay in 1892 and enjoyed a distinguished career in the Church of Scotland that saw him awarded St Andrews University's highest degree, the Doctorate of Divinity, in 1919. But his lasting fame may well remain his authorship of golf's first commercially successful book (first-edition copies now sell for as much as £8000). Rev. Forgan's advice to beginners is as relevant today as when it was written 129 years ago:

> In your earlier attempts you may 'miss the globe' and break a club alternately, but that is only what everyone does. Paying no heed to such trifles, therefore, play systematically from the first; never 'press' to achieve impossibilities or retrieve disasters; keep down your excitement, and play thoughtfully and with coolness; be neither timid nor rash, and confide in the advice of a trustworthy guide; do not blame your caddie or your clubs when the blame is your own; cultivate a graceful and easy style; and, finally, keep your eye on your ball every stroke; and, notwithstanding many preliminary discouragements, you will ere long be smitten with 'the epidemic of the club and ball,' and become enamoured of a health-giving pastime that will be enjoyed by you even to a green old age.

Incidentally, his wife Grace is also widely-recognised for her own special contribution to the nation's spiritual life – she is credited with the establishment of the World Day of Prayer in Scotland in 1929.

The Duffers' Golf Club Papers (1891)
By Dr Valentine Stone

Tucked away in the reference section of the Montrose Library is a copy of one of golf's rarest, and funniest, books. Published anonymously in 1891, it first appeared as a serial in the *Montrose Standard*. On the rare occasions that copies of the book go on the auction block, the author is listed as Dr Stone. This can only be Dr Valentine Stone, a member of the Royal Albert from 1883, Honorary Secretary of the club for a period and also a Provost of Montrose. He was the winner of the first handicap

Valentine Stone photographed as Town Provost, 1910. Courtesy of Angus Council.

competition for the Foote-Millar trophy in 1889, playing off a handicap of 8.

The Duffers Golf Club Papers is a comic account of the golfing tribulations of eight high-handicap members of the 'Prince Consort' Golf Club (a thinly-veiled reference to the Royal Albert of course). Since, due to their inferior golf games, they are normally 'relegated to an obscurity far in excess of their demerits', they decide to start their own club, in which 'they would be of the first importance'. Membership, it is decided, will be restricted to golfers with an average score of between 95 and 110. And each player was expected to be ready to 'go half-a-crown on every match'.

The original members consist of two ministers, two doctors, two lawyers and two landed gentry (presumably a reflection of the social make-up of the club at the time*)*. *The Duffers' Golf Club Papers* tells the story of three club matches – played in Montrose, Stonehaven and St Andrews – interspersed with accounts of various drinking sessions.

Though fictional, the author says the characters and incidents are drawn from life, so we can assume that *The Duffers' Golf Club Papers* provide us with a fairly realistic, if comically-exaggerated, flavour of how golf was enjoyed in the Royal Albert 120 years ago.

In the first chapter, it is recommended by one of the members – dubbed the 'Laird' – that the club meet regularly on Saturdays with a gathering (drinking session) after the match, a suggestion that alarms the 'Howler', one of the ministers: 'We have to look over our sermon' he says. 'And besides it doesn't quite do for us to be enjoying ourselves so near Sunday.'

Another central character is Willie Cushat, 'the club steward, greenkeeper, ball and clubmaker, local professional and general factotum to the club'. Cushat can only be Bob Dow, professional at the Royal Albert from 1863 to 1898, and the portrait is a deeply affectionate, if somewhat condescending one. According to the narrator, Cushat is said to 'combine the wisdom of the serpent with the harmlessness of the dove'. He caddies for the Laird and keeps 'things pretty smooth by minimising all the bad shots, and exaggerating the merits of the good ones'.

Dr Stone also makes the Laird a vivid character: 'Being too stout for long driving, he naturally has a very strong opinion that the short game is of the greatest importance.' The Laird is also particularly proud of a putter bought in St Andrews from Tom Morris (a notoriously bad putter).

The match in Montrose provides a useful insight into the routing of the course in 1891, as well as the challenges offered by the most fearsome hazard on the course at the time – a massive bunker on the infamous gully hole (the dip in front of the present 16th green). It overwhelms the pair of doctors who are playing a foursomes match against the 'Laird' and the 'Pleader', as one of the lawyers is nicknamed:

> *After several clouds of sand had been sent up, apparently without effect, the Medicos emerged from the recesses of the bunker looking very hot and not very amiable, with the ball in the caddy's pocket.*

The Laird, however, ultimately loses the match on the 17th hole when he 'studied a putt till he was quite bewildered'.

From *The Duffers' Golf Club Papers* it is clear that Bob Dow served drinks in the clubhouse while his wife cooked tea. Apparently collops (a dish sometimes made with mince and oatmeal) were often on the menu, so the gentlemen made sure to place a special order of fresh fish the morning of their match. But nothing can help their golf game, as the Laird laments when he bursts, rather suddenly, into song:

> *We've tried by lunch the luck to turn*
> *With nips our throats have made to burn*
> *We've stopped our smoke, but all in vain,*
> *Result the same, we fail again.*
> *A hundred yards we cannot get*
> *And hang it all! We're duffers yet.*
> *Duffers yet, duffers yet*

The match in Stonehaven is marred by the retirement of the Pleader, who takes one look at the steep climbs required and retires to the clubhouse with a bottle of whisky. His place is taken by Cushat/Dow (who had been caddying). He is equally unimpressed with the terrain:

> *'Weel, I've been on mony a gowf coorse,' he says, 'but this palls the deevil.'*

St Andrews offers an entirely different challenge – instead of insurmountable hills there are drunken caddies who end up in fisticuffs with each other! On the way home the party stops in Dundee for dinner and some 'burlesque theatre'. In a reflection of social niceties of the time, Cushat is not invited to join the group for dinner but is offered a ticket to the performance, which he is at first reluctant to accept:

> *'Mercy be here the theatre,' he says, 'Din ye no ken' at I'm a*
> *deykin o' a kirk; I wad hae ta geng afore the Session if it wis kent.'*

The Laird convinces Cushat to go, but again they take their seats in different parts of the theatre.

The Duffers' Golf Club Papers is one of the first comic golf stories ever published, still one of the most engaging, and certainly among the most valuable. At auction in London in 2007, a copy sold for £9200 while, in New York, a single copy sold for $16,000. Readers might be advised to save themselves some money and join the Montrose Library!

A Day on the Ladies Links (1891)
Dr Valentine Stone

This ten-page account, included at the end of *The Duffers' Golf Club Papers*, is likely the first literary description of women's golf. Written only two years after the founding of the Montrose Ladies Golf Club, itself one of the first ladies' clubs in the world, it captures – intentionally or not – not only the condescending attitude of the men but also the real enthusiasm that women in Montrose had for the game.

The story is set on the first Wednesday in September, the day of 'the monthly competition for the gold medal'. A tent has been erected near the 'Prince Consort' Clubhouse (this is the Royal Albert's short-lived clubhouse near the Stone Bridge) so that tea can be served afterwards. This allowed the ladies to 'indulge in a good many sneers and contemptuous remarks upon the churlishness and shabbiness of the Prince Consort people, who, they considered, ought to have been only too glad to throw their Club open and place its resources at the disposal of what an irreverent youth has called, the Sister Club'.

The narrator (Dr Stone was a member of the Royal Albert of course) thinks this a bit harsh on the men as two Prince Consort members actually serve as the Secretary and the Treasurer (as Royal Albert members did at the non-fictional Montrose Ladies Club).

Women's golf was, at the time, almost entirely an upper class endeavour and we find that a Miss Fatkey, apparently one of the best players, 'has a putter with a gold top, and a shield with her crest and monograph let into the shaft'. It was probably the only club she used. Except for a few pioneering souls, ladies were not playing 'long golf' just yet and the course their Medal is played on is clearly a longish putting course, no doubt similar in length to the 'Himalayas' in St Andrews today, where the Ladies Putting Club still holds regular competitions. Miss Fatkey achieves a two-round total of 109, about 3 per hole.

The contest is taken seriously enough by most, and each group is assigned a 'marker' – brothers, fiancés and other interested men – to take down the scores and adjudicate on the rules. A running joke in the story is that the male markers are run roughshod over by the competitors, whose interpretation of the Rules of Golf is more flexible:

> *At the next hole after a stroke had been played, Miss Shortly's dress, which was rather long, swept her ball a foot or two from its place. It so happened that its new place was much more favourable than before and the marker said it ought to be replaced in its original position. . . . Miss Talby, on the other hand, was magnanimous enough to call it a rub of the green, and suggested that it should be played from where it lay, adding that if she was pleased, no one else had a right to object.*

A couple of competitors are mocked for trying to attract the attention of a handsome military man, 'more to her style and grace than to her play'. But others are obviously keen to win. After spending a round behind a Tilly Slowgo, one of the better players laments:

> *'Oh I wish I were a man and could swear aloud as much as I liked. I should feel ever so much more comfortable.'*

More than fifty retire to the tent for tea after the two rounds, which take about an hour each to play. They wouldn't need to use the tent much longer. The narrator mentions that it is 'seriously proposed by the ladies to get up a . . . Clubhouse of their own'. That would happen, in reality, in 1895.

*　　*　　*

It is perhaps no accident that so much important early golf writing has a link to Montrose, for the town has long mixed literary and golfing pursuits. The famous Marquis of Montrose – he of the first recorded caddie and golfing honeymoon – was also a gifted poet. And between the great wars of the twentieth century, a cluster of Scotland's finest writers – who lived in Montrose and helped spearhead the Scottish Literary Renaissance – also tried their hand at golf. The novelist Willa Muir, a former pupil of the Academy, was one of them (she taught her husband Edwin, the renowned poet, to play) and looking back on the period she remembered how the lure of the links at Montrose appealed to a creative eye:

> *The great round of sky, the wide links with their stretches of thyme and eyebright, the wild North Sea beating on Sand Dunes held together by tough pink liquorice and marram grass . . . were it not a setting where the wind of the spirit had freedom to blow?*

CHAPTER 9

The Professionals

'Slacken yersel a bit and sit weel down tae yer ba'.

Golf advice attributed to Bob Dow

In recent years the club professionals in Montrose have been engaged by the Links Trust and have served all the clubs of the town. But in the period 1864 to 1910, the Royal Albert hired its own club professionals – three remarkable men who would become famous well beyond the confines of the Montrose.

Bob Dow playing on the Montrose Links.

Bob Dow

Measured by the influence he had on the sport in Montrose, and in Scotland, Dow had only one peer during his long period as a club professional – his close friend Old Tom Morris in St Andrews.

Dow does not appear in golf's record books as a player. Though certainly good enough to enter, he seems to have shown a complete disinterest in playing in the fledgling Open Championship (the first one was held at Prestwick – a long way from Montrose – when Dow was already twenty-eight).

But Dow was a frequent participant in the contests that really mattered to the golfing public at the time – the challenge matches between professionals (and sometimes their amateur partners). Looking back on Dow's eventful life, the *Montrose Review* commented:

For over 30 years he had few, if any, equals as a golfer in Montrose, and in the earlier days of his golfing career he did well in tournaments alongside the "giants" of the game .He attended the first professional gathering at Hoylake, and in company with such men as old and young Tom Morris, the Andersons, the Grants, the Straths, the Dunns, he appeared on greens scattered over the length of Scotland.

The matches between Dow and Tom Morris Sr were almost annual fixtures on the sporting calendar, and were followed with great interest across the country. The *Times* of London, as we shall see, devoted several inches of column space to their last match, held in 1893, when both Dow and Morris were in their 60s!

Bob Dow was born in Fyvie in Aberdeenshire in 1832 and his family moved to Montrose in 1840. At a young age he began an apprenticeship as a shoemaker in the town but, as the *Standard* reported on the occasion of his retiral, 'he took kindly to golfing . . . [and] availed himself of every opportunity to become proficient in the game'.

The first reference we have in the Royal Albert minutes of Bob Dow is in 1863, when he replaces Thomas Grundison as 'the man who keeps the green' at a salary of £3 a year. When the club acquired its first clubhouse in 1865, Dow was appointed club keeper and professional, and he was still to have oversight of the course, responsible for grass cutting and setting the holes for play under, it seems, the direction of a greens committee.

Perhaps the best contemporary description we have of Dow's all-important role comes from *The Duffers' Golf Club Papers*. In that comic account of life at the Royal Albert in 1891 (see the chapter on the 'Montrose Masterpieces') the professional is described as: 'the club steward, greenkeeper, ball and club-maker, local professional and general factotum to the club'.

Dow and his wife took up residence in part of the clubhouse soon after it opened. There are only fleeting references in the minutes to Mrs Dow, but she seems to have been equally-highly regarded. She must have provided food on occasions while her husband served the drinks. She makes an appearance in *The Duffers' Golf Club Papers*, serving up lunch for a golfing party. As for Bob Dow's salary, it increased steadily to £20 in 1873, in recognition of his growing worth to the club as golf teacher, caddie master, club keeper and greenkeeper. In 1877 he also received a £3 gratuity from the club.

Possibly Bob's early career as a shoemaker gave him the skills that would help in his clubmaking role, all-important in an age when clubs broke routinely and needed to be repaired or replaced. According to the minutes, a new workshop was built at the clubhouse in 1877, one that seems to have been constructed by Dow himself. The club later lends a mould out to Dow for making golf balls; in return for an annual payment of £1, he was allowed to use the mould and sell balls to members and other local golfers.

In his prime, Dow was almost certainly the best player in Montrose. He is recorded twice only in club minutes as a participant in Royal Albert Medal competitions, beating the field in 1874 and 1877 when he was already in his 40s (as a professional he did not of course actually receive the Medal). In 1881, as he neared his 50th birthday, he set the course record with a score of 71 strokes. The *Standard* in 1898 recalled:

> *His most remarkable feats have been in taking the first or 'post' hole of 259 yards, and the tenth or 'magazine' hole of 246 yards in one stroke. He is wont to say that Tom Morris has done this at St Andrews only one time more than his twice.*

In September 1871, the *Review* gave a blow-by-blow account of one of the many confrontations between Dow and Tom Morris, and this provides us with vivid insights into how the game was played at the time, by two of Scotland's finest:

Postcard showing the famous friends and golfing rivals, Tom Morris and Bob Dow. Courtesy of William Coull.

PROFESSIONAL GOLF MATCH – On Saturday, a match of two rounds on the short course was played between Tom Morris, St Andrews, and Bob Dow, Montrose. The stakes were £8 a-side. Play commenced shortly after eleven.

In the first round, the first three holes were halved; and the fourth was taken by Morris with a three against Dow's four. The next hole was halved and at the sixth or 'girdle' hole, Dow placed his ball on the putting green with his second shot while Morris played over and lay in a whin. In playing out, he was too strong and had to play two more than Dow. Dow laid his third within a foot . . . but missing the short putt, the ball went round the hole, 'stymieing' Morris whose ball was about nine inches behind. Morris took his turn, and lifting the ball over Dow's, dropped it clean in the hole, and thus securing a half.

Dow takes the next hole, the playing on both sides being rather inferior. Dow also took the next and the ninth was halved. In playing off the tee at the tenth, Dow drew his ball and dropped it on top of a dwelling house and ultimately had to give up the hole. . . .

> *The eighteenth [went] to Tom, finishing all square on the round,
> the play on the whole being somewhat loose. After a short interval
> for refreshments, they started on the second round.*

Tom eventually won the match in the second round by 5 & 4. The stakes
for this match played over 32 holes in a morning were considerable (and
there would have been many more side stakes among the watching
golfers). Tom in the afternoon then played another match – he went on
to play and defeat Royal Albert member George Keith, who was
'allowed a stroke at every alternate hole' – making a total of 49 holes
that day.

This kind of golf marathon seems to have been routine also for Bob
Dow, who according to another newspaper report was always ready to
'take his five rounds a day'. Even at the age of sixty-six years, the
Standard reported that Dow was 'still able to take a couple of rounds a
day on the links with perfect freedom, when occasion demands, often
giving younger and more powerful opponents a tussle for victory'.

His close friendship with Tom Morris may have been based, in part,
on similar personality traits. Like Old Tom, the Dow portrayed in *The
Duffers' Golf Club Papers* is a faithful churchgoer.

He also seems to have shared Old Tom's legendary patience as a
teacher. Near the end of Dow's life, an American golf magazine published this anecdote about one of the few times his patience wore out:

> *Old Bob Dow on the Montrose links in Scotland was a mild
> tempered man enough and patient was not the word for him.
> Once, however, he did nearly lose his shirt. He was teaching a
> young and fair Juno from the South who by her demeanor seemed
> to think golf should come to her rather than the other way round.
> Bob tried and tried but could make no impression. At last he
> exclaimed, 'Dinna haud yersel sae stiff-like, wumman, slacken
> yersel a bit and sit weel down tae yer ba'.*

The very reference to 'Old Bob Dow' is another confirmation that he,
like Old Tom, was a revered fixture in the sport, whose fame had travelled over the oceans to the many places where the game was then taking
root.

Bob Dow did not only make a contribution to the Royal Albert members. At least three of the newly formed clubs in the town benefited
hugely from his advice and support – and his employers, to their credit,
seemed content to allow him to take on that role.

The newly-formed Victoria Golf Club, for example, paid him an
annual retainer of £1 'for making holes at the various competitions . . .
and putting the club's flags in the holes every Monday, Wednesday and
Thursday during the summer'. For a time they used a room in the
Southfield clubhouse by arrangement with Bob Dow, most probably just
a place to store their boxes.

The Star Golf Club assembled in Bob Dow's rooms on the links before and after play, and Bob himself was a key member (and Captain) of the Union Golf Club set up in 1865, which becomes a flourishing club for a period.

Bob Mackie, speaking at the Victoria Club's Jubilee celebration dinner in 1921, fondly remembered a man he calls 'our old friend' and recalls his part in a memorable challenge match at North Berwick against one of the best players of the time.

> *Clearly, I can see the Royal Albert clubhouse when Bob was a vigorous man, and his wife, one of the sonsiest and rosiest of women. . . . A fine player was he – not exactly what one would call a terribly long driver, but he was always straight and was a grand putter, especially at holing a long curly one. Bob had the distinction of playing in the game in which was made the most brilliant shot on record. It was a 36 hole match over North Berwick between Bob and Willie Park. Bob was dormy one, and at the last hole – a short one – he played his cleek shot to within six inches of the hole. Willie's only chance of halving the hole, therefore, was to hole out from the tee. He took his cleek and did it.*

Bob Dow may justly be called the 'Grand Old Man' of Montrose golf, but his most important legacy may well be found in that long line of Montrose golfers whom he first encountered as caddies and then taught to play the game.

Alex Findlay was the first of these golfers – almost all members of the Union Golf Club and later of the Mercantile Club – to take his golfing talents abroad. He went to America where he did so much to launch the game there, and he was followed by four of his brothers. There was also Charles Burgess and all seven of his sister's family, the Nicolls, and many others. What is remarkable is how all of them are described in various accounts as great gentlemen and true sportsmen. That may be Bob's greatest legacy to golf in Montrose and around the world.

In 1888, in planning the tournament to mark the opening of the new Circular Course, the Royal Albert agreed that a suitable gift (not exceed-ing £10) be acquired to mark Bob Dow's twenty-five years service to the club. According to the *Review*, at the conclusion of the prize-giving ceremony, Dow was called out in front of his fellow professionals – the finest golfers in Scotland – and club member Alexander Lyell said he had a pleasant duty to perform:

> *Namely, to present, on behalf of the committee of Royal Albert, a silver watch to their local professional, Bob Dow (loud applause). Dow had been green keeper in Montrose for 25 years; and this being what may be called his silver wedding, the committee thought it only fitting to present him with a handsome silver watch.*

In 1892, the club Council accepted Dow's application for a week's leave of absence – possibly the first holiday entitlement he had received – and 'was empowered to grant such leave in future, the time however being limited to one week'.

Dow's swansong as a player came in the remarkable challenge matches with Old Tom Morris in 1893. They are remarkable not for the level of play (which was obviously very high) but for the interest they received. They are arguably the first senior professional matches on record, and that they should garner national attention is an indication of the stature Dow had in the golf world. According to the *Times* Dow seems to have given a good account of himself despite ending up on the losing end:

GOLF.
PROFESSIONAL MATCH.

Yesterday the first of the home-and-home professional matches between the veteran players Tom Morris, St. Andrews, and Bob Dow, Montrose, was played over the St. Andrews links before a good gathering of spectators. The match consisted of two rounds. Beautiful, clear weather favoured the play and the links were found in the best condition. In the first round the play was disappointing. Morris especially was in bad form, did not play his game, and repeatedly lost himself in putting. Dow, on the other hand, was very deadly in his short game. At the outset Morris had the advantage, but Dow soon equalized matters, was one ahead at the turn, and came in three ahead at the end of the first round. The second round was played during the afternoon, when the game took a complete change and showed the glorious uncertainty of golf. Morris quickly proved himself a formidable antagonist, he had the game square at the end hole, and, continuing his fine game while that of Dow fell off, became winner of the match by five and three to play. The return match will be played at Montrose to-day.

Dow retired in 1898, an event reported at length in the *Review*:

> *The retirement of Bob Dow . . . after thirty five years of faithful service, severs a link which binds the past and present history of golf in Montrose. . . . Bob has golfed on Montrose Links for upwards of fifty-seven years, and in his career has traversed the links for, it is estimated, 92,100 miles. This estimate is at the lowest account by a gentleman who has gone carefully into the matter, and does not take into account the many journeys 'up town' and over the private course at Usan, where Bob was frequently a welcome visitor.*

Old Tom playing a hole on the South LInks with Bob Dow, wearing the bowler hat, watching him play.

Usan House where Bob Dow was often a guest of Royal Albert member, George Keith.

(Incidentally this is the only-known mention of a private golf course at Usan – an estate about two miles south of the town – which must have been created by George Keith, a former Captain of the Royal Albert who often partnered Bob Dow in challenge matches. No trace of that course survives but, if a course was ever to be laid out again on that promontory, it would command the most magnificent sea views of any course in Scotland.)

The club moved quickly to set up a committee to circulate members for subscriptions for a retiral fund, essentially a pension for the most valued servant in club history, in an age when there was no state pension and the workhouse was the only location for the destitute. A sum in excess of £130 was collected and, from early in 1899, the club paid Bob Dow ten shillings a week from that fund.

Bob Dow died on 26 November 1909 (less than a week before the demise of his great friend Tom Morris). There were handsome obituary notices in both of the local papers, celebrating his contribution to golf in Montrose.

The more we learn about Bob Dow, the more our appreciation grows. His name regrettably is not preserved in the name of a particular hole or on any trophy, an omission that present-day golfers in Montrose might do well to remedy in the future.

Portrait of Bob Dow that still hangs in the clubhouse.

Charles (Chay) Burgess

After Bob Dow's retirement, it took the club five years to hire its second professional – Charles Burgess. In many ways, Burgess' golfing life is even more extraordinary than his predecessor.

Born on Wellington Street in Montrose in 1873, and apprenticed as a stonemason at the tender age of eleven, Burgess would eventually become a golf teacher to the stars, and a friend of Bing Crosby and American baseball legend Babe Ruth.

And his coaching of a young teenager in Boston – Francis Ouimet – would change the course of golf history.

However Burgess' first taste of fame came not in golf, but in football. He won a spot on the Montrose team as a right back at the age of fifteen, receiving a cap for Scotland (against Ireland) three years later. He then played professionally with Dundee, Millwall, Newcastle and Portsmouth. An indication of his stature is reflected by a Portsmouth newspaper account of his violent return to Millwall while in opposition colours:

> *Former Millwall idol Burgess, making his debut for Portsmouth, was booed every time he touched the ball, with supporters regarding his signing for the south coast club . . . a gross act of desertion. Tempers continued to rise in the 6,000 crowd and when Portsmouth's Smith placed the ball for a corner kick close by the main stand, he was felled by a stone thrown at him a spectator. . . . After the final whistle Portsmouth players were forced to run the gauntlet through incensed spectators.*

Chay Burgess in his Montrose F.C. strip. Courtesy of William Coull.

Burgess earned £4 a week at the height of his football career, but he decided to give it up in 1903 for a more stable family life in Montrose. A member of the Mercantile, Burgess had also been an exceptional golfer from an early age, receiving tutoring from both Bob Dow and Tom Morris in his youth. When he returned to Montrose, the Royal Albert offered him the professional's job with the following salary and duties:

1. *The salary to be at the rate of £40 per annum.*
2. *The club keeper to keep the greens (five in number) on the South part of the course.*
3. *The club keeper not to go away for a day without the Secretary's consent.*
4. *The club keeper to keep himself free until 5pm for engagements with members of the club.*
5. *The club keeper to keep a register of Caddies.*
6. *The club keeper to keep the ground within the railings tidy and to take a general oversight of all clubs not commonly in use.*
7. *Two shillings and sixpence to be the charge for one round with the club keeper and four shillings for two rounds.*

But it was also agreed that Burgess could still play football for Montrose on Saturday afternoons!

By this time, Burgess was supplementing his income from the Royal Albert with a stipend from the Town as head greenkeeper. In this role, he prepared the course for two major tournaments in 1905 (which he also played in).

The tournaments attracted virtually all of the leading golfers of the time. The Royal Albert, though they might admire the golfing skills of these professionals, were very much of the era that held 'amateur gentlemen' in highest esteem and were not prepared to let the professionals have the use of their facilities. Charles instead arranged for them the use of the Mercantile clubhouse. But it was outside the soon-to-be-opened new Royal Albert clubhouse that a photograph was taken, showing Burgess with Harry Vardon, six-times Open champion and James Braid, a five-times winner.

Burgess's golf was first class at the time (he won the Montrose Links Championship in 1905 and he earned a prize in one of the professional tournaments), but over the next three years he seems to have focused on developing his skills as a teacher. According to his biographer (great-grandson Charles D. Burgess) Chay 'taught a pendulum swing featuring a short backstroke and had his pupils envision the motion of a grand-father clock until they gained confidence'.

There is no reason to think that Burgess's stint with the Royal Albert wasn't largely a happy one. But that changes in 1908, with the arrival of the Earl of Southesk as captain. The minute of April 1908 reports that:

> *The Chairman on behalf of the Committee then brought forward the question of whether the Club Keeper (Charles Burgess) was in all respects satisfactory – remarking that the present circumstances were so well known that it was hardly necessary to enter into details.*

Within a week, Charles Burgess had resigned, with an equally mysterious letter: 'For certain reasons, I tender my resignation as club keeper and Professional for Royal Albert Golf Club and as arranged will leave one month from this date.'

It is frustrating for us that references to the reasons – 'so well known that it was hardly necessary to enter into detail' – are not explained by either party. Burgess's great grandson speculates that class friction may have had something to do with it. Chay Burgess was a former trade unionist and an active member of the newly formed Professional Golfers Association, and this may not have sat easily with some of the land-owning gentry who were club members. Chay was also earning extra money teaching golfers from the other clubs, and may have been accused of neglecting Royal Albert members.

Royal Albert professional Charles Burgess with Harry Vardon and James Braid, at the 1905 professional tournament in Montrose. Courtesy of William Coull.

Francis Ouimet, Chay Burgess's pupil, being hoisted on the shoulders of spectators after the US Open victory.

But we don't really know the true story. Whatever the reasons for Burgess's departure, the Royal Albert's loss soon turned into America's gain. Alex Findlay, who happened to be paying a visit to his home town that same year, persuaded Burgess to take up a post at the Woodlands Golf Club in Boston, Massachusetts.

Burgess would stay at Woodlands for thirty-two years, and this part of his story is told in considerable detail in *Golf Links: Chay Burgess, Francis Ouimet, and the Bringing of Golf to America*. That it was a happy association is evident from the gift he received on his twentieth anniversary with the club – $2000 in gold!

Burgess became famous as a golf instructor, and his work with one of his first pupils changed golf for ever. A 15-year-old high school student named Francis Ouimet caught the eye of Burgess, who encouraged and tutored him every step of the way. At the age of 20, playing as an amateur, Ouimet put Burgess's lessons to spectacular use, stunning the sporting world by tieing for the lead after 72 holes of the 1913 United States Open.

Ouimet then won the 18-hole playoff with British golf legends Harry Vardon and Ted Ray, considered the best players in the world at the time. The amazing upset, later depicted in a Hollywood film as *The Greatest Game Ever Played*, is widely credited with being responsible for a surge of interest in golf in the United States.

Fred Findlay

Fred Findlay became professional of the Royal Albert on the departure of his good friend Charles Burgess. Findlay would also make his mark overseas – becoming an important pioneer of golf in both Australia and America.

He belonged to a remarkable golfing family. All were members of the Mercantile Club and all eventually emigrated to work as golf professionals.

Fred was a good golfer in his own right, breaking the course record with a 71 in 1892. He was only 20, the Bandmaster of the Forfar and Kincardine Artillery Militia.

His playing career might have reached greater heights if it hadn't been hampered by a hand injury and his peak playing years were no doubt behind him when the Royal Albert turned to him. In May 1908, Findlay accepted the post, holding out for an annual salary of £30, 'with free house, fire and light'. However, within eighteen months he wrote to the committee offering his resignation and the club accepted it 'with great regret . . . and the committee were instructed to give Findlay an excellent testimonial'.

This particular parting was on the best of terms. Fred's brother Alf had emigrated to Australia and had become the first professional of the Victoria Golf Club in Melbourne in 1906, and he contacted Fred to take up a similar post at the nearby Metropolitan Golf Club. Family health reasons may also have contributed to the decision as his son Freddie suffered from ill health (he would die in Melbourne at the age of sixteen).

The Metropolitan Club can be numbered alongside Victoria and Royal Melbourne as one of the most prestigious clubs in Australia. Fred's record of his service there reveals much about what he had learnt from Bob Dow, and from his short period as the Royal Albert professional. Metropolitan's club history takes up Fred's story:

> Findlay, a vigorous man and witty, if you could understand his burr, brought to his job a mixture of iron discipline towards staff and courtesy to members. . . . The new pro is described as a great character, a clever club maker and a good teacher. Evidence of his club making still exists. He was the master of the art of taking a block of persimmon and chiselling, rasping and sanding it to shape. A brass base-plate was fitted and screwed; F. Findlay was stamped on top and coats of shellac were applied until the gleaming head was ready for the hickory shaft. After the junction was whipped with strong thread, a grip of soft leather was spiralled on and fastened into place. All that for five shillings. The professional stored and cleaned members' clubs for three shillings a month in 1920 and charged four shillings an hour for lessons or six shillings for advice during the round.

NOTES ON GOLF.

Fred Findlay has now the honour of being record-holder of Montrose course, his splendid total of 71 being the lowest in which the round has yet been completed. The play throughout was excellent, the iron approaches being especially a treat to witness.

Keillor's low score of last week may be compared with the record-holder's, and when the best of both are taken it will be found that the score is 68. No fewer than twelve of the holes were done at the same number of strokes. The scores were :—

KEILLOR.

Out, 5 3 4 5 4 4 4 3 4—36 ; in, 5 3 3 5 4 4 3 4 5—36—72.

FINDLAY.

Out, 5 3 5 5 2 3 4 3 4—34 ; in, 6 3 3 5 4 4 4 3 5—37—71.

Newspaper report of 20 year old Fred Findlays' new course record in 1892.

Findlay took on various other roles at Metropolitan – including caddie master – but his career took a decisive new turn when he also became the course curator. According to the club history:

> The extra work brought conflict with McMurtrie, the green keeper, who was sacked, it seems, when he bucked at the Scot's firm control.

This seems to have prompted Fred's interest in course design that developed further when he left Metropolitan in 1922 to join another brother, Alexander (known as A.J.), in America.

After no doubt being tutored in golf by Bob Dow, the eldest of the Findlay brothers – Alexander – had emigrated to the United States from Montrose in the early 1880s to manage a ranch in Nebraska. He had taken his golf clubs on the voyage and while in Nebraska laid out six holes in what may have been the only golf course in America in 1885. A decade later, as golf took off in the United States, Findlay became one of

Photograph of early Australian professions. Fred Findlay is on the left hand end of the middle row. Courtesy of Metropolitan Golf Club.

Course record scorecard from 1918 showing that Fred remained a top golfer well into his 40s. Courtesy of Metropolitan Golf Club.

the most prolific course designers of the day, laying out more than one hundred courses in all. He also promoted the game tirelessly, playing a celebrated series of golf exhibitions with the great Henry Vardon. In 1926 he visited the Vatican where he tried unsuccessfully to establish a 6-hole golf course!

Fred Findlay joined his illustrious brother in the USA and followed in his footsteps, designing 37 courses of his own, many of them still considered classics, primarily in Virginia. He died a wealthy man in Florida, at the ripe old age of 94, yet another successful Montrose protegeé of the great Bob Dow.

Fred Findlay in his later days in America. Courtesy of Metropolitan Golf Club.

CHAPTER 10

The 'Cadies'

That the allowance to cadies be 6d for the round of 18 holes, and 1s per day. Should a boy refuse to carry to any member, his name to be taken off the list.

Royal Albert Golf Club Minutes, 1870

As the Marquis of Montrose is the first golfer on record to hire someone to carry his clubs, we know caddies have been used on the links of Montrose for several hundred years.

Certainly no gentleman from the Royal Albert in the nineteenth century would be expected to carry his own clubs. He wouldn't even have a canvas bag to hold them until near the end of the century when its use became commonplace. Instead, his caddie would carry his clubs under his arm.

The Montrose Golf Rules adopted in 1830 state that:

Parties are at liberty to ask advice for directions from their partners, or cadies, in playing, but not from onlookers, whose observations on the play are not to be listened to; and while the one party is prohibited from walking before the other, it is understood, that no spectator shall interfere in the most distant manner with the game while playing.

So who were these early caddies? A friend or club member might occasionally carry a gentleman's clubs but it was probably local boys who were caddies – boys who had left school or had given school up at an early age or were simply skipping classes and sought to earn a few pence on the links. Many caddies would try the game themselves and some would become really good at it, often much better golfers than the players they caddied for. That was very much the case in clubs all across Scotland in this period.

St Andrews was something of an exception. There, many early golf professionals caddied as well, often for the same gentlemen, and would of course provide expert advice along the way. We know from the depiction of Willie Cushat, the professional in the *Duffers' Golf Club Papers*,

that in Montrose Bob Dow would sometimes be engaged, and that it was accepted that this would give his employer a considerable advantage. When the 'Laird' hires Willie (whose character is based on Bob Dow) to caddie for him, his opponents consider this 'a bit of sharp practice on the Laird's part, for Willie was of great assistance to him'.

But most caddies in Montrose were much younger, as indicated by the repeated references to 'boys' in the club minutes. The earliest surviving cash-book of the club from 1861 refers to payments made to 'fore cadies' but it is not until the club rules were revised in 1870 that we find the first specific rules for the employment of caddies by members:

> *That a list of cadies be posted on the walls of the clubhouse and that the forecaddies be taken alternatively from the list (provided they are not previously engaged). That the allowance to cadies be 6d for the round of 18 holes, and 1s per day. Should a boy refuse to carry to any member, his name to be taken off the list.*

In 1882, the club again tried to enforce the rule that only caddies on an approved list in the club be used.

The Caddie master was, of course, Bob Dow. In 1872, elementary education in Scotland was made compulsory, so all children by law would have to receive an education. Perhaps the club was mindful of this when,

This photograph, reported to be of a group of Montrose golfers, is dated the 1860s. It shows the golfer's dress of the period and caddies carrying the clubs under their arms. Courtesy of Angus Council.

that year, 'the Rev. Robertson proposed that Robert Dow be instructed to see that the cadies attend school in the evenings, which was agreed to'. This was also done at St Andrews.

The neglected education of caddies who found this (generally pleasant) employment a perfect excuse to skip school was one that exercised the minds of many golf clubs in the period, and without much success it must be said. Golfers themselves were more than a touch hypocritical over this issue; playing their competitions as they did in mid-week, boys were a cheaper alternative than an unemployed male.

In 1886, it was again asserted that Robert Dow 'have the sole charge of caddies and that a list of those who carry for the club be hung up in the clubroom'. Note here the first use of the modern spelling of 'caddies'. We may also infer that some members may have been using caddies not on the approved list, possibly to save a few pence.

After a stormy discussion of the issue, the club agreed there would be an increase in rates and resolved 'that the first round of 18 holes be 9d, the second round 6d and the third round 3d or 1/6 per day'. This payment of 1/6 for a total of 54 holes caddying in a day might seem a little inadequate (as well as being physically demanding), but taking relative costs into account, it is equivalent to around £7 today.

Reuben Williams, Caddie Master, outside the Starters Box, in about 1920. Courtesy of Eleanor Werninck.

Caddies would no doubt be boisterous on occasion while waiting to be taken and this seems to have annoyed some members in 1892, who asked that 'the caddies should be prohibited from assembling in front of the clubhouse'. Four years later, the club agreed that 'the rate of pay be 9d per round and that caddies are prohibited from entering the clubhouse and members shall on no account send them into the club for any purpose'.

It seems that caddies were to know their place but some of their number, having had free golf lessons from Robert Dow, would in time become golf professionals themselves and join the exodus of Scottish golfers taking the game to foreign shores and making their mark there; and it all began caddying for Royal Albert members on Montrose links.

The management of caddies was eventually regulated by the Town. A caddie shelter was constructed from funds raised at the Golf Course Improvement Bazaar of 1907, and caddie badges were introduced. On the eve of the First World War, caddies could finally earn a shilling a round, half that for the shorter Auxiliary course.

The Town engaged a separate Caddie Master – issuing him with a cap and jacket –

until the Second World War, after which the use of caddies seems to have declined dramatically. Not only were the economic times tough for golfers but the introduction of the trolley provided an inexpensive, if less colourful, alternative to the 'cadies' who had plied their trade on the links of Montrose for several centuries.

CHAPTER 11

The Clubhouse Sagas

'I dinna' ken fat they'll be wantin' next'

Willie Cushat (*The Duffers' Golf Club Papers*)

All golf clubs become absorbed by the issue of clubhouse facilities from time to time, but for the Royal Albert Golf Club it became a thoroughly troubling preoccupation. In a span of sixteen years, the club used no fewer than four buildings (including a temporary premises) following a vexing and occasionally farcical conflict within the club.

A Quiet Beginning: The Southfield Clubhouse 1866–1890

In its early years, the Montrose Golf Club, quite happily it seems, had no clubhouse at all, with members using one of Montose's many watering holes for refreshment. The granting of royal patronage and the influx of the more genteel members no doubt spurred the club into thinking about acquiring a clubhouse of its own.

The club would have been aware that golfers in other parts of Scotland were acquiring their own facilities. St Andrews, for example, had built its first clubhouse in 1854 (it had shared one for a time before that date). In addition to the obvious benefit of providing facilities at the golf course for members, a clubhouse would allow for the appointment of a professional and be a base from which caddies could operate.

In March 1865 the Town Council agreed that the club could lease, from the town's tenant on Southfield Farm, the 'cottage and pertinents on the southeast corner'. The rent was £4 a year.

In order to fund the improvements to what appears to have been a fairly run-down building, the club managed to raise £78 through a subscription appeal to members. This wasn't enough to cover a total rebuild of the cottage (as the Convenor of the clubhouse committee had wished) but it was enough to get started. Two small rooms were made into one more commodious space for members and an outside rail and well pump were replaced at a further cost of £10.

Also in 1865, the minutes make the first reference to a decision to employ a club professional, with plans made for him to live on the premises. Not more than £40 was to be spent 'in order to place the portion of the cottage to be occupied by Robert Dow which was in very decayed condition into habitable order, and also to provide blinds, locks, chimney cans and economical furnishings'. Those who had offered subscriptions were now to be asked to pay half.

This list of subscribers was also printed in the *Standard* which warmly welcomed the new development and referred to the cottage by what we can only assume was its original name:

> *We understand that this club has recently entered into arrangements for occupying the cottage on the Links, called the Golf House, which is to be converted into a clubhouse. The want of a suitable place of meeting has long been felt: and it is hoped that the proposed Club House will have the effect not only of stimulating local golfers to attend in greater numbers, on Tuesdays and Fridays, which are the usual days of meeting but also of inducing strangers to visit our splendid Links, which for golfing purposes are in some respects unsurpassed.*

The club managed to purchase the building from the Town Council in 1871 for £40. A major extension was then undertaken and it appears the club took out loans totalling £110 for the work.

Tradesmen's expenses for the renovations of the new clubhouse, carefully itemised in the minutes of 1865.

A water supply was installed in February 1881 and, possibly because the club added a drinking fountain available to local citizens, the Town Council agreed to pay half of the costs. Two years later, the fountain was leaking. The club also agreed to meet the costs of a new workshop put up by Robert Dow but it was to remain the club's property.

A Mystery Solved

The club would stay at Southfield until 1890. Yet as time has passed, its location has become something of a mystery.

In *Golf in Montrose*, William Coull speculates that it was located between the 1st and 17th holes of the Broomfield course, in the old stone cottage that remains as part of the present greenkeeper's sheds. But the building there does not appear to have been extended at any time.

So where was the clubhouse? A clue lies in the minutes of 1903, when it is mentioned that the Royal Albert was thinking of buying back, from Mr W.J. Sandford-Thomson, the 'old clubhouse' that was now known as 'The Villa'. This same property was the subject of an article in the *Review* in 1891, which states that the now grand summer residence incorporated the Royal Albert clubhouse.

The 1902 Ordinance Survey map on page 122 also clearly shows 'The Villa' positioned directly opposite the present Royal Montrose clubhouse.

The mystery is solved. The first clubhouse was actually located on the site of (indeed, forms the southernmost and original part of) 'Grey Harlings', the house that currently overlooks the 18th green.

This shows Caddie Master Bob Dow with some of the caddies outside the clubhouse sometime before 1890. Bob's daughter, aged nine, is kneeling at the front left.

A SUMMER RESIDENCE IN MONTROSE.

The above sketch represents what at one time was the Royal Albert Golf Clubhouse, but which now, by extensive additions and alterations, has been converted into a most desirable summer residence; When the Royal Albert Club erected their new Clubhouse near the Railway Bridge their old premises were purchased by Mr W. J. Sandford-Thompson, Balmanno House, Marykirk, and almost immediately the work of reconstruction and altera- tion was begun. Mr Thompson conceived the idea of fitting up the place specially as a summer residence to be let to those spending their holidays in Montrose, and with this end in view he spared no expense to make the place as comfortable as possible, and introduced every modern convenience he thought desirable. The result has been most satisfactory.

Montrose Review article from 1891 about the 'Villa', formerly the first Royal Albert Clubhouse.

Boothby's Battle: the "Stone Bridge" Clubhouse 1890–1906

In its first eighty years the club had made steady progress without facing any great crises. That now changed, as an ambitious and ultimately mis-guided proposal to build a new clubhouse in the South Links deeply divided the Royal Albert.

The campaign in favour of the new clubhouse seems to have been led by Capt. G.M. Boothby who had only joined the club two years previously. Given his name, occupation and passion for golf, it is very possible that he was the near relative of Major Robert Boothby, one of the Royal and Ancient Golf Club's most influential members and a great supporter and golfing partner of Old Tom Morris.

The younger Boothby commanded the Royal Artillery detachment in the nearby Panmure Barracks and certainly seems to have adopted a 'take no prisoners' approach to the clubhouse issue, pushing his ideas through despite a great deal of opposition from members of far longer standing. He would do Montrose a great service by donating the Boothby Championship Shield for the town's best player but his single-minded determination to erect a clubhouse in the South Links would turn out to be a blunder that would affect not only the club but all golfers in the town.

The saga begins rather innocently on 7 December 1888 at a meeting attended by only nine members. A proposal by Capt. Boothby 'that it is desirable that a new club house be built' was carried unanimously.

But then Boothby proposed that 'subject to the consent of the other clubs being got to the alteration of the tee, the site at the Stone Bridge be the site for the new Club house'.

This created a stir. Dr James Howden – a long-time member who had been Captain in 1875 – quite reasonably moved that such an important decision not be made until the following meeting, presumably so more members could be present, but he was outvoted. Boothby's motion passed by six votes to three.

That a controversy erupted and the legitimacy of these votes challenged is obvious from an ominous annotation in the margin of the minutes: 'Meeting held to be contrary to rules as so called.'

A special general meeting was called in March 1889, with Jameson Paton in the chair, to re-run the business of the previous meeting. This time the motion that 'a new clubhouse be built at all' was carried by ten votes to seven, with one abstention.

But there was only a tied vote when Boothby moved that the site of the new clubhouse be moved to the Stone Bridge. Half of those present wanted the new site to be built on or near the existing Southfield clubhouse. On what was becoming a very dramatic evening, the Chairman gave his casting vote for the motion.

That Jameson Paton, who was Club Treasurer at the time, was asked to chair the meeting at all adds a layer of intrigue though, as the owner of a mill in the town employing a thousand workers, he was probably Montrose's most highly-regarded citizen at this time and his chairmanship would be expected to be impartial.

Boothby then proposed that a committee be appointed to 'ascertain on what terms a sum not exceeding £1000 can be borrowed'. Five members handed the Secretary a letter of protest after that meeting and asked that it be recorded in the minutes:

> *The undersigned members protest against the resolution to erect a new clubhouse for the following reasons (1) because a new clubhouse is not required: because if additional accommodation should be desired, it could be added to the present clubhouse and (2) because the funds of the club do not warrant the erection of a new clubhouse.*

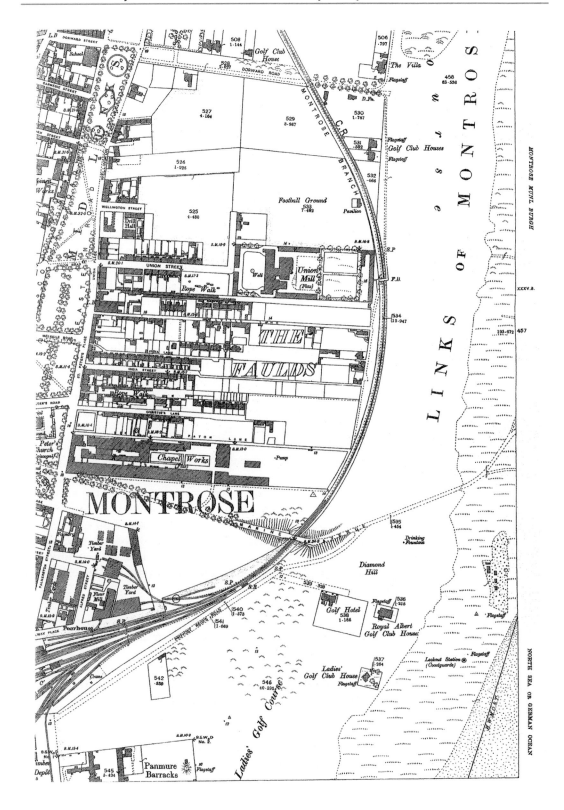

The new clubhouse photographed in 1891 by local photographer John Carr.

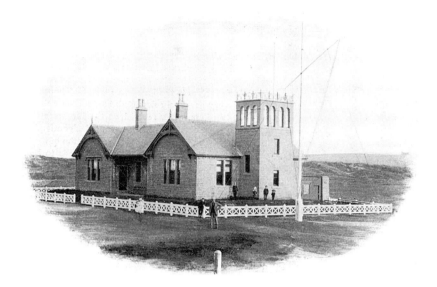

Opposite: The Ordnance Survey map of 1902 showing the location of the ill-fated Stone Bridge clubhouse, by now several hundred yards from the first tee.

These dissenters made a cogent case – the Treasurer at the next meeting reported that club funds stood at just over £13 – but it seemed that the Club Council had made their decision and were not to be swayed.

Now the situation soon turned from drama into farce. In a matter of a few weeks, both sides managed to get the Council to decide that its previous decisions were invalid.

First it was Dr Howden's turn. When the new clubhouse committee put forward its financing scheme, which was almost entirely dependent on loans, its proposals were soundly defeated by Dr Howden and his fellow dissidents. Instead they passed an amendment that 'under the existing rules, it was incompetent to apply the present funds or to borrow money to meet the cost of erecting a new club house', and 'that all proceedings that have been taken . . . are null and void'.

At the next meeting Capt. Boothby struck back, with a motion that proper procedures for voting on his motion at the last meeting had not been followed and that Howden's amendment should not have been adopted. This objection was 'accordingly sustained and the Secretary instructed to enter it in the minutes'.

Dr Howden and G. More Gordon (another former Captain) tried other blocking tactics but in vain, and a decision to lease a 1000-square-yard site at the Stone Bridge was pushed through.

Capt. Boothby, who had now become Club Captain as well, didn't waste any time. Only four months later, in April 1890, he reported that the new clubhouse would be ready by the July meeting.

Boothby had at last won the Clubhouse War, but at what cost? There were certainly casualties. The names of the members of the opposition group, active members all, now totally disappear from the minute book and most may well have resigned.

On the other hand, Capt. Boothby had reinforcements at the ready. No fewer than thirty new members were admitted in a matter of weeks, a recruitment drive that has no parallel in the history of the club.

This was an unprecedented upheaval and it seems that Bob Dow may well have shared the scepticism about the need for the new clubhouse (in which he would have to live). In the *Duffers' Golf Club Papers*, Willie Cushat, the colourful golf professional based on Dow, has this to say:

> '*I dinna' ken fat they'll be wantin' next. . . . If it hadna' been for a curn o' the new comers 'at werna' pleased wi' fat saired aulder and better players, we wid niver a' hard a wird aboot it.*'

If those were indeed Bob Dow's sentiments, he seems to have been right. Looking back, it is hard to fathom the rationale for seeking a site at the Stone Bridge area. It was in the far southwest corner of the links and, while golf was still played here, the main course was moving farther north. Indeed, the Stone Bridge was a substantial distance from the first tee of the new Circular Course that Tom Morris had just helped to arrange, and which had been the site of a major professional tournament that summer (the existing Southfield clubhouse was near the first tee!). Certainly the members voting in favour must have believed that the Town Council would never be able to take the South Links away from them. But whatever the reasons, it proved to be an expensive mistake.

The *Standard* offered a rather critical view of the plans for the new building in 1889, damning with rather faint praise:

> *The new Club House which the Albert Club propose building will be a handsome structure, and specially adapted for the requirements of golfers. The proposed edifice is rectangular in plan, divided into two parts or wings, one wing being specially set apart as a club room, a spacious apartment 39 feet by 20 wide, and lighted by five windows; the other containing a dining room 20 feet by 20 wide, and a kitchen. The central portion connecting these two wings contains two dressing rooms, lavatory etc., and in the front a verandah forms the entrance. The style of the building is what may be termed rural Gothic. Had its outline been more irregular, it would have presented a more picturesque appearance, and the addition of an extra foot in height would detract from its stunted appearance. It is a pity also that there is no efficient means for the disposal of the sewage, and having a cesspool for this purpose is strongly objected to in Montrose at least where we pride ourselves on our sanitary matters. Otherwise the plans are excellent, and when the building comes to be erected, it will be one well worthy of the splendid Links on which it is to stand.*

Funding the new clubhouse was always going to be challenging and the club agreed to accept loans of £25 from twelve members at a rate of

4%, and a loan of £100 from another member, Morton Campbell, at 3% interest which was only to be repaid after the other loans had been discharged. These were very generous gestures by members and may reflect the fact that the club was having difficulty borrowing money from other sources at similar rates of interest. Some of these loans were never to be fully repaid.

On balance, the members seemed to enjoy their new clubhouse with its vastly improved facilities (a handsome stag's head was donated by William Arbuthnott to improve the décor) but the costs continued to hang over their heads. Subscriptions were raised in April 1894 'to provide a fund for the reduction of debt', and it was resolved to make it a priority to repay the loans that members had given the club.

The club also determined to cut expenditure. Even the venerable Bob Dow's wages were cut to £25 a year; the stated reasons were that his workload had been reduced since the club had hired a domestic servant to help him run the clubhouse and the Town had taken over maintenance of the course. It was also noted that the Dows had been allowed to raise the price charged for lunch – from one shilling to one shilling and sixpence.

When Dow retired in 1898 and was replaced by Tom Russell and his wife, it seems that the needs of the clubhouse trumped any golf-related requirements of the job. The *Standard* reported that Russell 'is no golfer, but in the opinion of the club members, that is no disadvantage, seeing what they wished was a good cook. . . . He should soon learn to become proficient in the cleaning of cleeks etc.'.

The members had occupied the Stone Bridge clubhouse for less than ten years when they were forced to consider moving again. The Town Council, and the Victoria and Mercantile clubs all supported a realignment of the course that entailed moving the first hole even farther north. The starting tee would be adjacent to the Royal Albert's former clubhouse (i.e. where it is now). If there were recriminations in the club about the decision made in 1888, there is no mention of them in the minutes but there must have been some severe soul-searching at the very least.

The Town was also making clear its intentions to get rid of the South Links holes which would have left the Royal Albert with a clubhouse for golf that was not particularly near any golf ground.

To get itself out of this mess, the club resorted to a mild form of blackmail, offering to support the alterations to the course but only if the Town Council purchased the Stone Bridge clubhouse! Furthermore, this would have to be at 'a fair price to enable the club to build a new house near the proposed starting tee'.

When the Town turned them down the club became more petulant, this time refusing to participate in the professional tournament being held in 1902 to open the new course. It also kept back some of its contribution to the Town for the maintenance of the course, arguing it had to use that money to maintain the South Links holes the Town wanted to abandon. It even threatens to sue the Town if herring nets were put on the South Links course.

For a club that in its first eighty years had done so much to make Montrose links one of the finest in Scotland, this was definitely not its finest hour. The futility of the entire Stone Bridge episode was brought home at a meeting in September 1903 when David Carnegie suggested to his fellow members that they buy back the old clubhouse if Sandford-Thompson, the current owner, was interested in selling. (He wasn't!)

Finally, the Town saved the Royal Albert from its own folly. When the club dropped its asking price from £1150 to £800, the Town agreed to buy the Stone Bridge clubhouse if the Royal Albert would start paying its full share of the greenkeeping costs.

But even that price proved ludicrously high. It took the Town Council months to resell the building (though they advertised as far away as Edinburgh) and it eventually realised a loss of over £300. This loss was promptly applied to the books of the golf course, a substantial burden given that this amount exceeded the entire annual maintenance budget. In a very real sense, then, all of the golfers in the town suffered from Capt. Boothby's blunder.

Back North Again: The Traill Drive Clubhouse (1906–)

The Royal Albert Club Council, recognising the inevitable, had obviously been looking for new sites and when they finally unloaded the Stone Bridge clubhouse they immediately purchased a new vacant property less than fifty metres from their original clubhouse and next door to the Mercantile Golf Club. The cost was £50, but there was now the small matter of building a new clubhouse. 'Wood work' had been retrieved from the Stone Bridge clubroom (probably still visible on the walls of the front bar of the present clubhouse) but otherwise the club was again starting from scratch.

After debts were paid off following the sale of the Stone Bridge clubhouse, there was £160 left over. Members were given notice of a proposal to borrow £600 in the form of a bond from Alex Lawson, a shipmaster, from Ferryden. Why the club approached him is unclear other than he had funds available and he was presumably happy to receive interest on his capital. As it turned out, this bond was not to be fully repaid until the 1970s.

At the following AGM, Jameson Paton was again elected Captain, a good man to have at the helm at this time. The old Mercantile clubhouse (now known as the 'Golf Lodge', adjacent to 'Roo's Leap' restaurant) was secured as temporary club premises for the rest of the year at a rent of £45. More thought had been given to funding the new clubhouse, with members asked to take up £25 debentures at a rate of 4%. Seven members accepted the offer within a year, including More Gordon and his son of the same name who had been key figures in the campaign to stay at the Southfield clubhouse fifteen years earlier. Some divisions had clearly healed.

*The new clubhouse
in Traill Drive, in
view of the first tee.*

In an interesting sign of the times, the building committee were asked
to 'erect a shelter for bicycles and motor cars' and to contribute to the
making of the road in front of the clubhouse.

By September 1905, the clubhouse was nearing completion. The
Treasurer reported that total costs were likely to be £1730. There was a
deficit of £400 and the Treasurer was authorised to overdraw up to that
amount. Costs would have to be cut and annual subscriptions raised by a
whopping fifty percent, from £1 to £1 10s. A life membership at £25 was
also introduced.

Club Captain Jameson Paton was not present at that meeting but a letter was read from him offering a loan of £400, the exact amount of the
overdraft to be taken on by the club, on very generous terms. No interest
was to be paid until the first instalment was due on 1 April 1911, with
3% interest being applied at that date, rising to 5% only if the club failed
to repay on these terms. (One wonders if he regretted casting the deciding vote in favour of the move to the Stone Bridge clubhouse).

Meantime, the new clubhouse had to be managed to look after the
members' comforts, bearing in mind that a good number did not live in
the town. Mrs Burgess, wife of Charles and keeper of the clubhouse, was
granted £10 per year to hire a maid for 'the greater part of the year'.

The clubhouse initially included two furnished bedrooms that were to
be let out at a fixed price of 'bed and bath 3/6, Breakfast 2/-, Lunch 1/6

and dinner 2/6'. The Council also changed the curtains in the bedrooms from white to green, and, a year later, they took a really important decision – to replace the *Scotsman*, as the newspaper supplied daily, with the *Dundee Advertiser*!

In 1909, the club lost the services of Fred Findlay who had been appointed to replace Charles Burgess as Club Professional. Instead of hiring a new professional, the club approached Robert Winton, a local club maker, 'with a view to come to some arrangement with regard to supplying players for any members who may require them'. Mr and Mrs Clark were hired as housekeepers, on a salary of '£10 a year with a free house, fire, light and taxes'.

Jameson Paton died in 1910 and the club was due to repay the first instalment of £100 the following year, so it approached his trustees with a view to restructuring the loan – to no avail. Other debts were coming due as well. In the coming years, the club would struggle to find ways to juggle these obligations.

What mattered more was that members at last had a clubhouse that suited their needs and which was once again in view of the first tee!

CHAPTER 12

The Centenary Celebrations

Songs were sung by a number of gentlemen and the proceedings were of a most enjoyable character.

Montrose *Standard*, 22 July 1910

In July 1910, the club celebrated both its centenary and the confirmation that the new King, George V, had agreed to become the club's Royal Patron. The first mention of the club's centenary in the minutes comes in 1909 when it was agreed that the principal celebration should be a golf tournament in July followed by a banquet. They also decided to ask the Royal and Ancient to send a team to play a match with the club in Montrose; no more is heard of this idea so we can only assume the R&A was not able to accommodate them on this occasion.

The committee appointed drew up plans for a Centenary Tournament that was to be both a scratch and handicap event. In June, Patrick Dickson persuaded the club that members of the Montrose Ladies Golf Club should be allowed to compete in the Centenary Tournament and he offered to put up the prizes for the ladies.

The second development was that Captain Colin Neish presented a new trophy to be competed for, henceforth called the Centenary Cup.

Neither the Centenary Tournament nor the dinner that followed are reported in the club minutes but the *Standard*'s account of both is quite detailed. The tournament was open to all, and while many entrants were local, a good number came from clubs far and wide in Scotland. There were 141 players in total, which made it, to that point, the largest ever field to do battle over the Montrose links. And a battle it was to be, mainly with the elements, as the *Standard* reported:

Play started at eight, when the conditions were favourable but towards ten o'clock, torrential rains fell followed by brilliant sunshine, and later in the forenoon there was a fierce thunderstorm which recurred at intervals till afternoon, when a strong breeze rose and brilliant sunshine, with showers intervening, prevailed.

That a Carnoustie golfer, James Gillet, scored 74 and 76 in his two rounds that day to claim the scratch prize of two guineas is a tribute to his abilities. The lowest individual round was 73, scored by the eighteen-year-old J.C. Jessop of the local YMCA and Mercantile clubs, one of the town's finest golfers and uncle of a future Captain of Royal Montrose, Sandy Jessop. The handicap prize of five guineas went to a St Andrews University student, A.R.B. Collins.

The dinner in the clubhouse – referred to as a 'Smoking Concert' in the *Standard* – was attended by members and guests from local clubs and the Town Council. J.A. Lindsay, Captain of the Victoria Club, proposed the toast to the Royal Albert and made the following congratulatory remarks:

Golf in Montrose was practically entirely due to the Royal Albert. Until a comparatively recent time, the golf course was entirely maintained at the expense of the Royal Albert. Not only so but in the year 1888, the Royal Albert at their own expense formed the new circular course, opened with a fine tournament, the prizes for which were also provided by the club.

He concluded his speech by assuring the members 'that they would always get the esteem and gratitude of the whole community of Montrose'.

Captain Neish replied on behalf of the club. Other toasts were delivered to 'the Town Council' and 'Other Clubs' and the *Standard* reports that 'songs were sung by a number of gentlemen and the proceedings were of a most enjoyable character'.

GOLF AND DEMOCRACY.

As a holiday resort Montrose richly deserves success. It not only welcomes visitors; it is prepared for them, which is not quite the same thing. The municipality of the town and the Town Improvement Association have been lavish of expenditure to increase the attractions of the town. There are streets whose tree-lined expanse suggest the brightness of a Continental boulevard, and one long avenue in the Mid Links fringed with pleasant gardens provides an ideal setting for a promenade of fashion. The old town is undergoing a re-birth. It has passed its industrial meridian (its splendour is attested by the noble benefactions of its sons), and it is merging into "a place of recreation and repose." As such the late Sir Henry Campbell-Bannerman predicted a great future for Montrose. He was wont to say that he knew of no place in Scotland better fitted than Montrose for that purpose. If the prediction is fulfilled, it will be mainly due to golf. The gable-ends are disappearing; the links are expanding. There are now five courses, ample accommodation for the expert to shine and the duffer to play unafraid. Golf is at once a royal and a democratic game. Social caste does not obtrude on the links; and nowhere are there more democratic links than in Montrose, which is only to be expected in a town where the spirit of democracy is innate and aggressive. At one time, it is true, the links of Montrose were more exclusive, in the days when the Royal Albert Club was young. The Royal Albert is now approaching its centenary, and it is still a Club of somewhat patrician character. But alongside the pavilion of the Royal Albert is the equally stately pavilion of the Artisans Club. Separately housed, the players mingle on the links, and if a Royal Albert member occasionally grumbles at the changed condition of things, it is not because of snobbishness; his complaint merely means that the links are sometimes uncomfortably crowded. When they are crowded it is good for Montrose. The measure of the popularity of the links is the measure of the popularity of Montrose as a holiday resort.

An extract from the Montrose Review on golf and democracy, written to coincide with the Royal Albert centenary.

CHAPTER 13

Montrose Royal Albert Golf Club, 1910–1985

That a roll of honour of members of the club be prepared.

Motion by the Rev. Taylor at a meeting of the
Royal Albert Golf Club, 1915

This next period in the history of one of the world's oldest golf clubs is not as glorious as the first hundred years. There are occasions, however, when the club resurrects itself on the Montrose golfing stage, though rarely now on the national stage as it had often done in its first century.

Other clubs in the town were growing at a considerable rate as golf became more and more popular among both men and women. Yet the Royal Albert does not grow significantly in numbers in this period and, as a consequence, finds itself financially (and in a golfing sense too) out-muscled by the other clubs. The *Review* in 1910 may have got it right when it referred to the 'patrician' stance of the Royal Albert, which increasingly may have been out of step with changing times.

Its somewhat restrictive membership selection processes, still based on black ball balloting, did not help it to grow. Many upwardly-mobile men in the area were unwilling to undergo that particular test and instead sought membership of other clubs in the town. Nor did the 'Royal' have many of the best local golfers in this period within its membership; these were to be found mainly in the Mercantile and Victoria clubs.

The Royal Albert also suffered from the hangover of debts from the building of two clubhouses in sixteen years. More than a dozen different loans needed to be repaid, including £400 to the Paton estate which was only cleared off the club's books in 1933. Individual members who had loaned the club £25 each were offered life memberships in lieu of repayment, and some members took up this offer.

Others had to wait a long time for their money. It wasn't until 1953 that the descendents of Alexander Lawson demanded repayment of the bond taken out in 1906, yet the club still did not have the funds to meet its obligation. Their solution was to take out another bond from a some-what unusual source – the Montrose Natural History and Antiquarian

Society – which presumably had ample funds available. The Lawson Bond saga is eventually wound up around 1976.

A loan from Morton Campbell, also for funding the clubhouse, was *never* repaid, though the Club Council in the 1960s did try in vain to find his descendents.

With the finances in such a fragile state, it is not surprising that in the lead up to the First World War we find mention of only minor improvements and repairs. When it was found that the Robert Dow Pension Fund had an outstanding balance of £71, for example, the subscribers agreed that some of it could be used to paint the outside woodwork. The Captain's Board in the foyer of the clubhouse was erected in 1912 and the first telephone installed in 1913, with the charge for calling the Montrose Exchange to be two pence per call (junction and trunk calls extra).

In 1912, an Edinburgh architect was called in to examine dampness in the clubhouse and he concluded that 'the method of construction adopted in forming the asphalt flats on the roofs is bad, and as the stone used is of a porous nature, I am of the opinion that water is finding its way under the asphalt and so into the interior'. Almost a hundred years later, the problem is still being dealt with.

In 1912 there is also the first reference to a visiting party or society being granted the privileges of the clubhouse. However, as the first-ever group of this sort, the members of the Sanitary Congress were possibly not the most auspiciously-named!

British Amateur Championship

In 1886, Royal Albert had been one of twenty-four clubs to subscribe towards the purchase of the British Amateur Championship trophy – the same trophy that is competed for today. It appears that this contribution gave the club an entitlement to be represented on the committee that made the arrangements for the Championship.

Club representatives may not have attended all of these meetings from 1886 onwards but, from 1908–1913, the club had a very committed delegate in the form of C. Strachan Carnegie, who attended all of the meetings. He was very diligent in setting out – usually at some considerable length – his views on the organisation of the Championship for which he sought, and was invariably given, the club's approval.

For example, he told the club in 1908 that he was not in favour of the Championship being played on a rota of only five courses –

The Amateur Trophy, partly funded by the Royal Albert.

he felt that 'magnificent courses have sprung up all over Great Britain that would be suitable'. He was particularly not happy to see

> *Sandwich and Deal monopolising the Championships open and amateur. They are much the same links as the old North and South courses at Montrose and the accommodation is insufficient and inconvenient. Personally, I would not get a bed nearer than Ramsgate 7 miles away.*

He criticised Sandwich (the club is officially known as Royal St George's) as a course that, in his view, was not fit to host championships:

> *So many long approach shots are absolutely blind over a hillock, a defect which puts players from a distance, and not conversant with the lie of the ground, the distances or the hazards at a great disadvantage.*

Carnegie's strong views of the defects of the Sandwich course were obviously not shared by everyone, as Royal St George's has hosted the Amateur another eight times (and the Open Championship another nine!). However, the Amateur has, as Carnegie hoped, greatly expanded its horizons, having been played on 22 courses to date.

In 1920, Royal Albert's role in the administration of one of golf's great championships ended when all of the clubs involved agreed to cede complete responsibility for the arrangements to a committee of the R&A.

The First World War

On the outbreak of the First World War, all competitions were cancelled and many members joined up. Among the earliest to enlist seems to have been the Honorary Secretary and Treasurer, Thomas Lyell. The Council met in November 1914 to appoint a replacement as 'it is not known when he may return'. His replacement was H.G. Cowell, but he in turn had to be replaced less than a year later when he also joined His Majesty's forces.

The club still held general meetings throughout the war and, in 1915 the Rev. Taylor rather ominously proposed that 'a roll of honour of members of the club be prepared'. No evidence of this roll of honour has come to light and it is not known how many members were among the casualties. We do know that the Club Captain from 1914–16, the Earl of Dalhousie, received very severe wounds, and that Thomas Lyell and H.G. Cowell survived the conflict.

Austerity was the order of the day. Noting the 'the absence on military service of a large number of members of the club', the Royal Albert ceased paying their £5 contribution to the Town Council for representation on the Greens Committee. It also reduced the wages of the club keepers and even cancelled the subscription to the *Dundee Advertiser*!

The club continued its policy from the previous century of offering membership to officers of the armed forces. Officers of the Gordon Highlanders had been given membership when they were in Montrose for a month in 1912. During the war itself, however, there seems to have been little time for golf among those in service. Despite the fact that many Royal Flying Corps officers would have served at Montrose's military airfield – the first in Britain – there is no mention of any admission of airmen until one was admitted in 1919.

While the club obviously supported the war effort, it appears the Colonel of the 2/7th Argyll and Sutherland Highlanders (based in the town) overstepped the mark when he asked to take over the entire clubhouse for his officers. The Council were minded to recommend acceptance under certain conditions but, at a special general meeting of the club that followed a few days later, the request was rejected 'as it was within the knowledge of members that suitable accommodation could be obtained elsewhere, and that until efforts to obtain such were thoroughly exhausted they did not feel it encumbent on them to move further in the matter'.

In the run up to the Second World War, the club asked the advice of the Royal and Ancient Golf Club on how to treat the large number of officers serving at RAF Montrose. They were told that the R&A admitted RAF officers at Leuchars on payment of subscription only, no entry fee being charged. Presumably this is what Royal Albert decided to do in Montrose, though the minutes don't confirm that.

In 1937 the RAF Montrose Station Sports Secretary made an enquiry, 'whether the Officers Mess at this Unit could become a member collectively of your Golf Club' and concludes by saying that, if this were agreed, 'it would be heartily approved of by the considerable number of players on this station'. The club agreed that up to twelve officers could do so, on payment of ten guineas subscription. Any more in excess of this number would have to pay £15 15s.

The Lady Associates

Allowing officers of the armed forces to take up membership on favourable terms was quite acceptable, but allowing women to become members, or even to cross the threshold of the club, was another matter altogether.

A small but important step was taken in 1923 when R.C. Hoyer Millar, whose wife was a past Secretary of Montrose Ladies Golf Club, persuaded the Royal Albert to at least allow members to entertain women in the club dining room.

The following year he went further. While the club was still not prepared to allow women to become full members – that was a step too far for most golf clubs at the time – Hoyer Millar pushed a motion through the Club Council that created the new membership category of lady associates.

Wives, daughters and sisters of members could now automatically become members. Other women had to be voted in by the lady associates

A flight of training aircraft – Harts – from Montrose airfield around 1938. Directly underneath the flight is the South Links golf course (still used for golf at this time) and the former Royal Albert Stonebridge Clubhouse. Courtesy of Montrose Air Station Museum.

themselves, using similar admission procedures to those used by the men, including presumably the use of the black ball, though this is never mentioned. The ladies were to have exclusive use of the clubroom and cloakroom upstairs, and the dining room was the only location in which they could be served refreshments. Thirty-two associates were admitted en bloc in 1924.

Despite this encouraging start, the club seems to have taken a quite limited view of the role the lady associates could play in the club. Some of the ladies must have golfed, yet no competitions were held until at least 1930, when the ladies asked that part of their fifteen-shilling subscription be given back to them to allow them to affiliate to the Ladies' Golf Union, and thus be able to gain recognised handicaps. The club cautiously agreed that 2s 6d of the subscriptions could be used for this purpose, 'on a trial basis'.

The club continued to overlook the potential of the lady associates to help reinvigorate the club until 1950 when they were asked to form a joint committee to plan social and fundraising events. Even then, some members seemed concerned at the numbers of associates and various suggestions were made in 1959 to reduce them; these (thankfully) remained suggestions only.

Golf Between the Wars

The club considered, and then rejected, suggestions made in 1921 for winter competitions and instead made a few slight changes to the summer schedule. The golf programme at that time contained just seven events: the four Medals, which were stroke-play competitions; the Rangoon Cup, which was a bogey competition; and the Foote-Millar and Centenary trophies, which were handicap match-play.

Compared to other local clubs, this was a pretty thin programme. Fred Findlay's Mercantile membership card of 1910 shows that club offering its members over twenty competitions. This may well be one of the reasons for the Royal Albert's slow decline in terms of numbers and finance. It took the club until 1950 to appoint its first Match Secretary and to print its first fixture list for issue to members. Entry fees for club competitions were only introduced in 1939.

Nor did the Royal Albert join the Forfarshire County Golfing Association – the precursor of the present-day Angus County Golf Association – when it was first set up just after the First World War to provide clubs with both county competitions and links with the newly-formed Scottish Golf Union. Royal Albert waited three years before agreeing to join the Association. It hosted its first county match in the clubhouse in 1938.

In 1924 the club agreed to play Medal competitions on a Saturday for the first time and to delete a clause restricting play to between the hours of 9.00 a.m. and 5.00 p.m – clear signs that more members had full-time jobs and fewer now belonged to the leisured classes.

Facilities in the clubhouse continued to evolve, with electricity and a gas cooker arriving in the 1920s, and lockers in 1931, presumably replacing the old members' boxes.

Each club in these days was responsible for setting the handicaps of its members. In 1931, the club increased all members' handicaps by two strokes. No reason is offered for this in the minutes but, with the club taking such an arbitrary action, it might help to explain why there were moves around this time to set handicaps at all local clubs by some agreed method. The first step towards this did not materialise until 1951, however, when the Montrose Golf Association fixed the standard scratch for the championship course at 70 and recommended that the clubs add two strokes to all handicaps.

The Second World War

Golfers in Montrose still played on the courses in the First World War but in the Second World War the golf courses and the clubhouses were almost entirely within a restricted area, being adjacent to a serving RAF base that had to be defended against airborne attack. The base and the town were in fact to be subject to several bombing raids by the Luftwaffe and the beach area also had to be defended against possible invasion.

Royal Albert members played for the Original Gold Medal in April 1940 but that was the last competition held until the war ended. Members who lived during these challenging times do not recall much golf being played throughout the war years.

The club agreed from the outset of war to offer its facilities to the various Officers' Messes in and around the town. The Local Defence Unit – the precursor of the Home Guard to be affectionately nicknamed 'Dad's Army' – used the clubhouse as their base for a short period, but that arrangement was cancelled when a new HQ for the Montrose Platoon was found.

In July 1941, the club agreed to an unusual request from Lady Napier of FANY (First Aid and Nursing Yeomanry) 'that facilities be provided within Royal Albert Golf Club for the formation within the clubhouse premises of a Polish Officers Club'.

Specifically, Lady Napier asked for 'two rooms and the use of a bedroom upstairs for the accommodation of a FANY hostess'. Her organisation had marked the club as an ideal site, being opposite Grey Harlings where a large percentage of the Polish officers were quartered.

The club speedily approved the arrangement – by which it would receive £2 a week – subject to a number of conditions. Bar prices, for example, were to correspond with Montrose hotel lounge prices, and the Polish officers could only use their own liquor supplies for a large party if they gave advance notice to the Secretary. FANY were to meet any increased electricity and coal costs. They were also to be responsible for the blackout being rigorously observed.

It is not known for how long the Polish officers used the clubhouse but it seems they and the members happily co-existed for a few months at least. In 1942, the club offered membership to the officers of the Black Watch who were based in the area.

The Post-War Era

By this time the club had changed its practice of holding its meetings in the afternoons before playing for Medals. Instead, meetings were scheduled in the evenings, a reflection on the changed lifestyle of the typical member of the club. In 1952, the club also decided to reintroduce the practice that Captains should normally serve for two years.

Just over 150 years from the club's inception, the first typed minutes begin to appear in 1951 with the Secretary, Col. Scott Robinson, introducing this 'new' technology (he had a son who became an early golf professional in Sweden). He proved to be ahead of his time, as most of the following Secretaries reverted to hand-writing until typed minutes become the norm in the 1980s.

The front cover of the programme of events to celebrate the 150th anniversary of the Royal Albert Golf Club.

In trying revitalise itself, the club decided in 1952 to reintroduce junior members, but these would be restricted to 'boys and girls between the ages of 14 and 18 who are sons or daughters, grandsons or granddaughters or brothers or sisters of existing club members'. No lockers were to be made available and the juniors were allowed access to the dining room but not the clubroom. In 1957, the club reduced the entry age for juniors to 12.

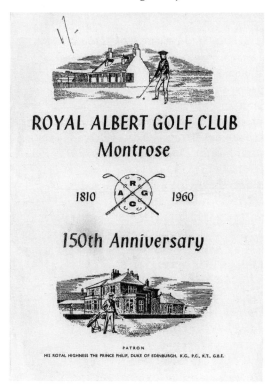

The 1950s also saw the introduction of two important new social activities. In 1951, there is the first mention of a 'Smoker' – an annual gathering to celebrate the prize-winners – which becomes a standard feature of the club calendar. In that year also, the club held a Christmas dance at the Park Hotel (presumably the clubhouse, before the later extensions were added, was too small to accommodate such a gathering). Within a short time, the annual Royal Albert Christmas Ball became one of the main social events in the town, bringing in some much-needed extra revenue; was held every year up to 1985.

The 150th Anniversary

The club celebrated its 150th anniversary in September 1960. It organised a series of golfing events spread over three days with the main event being an inter-club foursomes involving the eleven clubs who had participated in the 1857 Grand Match at St Andrews.

The inter-club foursomes on Sunday was followed by a dinner in the clubhouse attended by invited guests and members

End of the Black Ball

By the 1950s, membership of the club was still declining and may have reached a low point in 1957 with only 79 members (with an additional 37 lady associates). Nevertheless, the black ball procedure was still very much in place; the minutes of 1962 note that two membership applications (out of eight) were rejected because 'the ballot was found not clear'.

However, in 1968, the use of the black ball in balloting for membership finally ceased. The new arrangement for admitting members consisted simply of an application supported by a proposer, a seconder, and six sponsors. The end of the black ball ballot might possibly account for a temporary rise in membership. By 1969 there were 107 full members, 79 lady associates and 36 county and overseas members. Unfortunately, such a healthy membership position was not to be maintained for very long.

A few were members of exceptionally long standing. Canon E.W. Millar had been a member for seventy-four years starting in 1897, which would almost certainly make him the longest-serving member in the club's history. Huntley Cowell hit the half-century mark in 1959 and was offered honorary membership but the minutes record that

> *Mr Cowell who was present thanked the Captain and members for their expressions of goodwill, but declared that he did not wish to accept the nomination as an Honorary Member since he would be debarred from participating actively in the administrative affairs of the club.*

With more members of that calibre, the club's future would have been secure!

(It is perhaps a mere coincidence that the Royal Montrose's longest-serving member, having joined the 'Vicky' in 1953, was also 'a man of the cloth' – the much-loved Rev. Tom Long. Tom was born in 1909 and, much to the regret of his many friends, died in 2009 just a few months short of his 'centenary'.)

Caddie Cars, the Fairway Golf Ball Machine, and other Improvements

In 1951, the first caddie car shelter was added, funded largely through the generosity of member Charlie Cameron. It was not long, however, before the committee were trying to persuade members to keep this area tidy, even to the extent of providing parking lines and more hooks in 1957 in an attempt to bring order out of chaos.

In that same year, the cocktail bar was built in the main lounge and drinks were now served in the front clubroom – the men's bar – by means of a hatch. This seems to have been the first proper bar in the clubhouse, drinks having previously been served by the Steward from an area resembling an enlarged cupboard. On Sundays, members took drinks from a dresser in the early years and signed the appropriate chits. Central heating was first installed in 1961 with electric storage heaters.

Around this period, the club installed a Fairway Golf Ball machine. Members put in sixpence and pulled a lever; if three balls were viewed in the display, new golf balls could be claimed from the Steward. The top prize was three Dunlop 65 golf balls, while a Warwick ball was a lesser prize.

In the late 1960s the current flat-roofed extension to the clubhouse was added. While possibly not a fine example of architecture, it did offer the club the space to host large-scale dances, dinners and other social events in the clubhouse for the first time, and present-day members are grateful for that. Funding both of these improvements was to be a considerable challenge for members of this era.

The Albert Medal Resurfaces

In an earlier part of this account, we learnt that the Albert Medal had been mislaid early in the twentieth century. In 1911, R.C. Hoyer Millar, in whose care the medal was last seen, offered to purchase a replacement, but insisted that the club adopt a better system to record medals being passed from the winner to the Secretary for engraving, and back again.

Matters proceeded slowly and it was a year before the club submitted designs for the replacement. No cast had been taken of any medal (as was the case in St Andrews) and when the club presented Millar with an

The Albert Medal on display in the clubhouse.

estimate of over £16 (over £1000 in today's money) for a new Gold Medal, he objected to the cost. He offered to meet a share of the cost if the club met the rest. He also pointed out that the original Albert Medal was only gold-plated!

The minutes don't make clear whether a replacement was in fact purchased at that time but the members continued to play for the Albert Medal for most of the inter-war years. In 1952 it became the prize awarded to the winner of the first-ever club championship and continued to be used for that purpose until 1986.

Since the 1986 amalgamation, this Albert Medal has no longer been competed for but it is still on display in the clubhouse. While it's possible that the original medal re-surfaced at some point, it is more likely to be a replica.

George Robb, a Past Captain who won it on several occasions as club champion, recalls that it was spoken of by older members as a replacement for the original that went missing, so Hoyer Millar's offer to fund a replacement back in 1911 seems, after all, to have been taken up, though it is intriguing that the markings on this medal indicate it was made by an Edinburgh silversmith in the mid-nineteenth century.

The Royal Blackheath Matches

A significant new development on the playing front came in 1958, when the Royal Blackheath Golf Club invited the ten other clubs which had taken part in the 1857 Grand Match to a Centenary Tournament in London. The four-man team, from the Royal Albert, led by Vice-Captain Gordon Mortimer, returned with a fine gift from Royal Blackheath – a copy of the original programme for the 1857 match that is still proudly displayed in the clubhouse.

Participants in the first match at Blackheath in 1963. Courtesy of Peter Booth.

After Royal Blackheath had attended Royal Albert's 150th celebrations in 1960, one of their members, Richard Hawkins, brought a team of four Blackheath members to Montrose in October 1961 to play an inter-club match, following which he presented the King James Quaich to the club. He made the suggestion that there be an annual match between the clubs for the trophy – a suggestion that the committee were

very happy to endorse and, as a mark of the great esteem in which they held Richard Hawkins, they extended to him honorary membership of the Royal Albert.

The first match for this new trophy was held in Montrose in 1962. These matches have always been played on a holes-up basis – Montrose won the first match by 11 holes – and they were to continue until 1984. Then, after a hiatus of 23 years, the matches were resumed in 2007.

The early matches are fondly remembered and were the highlight of the golfing year for many Royal Albert members. When the matches were at home, there was usually a social function on the Saturday evening, open to all club members, to welcome their guests from London, followed by a dinner on the Sunday for the participants. In 1962, Herbert Booth, the immediate Past Captain, took some 16mm movie footage of the match in Montrose, shot both on the course and at the railway station on the Monday morning, when a local pipe band serenaded the departing Blackheath golfers until they had boarded the London train.

When it was an away match, the Royal Albert team boarded the sleeper train to London in the evening and emerged in Kings Cross station the following morning, well-fortified with the supplies they had taken on board to prepare them to do battle for the Quaich.

Other Competitions

In 1959, there was another reminder of the club's past history when the Dalhousie Golf Club in Carnoustie made contact with the Royal Albert to report that they had just discovered, in their clubhouse, the Forfarshire Cup. It had been presented by Charles Carnegie back in 1869 for annual competition between the clubs and competed for every year up to 1883. The Dalhousie club suggested that these matches might be resuscitated; the committee agreed to look at this but it was not until 1967 that the matches were resumed and they were then played most years up to 1985.

Regular inter-club matches were also introduced, for a time, closer to home with both Edzell and Arbroath Golf Clubs.

Finally, we end this account of the golf competitions of the Royal Albert where we began the story in 1818, with the Original Gold Medal; after 159 years, in 1977, the committee changed the rules. The Gold Medal was now to be competed for late in the season by all of the winners of the club's other Medals, and that is an arrangement that continues to the present time.

Fluctuating Finances

Finances of the club in the years after the Second World War fluctuated considerably and were influenced greatly by the performance of both the bar and gaming machines.

Alcohol consumption was, by present-day standards, quite considerable. In 1961, for example, 'bar drawings', as they were called, were over £2400 while total subscriptions by comparison were just over £368, and the club not surprisingly had a healthy surplus at that time.

Profit margins on bar sales were set pretty low; it seems that members expected to purchase drink at not much more than cost price. In 1958, for example, the bar profit was only 10%, and the club turned to local hotelier and member, Matt Todd, to advise on purchases and prices. Thanks to his efforts, the profit margin rose to 28% in 1958 but was again recorded as a disappointing 19% in 1963. Nor was the situation helped by what is described in 1957 as a 'bar subscription deficit' of £134 – the amount members owed in bar bills!

Nor presumably did the arrangements for the first Sunday opening of the bar in 1958 improve things. In deciding to serve drinks on a Sunday for the first time in its history, the club didn't want to pay extra wages to temporary staff or to impose on what was the club keeper's day off, so they adopted an 'honesty bar' approach:

> *It was resolved that a supply be purchased at retail price from the steward and be available in the club room with measures and a price list, that members be requested to make their own purchases and to conform to the hours.*

This arrangement lasted for some years but, perhaps inevitably, significant losses were found to have occurred, so eventually arrangements were made to staff the bar on a Sunday.

One new and, for a short period, important source of extra income was the profit from gaming machines. The first machine was introduced into the club in the early 1960s; in a relatively short time, there were two of them in place. As in many other golf clubs in this period, the profit on their operation was quite considerable and helped the club to meet the considerable costs of building the lounge extension to the clubhouse in the 1960s.

Unfortunately for the club finances, the popularity of gaming machines was quite short-lived and, by 1977, income from them was on the decline, and that decline continued into the 1980's. The large drop in income from this source was to add greatly to the club's financial problems in this period.

In spite of the valiant efforts of various Councils, the financial position of the club deteriorated alarmingly and deficits in excess of £4000 and £6000 were recorded in 1984 and 1985 respectively. These alarming statistics helped to persuade members that there was no alternative but to enter into discussions with other local clubs to discuss possible amalgamation.

Discussions proceeded slowly at the outset but then, in 1986, discussions with the Victoria Golf Club and North Links Ladies Golf Club rapidly reached a conclusion that was to produce a merged club – the Royal Montrose Golf Club.

The Club Keepers

The club was immensely fortunate to benefit from the services of a handful of long-serving club keepers and stewards, all of whom lived in the clubhouse itself.

Mr and Mrs W.R. Clark (1910–1925). Replacing Fred Findlay, the Clarks were employed at annual salary of £10 a year with 'a free house, fire, light and taxes'. The club met their request for an increase in wages two years later and awarded them £15 per annum. The Clarks appear to have given great service to the club – there is a total absence of complaints in the minutes from members about service in this period – and it was with great regret that the club accepted their resignation in 1925, 'owing to advancing years'.

Sergeant-Major Buchan and Mrs Buchan (1927–1952). The Buchans became valued club servants, so much so that the club paid Mr Buchan a bonus for a number of years, in part for maintaining the flower beds and gardens around the clubhouse in pristine condition. Mrs Buchan's catering was also very much in demand.

In 1948, the club had to respond to the demands put on establishments by the recently-passed Catering Wages Act, to set the wages of staff dispensing drinks at a certain minimum level. The Secretary was able to satisfy the official from the Board that 'the sale of liquor was a very minor activity of the club'. That may have been a considerable understatement and was to cause a later problem for the club.

The Buchans seemed happy with their lot and the club was very happy with them. When Mr Buchan took ill in 1951, the club appointed Mrs Buchan as his replacement but further ill-health caused them both to intimate their retirement in 1952. The club attempted, over a period of months, to find them alternative accommodation – even trying to find a replacement club keeper with whom they could exchange houses – but to no avail. The Council were eventually asked to re-house the Buchans, and the post was advertised at a salary of £50 per annum. Among the conditions of service was that the club keeper was to be available to members every day except a Sunday.

The club had been planning to give an honorarium to the Buchans for their long period of service but they both succumbed to ill health and died that year, so the club paid the sum of £50 to their surviving daughter. A rather sad postscript to this story is that Miss Buchan felt aggrieved that her parents had not been paid the minimum wage dictated by the 1948 Catering Wages Act and claimed arrears of wages. There was exchanged a series of letters between her solicitor and that engaged by the club; two years later the club reported to members that the claim 'had been successfully disposed of ', but also that the wages of the new club keeper would need to take account of the legislation.

Mrs Lily Stuart and Jack Stuart (1954–1970). Lily Stuart served the club for sixteen years, with her husband Jack undertaking occasional club maintenance at those times when his job as a salmon fisher allowed. Their son Ian Stuart has been a member of this club for many years and has fond recollections of his time as a resident in the clubhouse, especially the ready opportunities offered on his doorstep to hone his golfing skills.

The photograph below shows Ian's parents manning the new 'cocktail bar', and the Fairway Golf Ball Machine is also on display.

At this time, there was only limited catering, offered at the rather modest prices set by the committee in 1953:

High Tea	*– 3s*
Afternoon tea	*– 1/6d*
Tea & biscuits	*– 9d*
Biscuits & cheese	*– 3d*

A suggested increase by Mrs Stuart in 1960 of the price of tea and biscuits to one shilling prompted a letter of protest to the committee from some of the lady associates; the committee in its wisdom decided to leave prices as they were.

Mr and Mrs Tasker (1973–1984) were a popular couple with the members. Mrs Tasker was of Italian extraction and is remembered by members as a first-class cook who provided a range of delicious meals.

Lily and Jack Stuart. Courtesy of Ian Stuart.

Profiles of Key Figures

F.A. Milne

Fred Milne was the only golfer to be Captain, at separate times, of both the Royal Albert and Victoria clubs, and he also presented F.A. Milne trophies to both clubs that are still competed for today. The photograph opposite captures him dressed in a typical 1940s style.

Kathleen Copley (nee Lackie)

Kathleen was the daughter of Cathy Lackie, herself a good golfer and a leading figure in the Royal Albert Lady Associates and the wider world of ladies' golf in the UK, including involvement with the running of the Curtis Cup competitions.

Kathleen was a gifted young player who captained the Scottish girls' team in the early 60s. She soon made her mark in ladies' competitions in the Montrose and Angus area and became a regular county team player. In 1974, she reached the final of the Scottish Women's Amateur Championship at Nairn and had an epic duel with Dr Aileen Wilson (Haggs Castle) before losing at the 22nd hole.

She was capped for Scotland in 1974 and 1975. While living temporarily in Singapore, she also gained further international honours, representing that country for two successive years in the 1980s.

After her marriage, she served on the Scottish Ladies' Golfing Association executive, becoming chairman in 1990. She died in 2007 at the age of 63.

F.A. Milne. Courtesy of David Milne.

Kathleen Copley on the first tee at Montrose.

CHAPTER 14

The Victoria Golf Club, 1864–1986

Friendship Sincere and Loyalty True

Motto on the original Silver Medal of the
Victoria Golf Club, 1865

Though a junior partner in the history of Royal Montrose in terms of longevity, the Montrose Victoria Golf Club was in its own right one of the most venerable golf clubs in the world when it amalgamated with the Royal Albert in 1986.

Its story begins on 4 October 1864 when, according to the club minutes, nine gentlemen met in the Crown Hotel 'for the purpose of forming a new golf club'. James Allardice, publisher, was in the chair and stated that '13 gentlemen have agreed to become members with good prospect of raising that number to 25 or 30'. Entry money was fixed at two shillings and sixpence, and draft rules based on those of the Royal Albert were proposed. The naming of the club was delayed, although various suggestions (unrecorded) were made, and John Watson was elected as Captain.

Captain Watson was an interesting character. In 1864, he was a 70-year-old retired farmer who had come to live in the town. He was also noted as a poet – his book of verse *Samples of Common Sense* was published in 1875 – and he contributed articles on agriculture to several magazines.

The first meeting also appointed James Davidson, clerk, as Secretary and Treasurer and Allardice and David Sinclair, postmaster, as members of the new club's committee. Others present were James Crammond, iron founder, David Duncan, jeweller, Alexander Rodgers, bookseller, R. H. Warren, bandmaster, and Charles Irvine and David Smart, both shoemakers.

From the occupations of the first members, it is clear that the new club was filling a niche for those who were keen on golf but who on the social ladder fitted somewhere between the working men who had already set up their own golf clubs, and the members of the Royal Albert, which had become more exclusive since acquiring royal status.

Three days later a second meeting agreed that the name of the new club should be 'Montrose Victoria Golf Club'. A Silver Medal was to be competed for annually and David Duncan offered to make one for less than forty shillings.

The Medal was to be competed for on Thursday, 13 October at 1.30 p.m. but two members were given the right to compete together the following day if that time proved inconvenient (perhaps one of the first examples of an 'extra day score'). The office bearers were to procure a supply of flags (white with red edging) to denote the holes on competition days.

At a third meeting in the following week, eighteen rules were adopted (although these were later modified, initially following correspondence with the St Andrews, Perth and Musselburgh clubs). A motion was passed not to admit young men under the age of eighteen as members, and arrangements were agreed for the Medal and (importantly!) the sweepstake, which were to be played the next day.

The results of that first competition show a winning score of 102 strokes by Robert Williamson, three better than James Allardice. The highest scores were produced by Charles Irvine, having recorded 170 strokes to the 182 of his partner, David Smart, indicating that these men were probably relative newcomers to the sport. An account (almost certainly fictional) of the exploits of this final pairing provided much amusement when it was recounted many years later at the club's Jubilee dinner

The principal speaker at that dinner was R.W. (Bob) Mackie, a 'Vicky' member, then working as a journalist in Glasgow, who royally entertained the members with further recollections of this auspicious launching of a new club, drawing on both personal reminisences from older members and, at times, a mischievous imagination.

He recalled that the first meeting-place of the club was the Crown Hotel, a licensed establishment, though he disparagingly referred to it as a 'pussyfoot place, somewhere where families met to enjoy ginger beer and bridies, not a place for serious drinking'. Nevertheless, he recalled that it had some redeeming features, not least a buxom landlady who would marry one of the club's founding members, James Davidson, who 'became the Falstaffian and favourite proprietor of the Star Hotel'. Mackie also remembered:

> Charles Irvine, tall and straight with the hat and mien of a professor; and David Smart, strange of speech but a fine fellow for all that; and David Sinclair, whose fulminations often frightened me from the Post office, then situated under the Ball House.

Mackie makes the original members out to be a colourful lot but they were certainly strikingly effective in getting a new golf club off the ground.

By the time of the first annual meeting in 1865, twenty-seven members had been admitted and the first handicapped competition played. The

A team from the Victoria in one of their many inter-club matches, against on this occasion St Andrews University team in St Andrews.

prizewinners were those who 'took the greatest number off their score as averaged by the committee or those who came in fewest above their averaged score'. Later that year Bob Dow was admitted as the first honorary member and was 'to be paid one pound annually for the trouble in making holes in the golf course for the club's use at the various competitions'.

Eventually, the silver medal was delivered from the jewellers, with the motto 'Friendship Sincere and Loyalty True'. Captain Watson said he hoped

> *that sincerity in friendship will be the cement to bind the members of it together and keep up the credit of the Royal game; and further, as a stimulant to players to improve the use of their clubs, and turn out on the Links on suitable occasions for air and exercise which are so conducive to health.*

Captain Watson specified a number of conditions for the playing for this medal including that 'a marker approved by the committee shall go with each squad of players to keep the scores and deliver same to the Secretary at the close of play'. This was accepted only after a vote, since the players themselves were to pay the attendant expense, and was a practice retained until voted out in 1876. Robert Williamson was the first winner of this Captain's Medal (taking exactly 100 strokes) on 27 September 1865.

In what was a breathless first year, the Victoria also conducted their first inter-club match. Though not recorded in the club minutes, the *Standard* carried the following report:

October 13th 1865: friendly match between 10 members of the
Union and an equal number of the Victoria club. It had been
arranged that the match be decided by holes and it was observed
by the scores that the Union won the match by 4. If the match had
been decided by strokes, the Victoria would have been the victors.

This may, in fact, be the earliest reference to an inter-club match in
Montrose.

By the end of the 1860s the club was thriving, having admitted almost
one hundred members; perhaps it had grown too quickly, for in 1873 it
was argued by some that membership must be restricted to fifty 'as
accommodation would be severely enough taxed'. Finances were healthy
too, having risen to a 'most satisfactory' £15 by 1873. The committee
reported 'the greatest of pleasure in knowing that there is not a single
defaulter as regard payment of subscriptions and entries', and that 'the
utmost harmony has prevailed and the Victoria Golf Club was never
more prosperous'. Many Club Treasurers today would be delighted to
make such a report!

A Place of Their Own

Although meetings were now held in the Star Hotel, the Club was looking to establish a base elsewhere. Attempts to rent part of the Royal
Albert's Southfield clubhouse failed to bear fruit although a room was
taken for a period in which to store their boxes. In 1872 the Committee
reported:

They visited a house lately built at the foot of Melville Lane facing
the links, in which they are offered a room for the exclusive use of
the Club. 13 feet square, airy, well lighted and of easy access
commanding an excellent view of the green at a yearly rental of
two pounds. If desired the services of a person occupying the
ground floor can be secured for cleaning out the room.

The minutes record that the new clubhouse was 'to be shut by 10 o'clock
in the summer and one hour after sunset in the winter' and noted the
club's thanks to Mr Smart for the gift of 'a very handsome snuff box to
lie on the table for the general use of members'. In Mackie's account of
these early years, he said that 'for many a day, I believe, the snuff box
was there and was freely used by those who sought refreshment and
inspiration through this olfactory organ'.

In 1874, the rented house 'at the Folds' (presumably a mis-spelling of
Faulds) was purchased by the club, for £150. Most (but not all) of the
committee agreed to take a share or shares and a trust was formed of five
shareholding members. In the early 1880s a clubhouse keeper was
engaged with 'the privilege of occupying two rooms rent free but pay his
own gas and taxes'.

The first Victoria clubhouse in Faulds Road, now a private residence.

Although the costs of the clubhouse appear remarkably low by twenty-first century standards, it was still a considerable financial outlay by a fledgling club. Despite a sharp increase in the annual subscription and entry monies (the latter rose to more than seven shillings by 1882), an overdraught of £18 was taken from the Bank of Scotland to cover the cost of alterations that had been found to be more expensive than the estimate. Another overdraft was approved in 1884 in order to pay the immediate demands of the club purveyor (of refreshments).

'Song and Sentiment Abounding'

This latter situation was no doubt viewed with particular concern since, if the content of the minute book is a suitable measure, the social arrangements within the club were at least as important as the golfing ones! An 'annual supper' (in the Crown Hotel) is mentioned as early as 1865, and by 1869 the annual 'convivial' was to be upgraded to a formal dinner. In subsequent years the event would be described as 'a most harmonious and happy evening . . . with song and sentiment abounding'.

As the clubhouse was established so the 'Refreshment Department', as it was called, became sufficiently important for its own treasurer to be appointed in 1875. John Webster was appointed purveyor to the club and it was agreed that dearer whisky be kept and priced at four pennies per glass (or two pennies per nip). Bob Mackie recalled:

> *In those days, every member carried a key of the liquor safe. If he wanted a drink, he unlocked the press, measured out what was required and deposited the amount for the price in a receptacle provided for that purpose.*

It seems, however, that some members might have been in the habit of obtaining their liquor at even lower cost since 'serious deficiency in the refreshment department' was reported to the 1879 AGM, whereupon the committee agreed on a weekly stock-take for three months. Even so, five years later, a large quantity of liquor was being removed without payment and a radical motion to cease purchase of alcohol altogether was briefly considered before being withdrawn: this motion, it is recorded, 'led to a full scale debate, during which the Chairman had to call certain members to order for unparliamentary and uncalled-for aspersions', a clear illustration of the dangers of threatening to deny golfers their after-game 'nip'.

Club golfing competition results (when recorded) show a steady improvement in scoring over this period. The Silver Medal of the Club, which might be considered as the original Club Championship, was won with scores of 102 (in 1864), 101 (1865), 98 (1867), 93 (1872), 89 (1873) and 87 (1876). A similar trend is seen for the Captain's Medal from 1865 although it must be remembered that the many course changes may have had an influence on the better scoring. To these competitions were added a monthly Victoria Cross or Badge (1869), the Walker Handicap Medal (1870), a monthly competition for a gold cross gifted by Captain Japp (1878), the Whiteman Cup (1882) and numerous sweepstakes and matches for prizes donated by members.

Somewhat curiously, matches between married and single members also feature regularly during this period. In 1880 members of the late Prince of Wales Golf Club were admitted to membership and the medal of that club was presented to the Victoria. (The Prince of Wales Club had its own unique heritage, initially restricted to men who had never played golf before!)

After the first-recorded match against the Union in 1865, no further mention is made of a match against another club until a resolution in March 1872 to seek a friendly, ten-a-side match with the Royal Albert, although the outcome is not recorded. Early match arrangements are also recorded with St Andrews Thistle (1874), the Union Club (1877), Aberdeen Bon Accord (1878), Forfar (1882), Arbroath (1882), the Mercantile (1883), Broughty Ferry (1883) and Aberdeen Victoria (1886).

A New Era

A major development for the club came in 1895 with the acquisition of the new clubhouse, the building overlooking the East Links and now the site of Roo's Leap restaurant.

We know little about the details of the purchase of this property because the minutes from the period are lost (though Mackie refers to a 'somewhat protracted and stormy search for a site').

We do know that John Sim, a long-standing member, was the architect of the new building. A number of members took up debentures to help

fund construction and, as the Victoria was by now a club with a sizeable membership, it was better able to meet this financial obligation.

Junior membership was introduced in 1906 at a reduced subscription of five shillings per annum. A corresponding motion to the 1909 annual meeting regarding a ladies' section was, however, 'summarily negatived', though the same meeting had a 'lengthy discussion' on the question of introducing a billiard table! The club seems to have reconsidered the issue of a ladies' section the following year following complaints from some of the members, but no ladies' section was ever formed.

Arrangements for golf were periodically reviewed and in 1902 it was agreed that five hundred copies of the latest version of the rules be 'printed, sewn, red cloth bound and include office bearers, all Captains and trophies with past and present winners and given free to all members'.

Inter-club matches remain a feature of the golfing and social calendar. In 1906 it was resolved:

> When a match is played here between this and another club the visiting team shall be entertained to suitable refreshment after and, if advisable, also before the match, and at each or any of these reflections one round of liquor shall be provided. Further, that every member of this club who takes part in the match shall pay the sum of 2/6 to repay the cost of the entertainment.

However it seems that not all members were always upholding the expected standards. The Secretary's report to the 1913 AGM includes a reference to

> a coterie of the indifferent golfers persistently indulging in a low game of chance . . . the usually euphonious golfing expressions giving place to vulgarisms such as 'dead cinches', 'cast iron threes' and many others more forcible than polite.

In regard to the financial position of the club, the Committee appears to be most frequently occupied with discussions on the arrangements for the cost of upkeep of the golf course. The original agreement was that this would be split evenly between the Town Council and the golf clubs but the contentious question became what proportion each club would bear. In addition to an annual maintenance subscription the associated costs are noted as including a horse-mower (£25 in 1902), a shelter on the course (1903) and £3 towards the cost of the 1909 Scottish Professional tournament (for which the Victoria was the headquarters for the duration).

Although undoubtedly not the only factor, these costs contributed to the calling of a special meeting in December 1906 to discuss 'the best means of relieving the pecuniary stress under which the club is labouring'. Subscriptions were increased yet again, to more than twelve shillings, honoraria for the Secretary and Treasurer were withdrawn and the club keeper's salary reduced by £5. Drastic actions indeed!

Thereafter the club appears to enjoy a period of relative financial stability. In 1911, the Treasurer reported a healthy balance and an abnormally high profit from the bar. He reasoned:

> This was not altogether derived from the unlimited consumption of alcohol on the part of the members but might be attributed to

the better profits obtained from the sale of the more effeminate beverages and a greater inclination toward drinking on the part of the teetotal members.

This state of affairs seems to have continued through the First World War and the 1916 report admits that gambling in the clubhouse – so criticised just three years before – was now helpful to the bottom line!

The winter games of chance still hold their sway amongst a very select body of patrons and it is largely due to their patronage of the 19th hole that the treasurer is able to record so favourable a report as to the Club's finances.

A poem about the horrors of the war, specially appended to the minutes of the Victoria Golf Club in 1921.

Despite the sometimes-precarious financial situation, the club continued to develop the clubhouse gradually and repay some of the loans due from the original construction. In 1902 the Committee agreed to install gas lighting in the dwelling house and after a heated debate electric light was approved for the clubrooms. Telephones arrived in 1906 in the form of a 'shared 10 party line with two free calls per diem' at an annual cost of just over £3.

The Committee, however, felt unable to support the suggested purchase of a piano (twelve guineas in 1906) and recommended to the proposer that individual members be invited to subscribe (which they obviously did, since a later record shows agreement to loan the instrument to the Royal Albert for their centenary celebration).

While activities were naturally curtailed during the war, a few competitions and matches are reported each year along with more sombre news and resolutions for the club to contribute to the war effort. Recovery from this difficult period seems to have taken some time for it is not until September 1920 that Bob Mackie is approached to write a history of the club for presentation at a Jubilee Dinner. This dinner took place in the clubhouse on the evening of 13 April 1921 and was widely reported at the time.

The full programme of entertainment that followed Mackie's humorous account of the club's origin is set out below. If we have difficulty nowadays understanding why it took three years after the end of the war for the spirits of local golfers to revive and celebrate this Jubilee, the poem 'The Forfar Bus',

THE FORFAR 'BUS

On the Forfar 'bus in a morn of spring,
    A nipping wind and the frost's sharp sting;
And I can't tell why, but you want to sing
    If your heart's like the heart o' me.
The folks in the 'bus, they stretch their legs,
    And talk of the fall in the price of eggs,
Of milk by the pint, and butter in kegs,
    With—"Drop in some day to your tea."

And my mind goes back to the days that were—
    Days of turmoil and days of stir,
And a 'bus from Albert to Pozieres,
    And fellows that rode with me.
We cursed the night, and we cursed the wet;
    We envied the luck of the men we met
Coming out of the trenches at Courcelette—
    A deuce of a place to be.

The Forfar 'bus brought me back once more
    As the clock at the Pillars was striking four;
Though the wind may blow and the rain may pour,
    There's a chair and a fire for me.
But the lads that jumped off at the duckboard track—
    (Cold was the night, and heavy the pack)—
They didn't join on when the 'bus went back—
    And they'll never come in to their tea.

THE WAYFARER.

appended specially to the club minute, spells out in poignant terms the heavy toll of the war years on local communities.

Again, our account of the inter-war years is considerably hindered by lost minutes but the local newspapers recorded a period of golf, socials and a steady progress of a club that was important and influential in the local golfing scene. In the 1920s, Victoria teams competed in most County Championships and the club was among the founder members of the Forfarshire County Association in 1908, and one of its keenest supporters.

A Co-operative Spirit

We can resume the story of the Victoria in the immediate aftermath of another war when preparations for entertaining returning forces among members, were tinged with sadness regarding those who would not return. A Victory Trophy was purchased from the Lord Roberts Memorial workshops in Dundee using the residue of the 'Welcome Home Fund', and the Secretary was instructed to write to the Montrose Golf Association regarding the resumption of activities 'at a time when co-operation between the Montrose golf clubs seems of prime importance'.

At this time, golfing was hampered by the necessary course reconstruction after occupation by the Air Ministry, and members noted that 'the present course is quite unsuited to open competitions and therefore an early opening of the Medal course is of first importance'. A 1947 report by the head greenkeeper, L.H. Warne, suggested the reconstruction of the four north holes (6th to 9th) would cost about £3000 as well as noting sea encroachment at an alarming rate at the 6th. An exhibition match was arranged and Victoria members generously contributed £200 to a total of £720 raised. The match was played by four of the leading professionals of the day (Bill Shankland, Norman van Nida, Dai Rees and Jimmy Adams) in aid of St Dunstan's Institution for the War Blind.

The number of available prizes was increased when ex-Captain F.A. Milne – the only golfer to be Captain of both the Victoria and Royal Albert clubs – donated a trophy to the club in 1949. In 1953 a Mr Glennie offered a cup for possible use by the junior section (he had won said cup as runner-up in the Amateur Championship of India).

The Victoria, in common with the Royal Albert at this time, sought ways to strengthen its financial position. Among the issues it explored was how to attract younger golfers. A junior section was re-formed in 1948, and the minimum age for junior entry reduced to 12 years in 1958. There was a trial period of catering in 1950, with 'light teas on Wednesdays and Saturdays', but no demand was found for these. In 1954, a TV was purchased for the bar to attract members, with a donation box for viewing! Allowing the bar to be opened on a Sunday during summer months (1962) was another radical experiment.

In the late 1950s, the club regularly reported operating losses and, by the 1959 annual meeting, it was on the verge of going into debt. Whether

ANGUS HERALD, SATURDAY, JUNE 22, 1935.   **17**

Jessie Soutar, the wife of the Town Provost and a leading figure in the North Links Ladies club, is pictured presenting the Angus Championship team trophy to the Club Captain, W. A. Richmond, Bill Richmond's father, in 1935. Courtesy of Eileen Mowat.

NEW RECORD

W. C. RICHMOND GOES ROUND IN 67

Twenty-four-years-old Willie Richmond, Victoria, broke the Montrose course record in the first round of the Golf Association's annual scratch tournament on Wednesday night.

His record-breaking 67 included five " birdies." He went out in 35, having par figures all the way until the eighth, where he had a " birdie," but ran up a 5 at the ninth. He did the home half in a brilliant 32. After a 4 at the twelfth, he had " birdies " at the thirteenth, fourteenth, sixteenth and eighteenth.

directly connected or otherwise, the same meeting agreed 'that lady guests be admitted to the upstairs rooms but at the discretion of the council the bar should be reserved for members'.

Club amalgamation had been first mentioned as early as 1956 at a Council meeting as a means of addressing the financial difficulties of the club, but the time was still not ripe to pursue the idea.

Financial concerns aside, 'Vicky' members were thriving on the golf course. In 1954 the Scottish Golf Union requested information on junior member Tommy Frost for consideration for international trials: the club Council minuted their appreciation of the support 'the boy' was receiving but a motion to display a notice of recognition of his achievement was, oddly, not carried. Some eight years later, Frost is noted as having established a new course record of 65 for the Montrose championship course.

Another notable achievement was that of W.C. Richmond who, while playing in the 1958 'Tassie', returned a score of 68 at Carnoustie to establish a new amateur record and to equal that of professional Ben Hogan. And as the *Review* report of June 2 1960 on the previous page shows, he set another course record closer to home.

The Centenary

In October 1964 the club celebrated its centenary with a dinner in the clubhouse – it was really an extended 'smoker' – attended by a total of 75 members and guests from the other local clubs and Angus county. The 'well-kent' figure of Town Provost Willie Johnston was the guest of honour and Captain John Wallace was in the chair.

The toast to the club was proposed by Jack Smith, a well-known local journalist. In his speech, Jack remarked on the happy coincidence that, on the fiftieth anniversary celebrations held over until 1921, the same toast was delivered by Bob Mackie, another journalist and his predecessor as the writer of the weekly 'Gable Ender' column in the *Montrose Review*. He commented that on that occasion Bob spoke 'six columns' but he was not seeking to match that.

The three "Bills" in the photograph above taken at that Centenary Dinner (4th and 5th from the left, and 2nd from the right) – Messrs Tulloch, Lorimer, and Richmond – are happily still members of the club in 2009 (though their considerable golfing talents may have dimmed just a little over time!). Courtesy of Bill Lorimer.

The *Review* concluded its report on the dinner by reporting that a musical programme followed the presentation of prizes and the last of the company left the nineteenth hole 'in the wee sma' hoors'.

Other Golfing Achievements

The club continued to have its share of young and not-so-young talented golfers. Junior members John Laing, Alan Hemsley and Owen Taylor played for Scottish Boys and Youths at various times. T.D. (Tommy) Frost in 1959 and 1960 and Alan Hemsley in 1976 were County Champions.

Three young Victoria golfers – all happily still club members – who reached the semi-finals of the Montrose Open Championship in 1982. They are Mike Millar (left), Scott Paton (right) and Graham Hemsley, the eventual winner of the championship that year. Courtesy of Ally Hogg.

The premier team County competition for the Evening Telegraph County Cup – a four-man team event – was won by Montrose Victoria on six occasions in total, the most recent in 1984 when the Victoria team of Scott Paton, Neil Paton, Mike Miller and Graham Hemsley triumphed. A photograph of the 1974 team is displayed overleaf.

In a different kind of contest involving general knowledge, a team of Messrs Clark, Bisset, Elrick and Lakie reached the last four of Grampian TV's 'Top Team'.

Towards Amalgamation

The early 1980s seemed to start optimistically enough for the club, with the possibility of overspill memberships from Dundee, Broughty Ferry and Monifieth prompting a proposal to raise the qualification for country membership from 25 miles to 50 miles.

The victorious 1974 Angus Championship team comprising, from left to right, Lindsay Brown, Jim Watt, Graeme Paton and Bill Richmond is pictured opposite (top). Courtesy of Bill Richmond

However, within a very short time, the tone changed completely in light of increasing losses due to rising costs and falling revenue from the bar and 'fruit machine'. A specific catalyst for subsequent events seems to have been concerns regarding on-going financial support for the Montrose Links Trust that the clubs were to be called upon to meet. It was against this pessimistic financial background that discussions about possible amalgamations with other local clubs took place.

After 122 years of independent existence, the legacy of the Montrose Victoria Golf Club would live on in the Royal Montrose Golf Club. We cannot know if this prospect would have delighted or alarmed its founders. But perhaps this is the place to turn our thoughts to those remarkably energetic men. In his speech to the Victoria Jubilee dinner in 1921, Bob Mackie imagined them this way:

> *All gone to the Elysian fields . . . where maybe they are now competing in the veterans' Open championship, flying and playing from cloud to cloud, with sweet little cherubs for caddies, playing with their old earthly zeal and zest, and with a skill they never attained when they were members of this club, toiling and moiling, as they did, year after year, round the old courses of Montrose to the music of the grey North Sea.*

CHAPTER 15

The Ladies

Rain fell heavily in the forenoon, but notwithstanding that all the competitors turned out. Early in the afternoon and until evening thunder peals were frequently heard, preceded by vivid flashes of lightning, but the ladies continued to play in the heavy rain.

From a report in the *Scotsman* of the 1899
Montrose Ladies' Golf Tournament

Women in Montrose were among the early pioneers of ladies' golf in Britain and have also made an invaluable contribution to the development of the sport in the town. The heritage of ladies' golf at Royal Montrose has been greatly enriched by the merger with the vibrant North Links Ladies Golf Club, which was founded in 1927. But the club's support for women golfers dates much further back than that.

Montrose Ladies Golf Club

The Montrose Ladies Golf Club was formed in 1889, one of the first golf clubs for women in the world. It was also one of the most successful. Before the end of the century its membership already exceeded that of the Royal Albert. And its elaborate Montrose Ladies' Tournament was possibly the most popular celebration of women's golf anywhere.

The connections with the Royal Albert were strong from the very start. The new club consisted largely of wives and daughters of Royal Albert members, and it is from the Royal Albert that the ladies looked for their honorary secretaries and treasurers. Several Royal Albert members were 'associate members' and keenly took part in mixed competitions. Bob Dow, the Royal Albert's professional, set up and maintained their various courses until his retirement and also provided lessons.

The ladies quickly built and funded their own wooden clubhouse, near the Royal Albert's, and given the membership the new club attracted it is not likely that financing was much of an issue. According to the *Review*:

The opening of the clubhouse undoubtedly tended to popularise the Club in the district and there is now scarcely a castle or

*mansion house in north-eastern Forfarshire which is not
represented on the roll of the membership.*

For a few short years, the ladies had to be content playing on their own
putting course, as it was not yet widely accepted that women were capable of playing the full game. This was consistent with the practice of all
of the fledgling ladies' clubs in the country. An accurate visual picture of
what this early form of ladies' golf was like can still be had by visiting the
Himalayas putting green at St Andrews – still run by a women's club in
that town. For a literary description we need go no further than *A Day
on the Ladies' Links*, written by the Royal Albert's Valentine Stone in
1891 (see chapter on the 'Montrose Masterpieces').

It did not take long for women in Montrose (and in a few other towns)
to begin flexing their muscles. By 1893, they were playing on a 'Cleek
Course', probably a pitch and putt or par-3 course and they had already
inaugurated an inter-club match with their counterparts in Aberdeen.
And in 1895, a 9-hole driving course was opened which encircled the
putting course. This became the South Links Ladies' Course and, from
the following description in the *Review*, it was clearly a varied and interesting challenge:

*Early lady golfers
sometime before
1906 with their new
clubhouse and the
Royal Albert Stone
Bridge clubhouse in
the background.
Courtesy of William
Coull.*

*It starts from the Ladies Clubhouse and goes in a northerly
direction towards the Royal Albert Clubhouse, opposite which the*

first hole is located. The course is then continued along the bents, in the middle of natural hazards, to the lower lighthouse. The player has then to drive across a fine piece of links to the lookout and from thence northeasterly to the fringe of the ordinary short course. The next hole is in the bents and the ninth is near the south side of the Ladies Clubhouse, a circuit being thus almost completed. From two of the bents teeing grounds a very picturesque view is obtained of the sea and river, Scurdieness and the sands fringing Montrose Bay. The holes have been furnished with numbered zinc plates mounted on moveable iron rods and the teeing grounds are supplied with boxes of sand. . . .

[The third hole is] *about 50–60 yards. The character of the intervening ground necessitated playing with a cleek or iron. Rough undulating hillocks occupied the middle distance, a belt of whins and a small bunker defended the approach to the green and the green itself was on the slope of a hill, at the other side of which a hollow with rough grass trapped the shot which was too strong.*

The 1902 map on page 122 shows the location on the South Links of the ladies clubhouse and golf course, on ground now part of the GlaxoSmith Kline plant.

Like the men, the women had to keep an eye on the Town Council which had expressed its wish to rid the South Links of golf altogether. In a letter to the Council, as reported in the *Review*, the club noted that 'there is plenty of ground more suitable for footballers and others without breaking in upon any of the golf courses'.

The women were not, however, confined to the Ladies Courses. In 1896, there is mention of some women practising their long game on the regular Montrose course and having 'attained considerable proficiency in play'. At the 1897 Montrose Ladies' Tournament a mixed handicap competition was held on the 'gentlemen's driving course'. And in 1898, new hazards were laid out on their own driving course 'to render the course of a more sporting nature'.

By the end of the nineteenth century, the Montrose Ladies Golf Club was one of the premier clubs in Scotland with 150 members. The club held some of the earliest and most popular golf tournaments for women, beginning with a two-day event in 1891, which had expanded to three days by 1893, including a mixed competition on Wednesday afternoon. It was now regarded as the 'principal event of the summer season on Montrose links'. Two courses were laid out in this year, 'the object being to have them changed for different competitions'.

By 1895, the annual tournament was a week-long and attracted entries from all over Scotland, as well as from Cheltenham, Birmingham and London. In order to allow visitors unrestricted play on the ladies' putting and driving courses during this tournament week, a new putting course was laid out in 1898 so that one of the courses could be reserved for those taking part in the tournament. In addition to various handicap and scratch competitions, there were putting events (those were handicapped as well), longest drive contests (in 1905, a Miss Balfour won with a drive of 203 yards), and an 'Approach' competition, where both men and women aimed at some kind of target (though the men's tees were set 20 yards further away).

One year an innovative competition was held – an all-in (men and women) individual match-play scratch competition with ladies, regardless of ability, receiving two holes of a start when playing a man.

The costs of maintaining the Ladies' Courses were considerable and in 1901 the members asked the Town to help out, claiming that:

> *For the past two years they had been paying a lad from April to October 15 shillings per week and one day each month during the rest of the year.*

This meant that the ladies were paying more than the men. The Council agreed to take over the upkeep of the Ladies' Course with the ladies paying half the annual cost up to a sum of £30 per annum. The ladies offered 'their implements at half their first cost', but the Council refused, feeling that 'these might be handed over free of charge as they would be almost entirely used on the Ladies' Course'.

These women were a hardy lot. They preserved an unbroken record of playing monthly for the Paton Gold Medal (donated by George Paton of Mall House). In March 1898, although snow lay on the links to a considerable depth, two members resolved to play despite the difficulties they knew would be encountered. The round was completed, although finding the ball proved difficult on several occasions. Again, in January 1899, 'undeterred by 10 degrees of frost and with the Links covered with a white mantle of hoar frost', the monthly competition was held. In addition to their Medals, the ladies also often competed for a handicap bracelet.

The club boasted several outstanding golfers in these early years, as reflected by their regular thrashing of the Aberdeen Ladies Golf Club in their annual match. In 1898 Montrose's A. Gillies Smith established a record on the Ladies Course in Aberdeen with a 63. Montrose won the match 34–14. Gilllies Smith, who played off plus two, was also a member at North Berwick where she won the Ladies' Gold Medal eight of the first eleven times it was played for!

In 1903, Montrose's Miss Harvey finished a very creditable (and very wet) fourth in the first-ever Scottish Ladies' Championship at St Andrews. She had to endure an 18-hole playoff in the wind and rain for *third* place (she obviously lost). And Miss E. Renny Tailyour performed extremely well at the 1910 British Ladies' Championship at Westward Ho! before losing in the later rounds to the renowned Violet Hezlet.

Another contribution of the club was the development of the course that we would eventually know as the Broomfield. In 1905 the club

THE MONTROSE LADIES' TOURNAMENT.

The third day of the tournament was opened under the most inauspicious weather conditions. Rain fell heavily in the forenoon, but notwithstanding that all the competitors turned out. Early in the afternoon and until evening thunder peals were frequently heard, preceded by vivid flashes of lightning, but the ladies continued to play in the heavy rain. As a consequence the greens were very heavy. The following are the results up to last night:—

LADIES' HANDICAP COMPETITION ON PUTTING COURSE BY HOLES.

Fifth Round.—Miss Lee (2) beat Miss Burness (2); Miss E. Harvey (1) beat Miss M. Lyall (6); Miss L. Lyall (6) beat Miss J. Woodward (1); Miss Sandford-Thompson (5) beat Miss H. Stone (4.)

SEMI-FINAL.

Miss Lee beat Miss E. Harvey; Miss Sandford-Thompson beat Miss L. Lyall.

FINAL.

Miss Lee beat Miss Sandford-Thompson.

LADIES' COUPLE HANDICAP COMPETITION ON DRIVING COURSE BY HOLES.

THIRD ROUND.

Miss Harvey and Miss M. Harvey (1) beat Miss G. More Gordon and Miss L. Burness (2); Miss H. Stone and Miss H. H. Fernie (3) beat Miss E. Woodward and Miss M. Duncan (2); Misses Gillies Smith (0) beat Miss W. L. Smith and Miss J. R. Smith (4.)

SEMI-FINAL.

Misses Gillies Smith, a bye; Miss H. Stone and Miss H. H. Fernie beat Miss Harvey and Miss M. Harvey.

FINAL.

Misses Gillies Smith beat Miss H. Stone and Miss H. H. Fernie.

MIXED COUPLE COMPETITION ON DRIVING COURSE BY HOLES, WITHOUT HANDICAP.

SEMI-FINAL.

Miss Harvey and Mr A. Rae Smith beat Miss Watson and Mr F. J. Pullar; Miss A. Woodward and W. M. J. Paton beat Mrs Dickson and Rev. T. A. Cameron.

The following were the starters for the stroke competition:—Miss Duncan (0) and Miss E. Woodward (3); Lady F. Wolrige Gordon (10) and Miss More-Gordon (10); Mrs R. J. Muir (12) and Miss Lee (10); Mrs Yorke (13) and Miss G. More-Gordon (5); Miss Finlay (1) and Miss J. Woodward (0); Mrs Bevant (7) and Miss Sandford-Thompson (7); Mrs D'Arcy Simpson (13) and Mrs Stone (12); Miss Gillies Smith (owes 2) and Miss A. Gillies Smith (owes 1); Miss M. L. Smith (7) and Miss A. Woodward (0); Miss Duncan (5) and Miss J. R. Smith (16); Mrs Dickson (3) and Madame Philippe (10); Miss Robertson (7) and Mrs Simson (7); Mrs Armstrong Smythe (12) and Miss Woodward (10); Mrs Millar (7) and Miss Watson (5); Miss M. Harvey (3) and Miss E. Burness (10); Miss H. Stone (7) and Miss H. H. Fernie (3); Miss Harvey (0) and Miss E. Harvey (3); Miss Burness (12) and Miss F. Burness (10); Mrs Fernie (7) and Miss E. E. Fernie (5); Miss L. Burness (3) and Miss Black (15.) Miss A. Gillies Smith was first with 71 (plus 1)—72; Miss A. Woodward (scratch) was second with 74. The next best scores were:—Mrs Bevan, 82 (less 7)—75; Mrs Finlay, 78 (less 1)—77; Miss M. L. Smith, 82 (less 5)—77; Miss Gillies Smith, 76 (plus 2)—78; Mrs Simson, 85 (less 7)—78; Miss Duncan (scratch), 79; Mrs Dickson, 82 (less 3)—79; Miss Harvey (scratch), 79; Miss E. Woodward, 82 (less 3)—79; Miss H. H. Fernie, 82 (less 3)—79.

APPROACH COMPETITION.

For the approach competition there was an entry of thirty lady competitors and 18 gentlemen. The ladies' tee was twenty-five yards from the net, and the gentlemen's forty-five yards, whilst the flag was twenty-five yards beyond the net, making the distance fifty yards for the ladies and seventy for the gentlemen. The possible was 75 points, and Miss Gillies-Smith was 52 and Mr D. S. Campbell 58. The following are the results in the stroke competition:—

Ladies.—1, Miss Gillies-Smith, 52; 2, Mrs Dickson, 29, after a tie with Mrs R. H. Millar.

Gentlemen.—1, Mr D. S. Campbell, 58; 2, Mr W. A. Key, 54.

A report in the Scotsman on the elaborate week-long tournament of the Montrose Ladies Club in 1899

A group of lady golfers at the Stone Bridge clubhouse during a tournament week in the early years of the twentieth century. Courtesy of the Montrose Society.

Lady golfers in front of the South Links clubhouse circa 1930. Courtesy of Denis Rice whose mother is pictured in the centre of the group.

submitted a sketch plan to the Dean of Guild for 'a relief or auxiliary course of 9 holes' to be laid out on the North Links but retaining 'three holes to the south of the walk to the Pavilion'. This last request was refused but a 9-hole course was laid out, paid for by the Golf Course Improvement Bazaar held in the town in 1907. The ladies were a driving force behind the organisation of the Bazaar which was attended by Prime Minister Campbell-Bannerman, and which also paid for many improvements on the championship course.

The Montrose Ladies Golf Club now moved to the North Links to play on the new Auxiliary Course and they arranged for their wooden clubhouse to be transported intact on rollers to its new location, opposite the first tee of the Broomfield Course (and where it is still found today, though it is now used as a holiday home).

Nevertheless, golf on the South Links, which the ladies had done so much to preserve, continued for another generation and even spawned a new club – the South Links Golf Club.

The ladies also persuaded the Royal Albert to allow them to participate in the golf tournament held in 1910 to celebrate its centenary – the first time women were allowed to play in such a club event. It was only their due for the contribution they had already made to golf in the town in their first twenty years.

In 1939, a week before the outbreak of the Second World War, the Montrose Ladies Golf Club held a tournament to mark their Jubilee. This proved to be their last hurrah. On the outbreak of war, competitions ceased. Their clubhouse was commandeered by the army and was occupied first by British and then Polish troops. Sadly this fine Ladies Club never got going again after the war and was officially disbanded in 1947. But another golf club for ladies was already in being, and in much ruder health.

North Links Ladies Golf Club

On 16 June 1927, 'a meeting of Ladies favourable to forming a ladies golf club for competitive play on the North Links was held'. This meeting marked the launch of the North Links Ladies Golf Club.

From this somewhat terse opening sentence in their first minute, it is clear that the focus of this group was to be on serious golf.

Many of these women were wives, daughters or mothers of golfers who were members of the Mercantile, Victoria and Caledonia clubs – still resolutely all-male clubs – but a good number were also single working women. Captain Fotheringham of the Mercantile Club took the chair at the inaugural meeting and the first Captain appointed by the club was Miss Glory Adams, a woman of independent means living close to the course who at a later time became a Town Councillor of some renown.

At the first AGM in 1928, the club had a membership of forty-four and funds in hand totalling £183 – an impressive start for a new venture. They also had their first dispute, when Glory Adams, who would continue to be a strong influence in the club over many years, precipitated 'an animated discussion' by asserting this should be 'a business girls club'.

Members then debated 'whether married ladies were to be included as members'. Since a number of married women were already members, this suggestion from the Captain was presumably rejected and married women continued to be members, although for the first seven years of its existence it is noteworthy that the committee composition was overwhelmingly 'Misses'.

Glory Adams, first Captain of the North Links Ladies Golf Club. Courtesy of Angus Council.

The club would play all its competitions on Wednesdays – mainly in the evening – and on Saturday afternoons, unlike the members of the other ladies' club who were generally free of employment and able to play during the day. Within weeks of their first meeting, they had an extensive fixture list and had begun to acquire trophies for the various competitions playing on both the Championship and Auxiliary Courses.

The club was offered the use of the annexe of 'The Villa' as a clubhouse – the original Royal Albert clubhouse, and now part of 'Grey Harlings' – except for August and September when it was occupied by Lady Cockerill. When asked to allow its use in these months too, and to become President of the club, Lady Cockerill kindly agreed to both requests.

However, from their first general meeting, these resolute women were fixed on acquiring their own clubhouse as soon as possible. In April 1928, they agreed to devote their efforts to raising £503 – the estimated cost of a new building. This meant holding a series of whist drives, fancy dress balls, sales and bazaars over the next few years. As an example of their determination, the Town Council records indicate the club hired the Guild Hall for five dances in August 1928 alone.

The local building firm Perts built the new clubhouse – primarily a wooden structure to reduce costs – on ground just 100 yards east of their temporary home in 'The Villa'. An agreement was struck with Perts to pay around 50% of the building costs on occupation, and to pay off the balance in instalments with a moderate rate of interest. Perts clearly had no concerns about their ability to raise the funds and indeed the final payment of £50 was made in 1934. Their new clubhouse was ready in time to be the venue for their AGM in November 1929 – a remarkable achievement for this newly-formed club.

By 1935 membership had risen to seventy-six, plus thirty juniors. The entry fee for the juniors was set at a nominal one shilling and the junior section was allowed to keep all of its funds to finance junior golf.

Included in that early group of junior girls were Sybil Gibson (nee Cowie) and Jean Thomson (nee Archibald). Jean is still a member of Royal Montrose as we approach our bicentenary and Sybil a welcome visitor. The club member who seems to have done most to aid and encourage the juniors – arranging coaching, tournaments and inter-club matches – was Mrs Jessie Soutar, whose husband became Town Provost. There is a picture of her presenting a prize to a Victoria Club winner in 1935 on page 157.

SMILING CHAMPIONS OF THEIR SEX who took part in Montrose North Links Ladies versus Gentlemen's golf match over the medal course, Montrose, on Saturday.

A group of junior girls in the mid 1930s about to play Royal Albert men in a challenge match. From left to right, they are Nita Soutar (Mrs Soutar's other daughter), Nancy Donald, ?, Margaret Scott, Hilda Reid, Norma Milne, Jean Ross and Sybil Cowie. The picture perfectly captures not only the dress of the period, but the clear zest of the girls for the game. Courtesy of Eileen Mowat, daughter of Jessie Soutar.

In 1935, too, is the first reference to any contact with Montrose Ladies Golf Club, when a telephone call was received 'challenging the club to a two-ball foursomes'. This would be one in a large number of inter-club matches played each season – eleven in 1936 – and the North Links Ladies teams showed what formidable golfers they were by recording victories in most of them.

In 1935 the club asked for, and was given, representation on the Dean of Guild Committee that managed the courses, in recognition of their growing status by the other clubs, and they also joined the Montrose Golf Association when it was set up.

Representatives from the two ladies' clubs, along with the Royal Albert lady associates, formed a committee in 1937 to organise a one-day Ladies' Open competition, the Council agreeing to grant them courtesy of the course. The tournament, which comprised one round medal play, a two ball foursomes and a putting competition, attracted 49 entries. In 1938, there were 53 entries.

At each of the general meetings held 1937–39, the club took the unusual step of appointing Joint Captains. No explanation is offered, and in 1948 they decided to revert to a sole captain again but joint captaincy was certainly an innovative idea.

In April 1940, the club committee met as usual to make their plans for the summer golf season. However, following the note of that meeting in the minutes, we find this brief statement:

> *Clubhouse requisitioned by Military Authorities as from 5th May 1940.*
> *Members were asked to empty lockers.*
> *Inventory of effects was taken.*
> *These are stored with Mr C Mitchell, Grocer, Union Street.*

The North Links clubhouse was now located within a restricted military area for the duration of the war and used for a time as a billet for Polish troops.

The club was restarted in 1947 and Mr Mitchell was paid £6, one pound for each of the years he had stored their furniture.

In spite of this nine-year gap, members were soon back to the energetic pursuit of their business and golfing affairs, though the request from the LGU for a half-entry fee when the club sought to rejoin that organisation was queried, as 'our club has been commandeered and the circumstances were unusual'. We don't know if the LGU accepted this special plea – it most certainly should have!

In 1951 and 1952 the club was presented with trophies and £30 from the now defunct Montrose Ladies Golf Club.

The club continued to flourish until 1986 when it amalgamated with the Royal Montrose Golf Club. Amalgamation was agreed at a general meeting in 1986. It was a very difficult decision for the members to take. For fifty years, this ladies' club had flourished and enjoyed many happy years of fellowship both on the golf course and back in the clubhouse. Royal Montrose's male members soon realised how fortunate it was that the ladies agreed to the amalgamation, bringing to their new club the same energy and determination that had made the North Links Ladies Golf Club such a success.

Several members are named in minutes as 'having brought honour to the club by their successes both locally and nationally'. Carol Hay, Elizabeth Richardson and Kathleen Sutherland were all selected for Angus Ladies' County team with Kathleen being County Champion many times. Kathleen also had the distinction of being Club Champion on each of the last twelve years of the club's existence, from 1975–1986, a quite remarkable achievement for a member who went on to have many more golfing achievements as a Royal Montrose member.

The 1976 Angus county team with three Montrose golfers – Kathleen Lackie, Carol Diack (nee Hay) and Kathleen Sutherland – from the far left in the back row. Courtesy of Angus County Ladies Golf Association.

CHAPTER 16

'A Golf Ground Unequalled': Evolution of the Montrose Links

The Links [at Montrose] extends between the town and the German Ocean, and is a very fine course. . . . The play is diversified by bunkers and whins whilst the turf admits a very correct short game.

W.H. Farnie, *A Golfer's Manual*, 1857

During their campaign for royal patronage, the members of the Montrose Golf Club made a forthright claim. It is found in the letter sent in 1845 to William Gladstone, seeking his assistance:

You are probably aware we possess a golf ground unequalled by any in Scotland.

This was not an idle boast. For there is plenty of evidence to suggest that at the time of the letter, and perhaps for centuries before, Montrose could well have been the best place in the world to play the royal and ancient game.

Certainly, golfers in Montrose have always been spoilt for choice and the evolution of the golf course has been marked by a restless rearrangement of the holes they play that continues even to this day. Sometimes those changes have been a matter of making a virtue out of necessity. But just as often it has been due to the uniquely abundant, yet highly accessible linksland that Montrose has always enjoyed and which for centuries distinguished it from other golf towns.

It was a feature that struck the contributors to some of the earliest books about Scotland.

'There is here a great flat area of fields extending for two miles', reads the descriptive text about Montrose in the first atlas of Scotland, published in 1654. The relatively gentle, but sporting nature of much of the

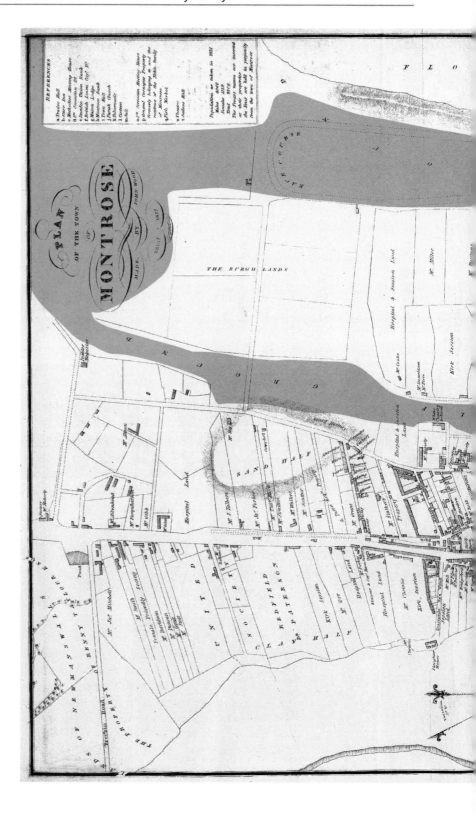

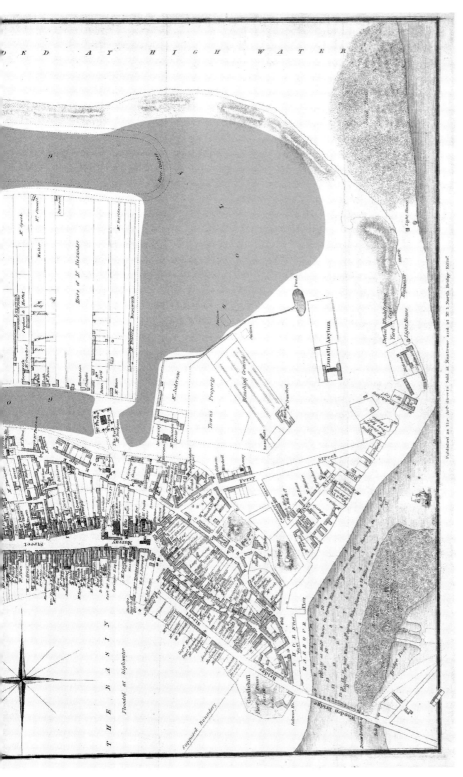

The 1822 'Wood' map of Montrose, with the area used for golf in the early years highlighted. Courtesy of Angus Council.

linksland at Montrose (the strips of high dunes next to the sea was another matter, as we shall see) made it ideal for sports of all kinds.

We have seen in Chapter One how the poet Arthur Johnstone, also writing in the seventeenth century, depicted an idyllic scene of youths riding horses, wrestling and playing ball games (including golf) on the links. In later centuries the links would be used for football and cricket.

In his pioneering book, *Golf in Montrose*, William Coull imagines the essence of golf in these early days in a way that is not easily bettered:

> We pass the old Celtic Kirk with its shell-covered Bell Tower, and take the path between the gravestones in the old kirkyard, carrying our few, loose, wooden clubs. We pass a line of crofts that run from Fishmarket Wynd (George Street) to the area that is now Mount Road and Dorward Place. We have reached the golfing ground – the virgin links upon which little building has taken place; there is no Academy, no St Peter's Church, Chapel Works or Union Mill, no ropeworks, soapworks or houses; only grass, saffron-flowered whins and the ubiquitous rabbits, bobbing to the skylarks' song. . . .
>
> We are in what will eventually be known as the Mid Links and the game commences. Here and there a branch of broom or gorse protrudes from a hole in the ground, marking its position.
> . . .
> We use a wooden club for all our shots, even from the natural sandy holes which are on the course. The more proficient players can hit the feather-filled balls incredible distances – 200 yards not being unusual.
>
> After putting the ball into the hole we proceed to hit it towards the next hole. There are no special 'greens' or 'tees'. Having played over a fair part of the Links, perhaps upwards of a mile in length, we return to the starting point using the same holes as played formerly.

By the time the Montrose Golf Club was established in 1810, the centuries-old golfing areas that Coull describes were being encroached upon. But there was still an enormous amount of golf ground to choose from, as we can see from the *Wood's Town Atlas* of 1822 on pages 172–173.

The map shows that the accepted golfing grounds of the town stretched north from St Peter's Church, and also included the entire coastal region from the current championship course right down to where the GlaxoSmithKline plant is today. In fact, there was yet another golfing ground, just north of the map that linked these two areas together. It made for a gigantic arch, a near oval really, within which it was possible to make dozens of golf holes. This was likely the most ample and accessible golfing ground in the world.

Such abundance meant almost endless flexibility. On Medal days, golfers needed to be told exactly which holes they were to play. The Montrose Golf Club minutes of 24 June 1818 record the Captain's instructions for that year:

> *The members shall start at Mr Paterson's holes, play round the course to the hole at the foot of the Bleaching Green and out again to the Brander, after which return to the hole at the foot of the Bleaching Green making in all 17 holes.*

With the help of the 1822 map, we can roughly trace this early routing. We can see that the home of Mr Paterson, the Old Kirk's minister at the time, was located at the foot of New Wynd, adjacent to the present Links Hotel. So we know these early golfers started just north of what is now St Mary's and St Peter's Church (where many would have been members) and then played northwards up what is now the Mid Links and on to those parts of the present course that have been played for possibly 500 years.

A view from the Academy northwards towards St Mary's and St Peter's and that part of the Mid Links used for golf. Courtesy of Angus Council.

Quite likely they played in a clockwise direction along today's 13th, 11th and 10th fairways, turning southwards just before they reached the high dunes – in those days more frequently called 'the bents' – next to the sea. Following the current 17th fairway (or perhaps the 2nd on the Broomfield) they would continue through the East Links (next to today's Seafront Splash) before veering west again to the 'bleaching ground'

that was leased out to local weavers by the Town. From the Captain's instructions, we know the golfers returned to the 'brander' (as a drain was then called) and then back again to the final green to make up the 17 holes, which was the traditional length of a round in Montrose until the 1860s.

This was a startlingly long course, given the feathery ball and equipment then in use, certainly over 6000 yards.

It would be a mistake to think this, or any other routing from the era, was in any way permanent. Only seven years later a different Captain was instructing golfers to play in an entirely different direction, starting (not ending) in the South Links and 'playing round to the ewe hillock [near today's 12th hole], returning to the bents and come in to Cook's Hole'.

Mr Cook's property was at the foot of Carnegie Street, and William Coull speculates that to get from the 'bents' to the Mid Links they may well have played along 'Wallie Green', the old name for the lower part of Dorward Road, which now links the clubhouses to the town centre. Its unusual width would suggest that it was originally a golf hole. Wallie was the name for a well, so its name may have meant a fairway with a well on it.

Again, this was an exceptionally long course. The next year, the club Secretary sent the following list of the holes to the Thistle Club in Leith in response to their request for more information about the Montrose links:

List of the holes and respective distance of each

1st hole	485 yards	8th hole	382 yards
2nd "	336 "	9th "	264 "
3rd "	308 "	10th "	322 "
4th "	441 "	11th "	483 "
5th "	388 "	12th "	457 "
6th "	388 "	13th "	424 "
7th "	331 "	14th "	469 "

The average hole is a whopping 391 yards (about thirty yards per hole longer than on today's championship course!). Little wonder that no early Gold Medal winner, using the feathery ball, was returning a score below 100 strokes over 17 holes.

It cannot be stressed too much how unusual Montrose's links were. With fourteen distinct fairways, Montrose had significantly more golfing area than the other main golf centres in Scotland. St Andrews had but ten holes (with eight played to twice); Musselburgh had eight; Aberdeen had seven; and Perth, Brunstfield, Glasgow and North Berwick each had six. Blackheath and Leith had only five.

This monster of a course certainly generated good golfers. We have seen in an earlier chapter how Montrose players defeated a crack team from the Honourable Company of Edinburgh Golfers in a celebrated challenge match in 1827. Four years later, David Duncan, a gentleman farmer from just outside the town, shocked St Andrews by winning their Gold Medal. A report on the competition appeared in the London-based *Sporting Magazine*:

> *The annual contest amongst celebrated golf players in Scotland excited unusual interest. . . . The old proverb in the racing world, that 'odds never beat a horse that could win' was fully exemplified on this occasion: and a gentleman from North of the Tay, whose performances were not greatly rated by the greater artists at Golf, contrived by superior skill to walk off with the golden prize, to the most utter dismay and disappointment of the entire field.*

The First Keepers of the Green

Though sheep would have helped keep the whins and grass down, it would have been a daunting task to ensure that three miles of golfing ground was maintained in some kind of order. Even inserting the holes would have been a chore, as it was not until 1825 that the club received 'an instrument for making holes on the green', a gift of James Cruickshank of Langley Park, a member of the Keithock Club. Cruickshank was one of the local gentry who we surmise couldn't quite bring himself to join the Montrose Golf Club – but nevertheless expected it to keep the links decently presented!

That responsibility seems to have fallen mostly on the shoulders of the indefatigable Patrick Mason, a four-times Captain of the Montrose Golf Club, who as early as 1820 was commended in the minutes 'for his unremitting attention to the golf course'. In 1822 he was again singled out for 'having devised and effected the present extended golf course', making him the first recorded course designer at Montrose.

Mason was no doubt also put in charge of the first paid greenkeepers. The first mention of one is in 1830, when it was 'proposed and carried that David Marshall should keep the golf course in repair and that, if properly kept, he shall receive one shilling per week'.

But maintaining the course also meant keeping others at bay, and here Patrick Mason was again praised 'for having manfully and successfully resisted every encroachment on the rights and privileges of the Golf Club'.

Why the club should have any rights and privileges at all must have seemed baffling to non-golfers. After all, the links were common land that by law anyone could enjoy. Yet the fledgling club was already telling others what they could and couldn't do. In 1818, a Mr Maberly, operator of a weaving works in Mill Street, was allowed to cut a drain eastwards across what is now the Mid Links but only after promising that 'the Golf Course should sustain no injury by the said drain'.

The Town Council did not always think much of these self-proclaimed rights and privileges, and in 1832 it announced plans to build a new Trades' School north of St Peter's Church. The club protested that the proposed site was on 'one of the finest pieces of the links' and on this occasion they were supported by 'the other club', the Keithock.

At first, the Council was dismissive, stating that it did not 'recognise such bodies as the Medal Holders and members of the Golf Clubs'. However, these golfers were not without influence. They commissioned a lawyer to draw up a schedule of protest and the Council was soon forced to give way and build the Trades' School behind the Academy.

Golf on the Mid Links was saved, but only temporarily.

The Invincibles!

About fifteen years later another threat arose that even the newly chris-tened Royal Albert Golf Club, with its sudden influx of aristocratic members, could not counter. The Aberdeen Railway Company proposed to build a terminus in Montrose, which would entail track cutting across the course. The club had some initial success. A petition was sent to the local Radical MP, Joseph Hume, to fight against the Bill going through Parliament. He seems to have succeeded in forcing some changes onto the proposed route but no one could stand in the way of progress.

This railway is no longer in use, but its route can be observed on the map opposite and its passage can be traced by following today's Whinfield and Faulds Roads. It would have then veered west towards Erskine Street into what was then Caledonian Station. Today it's a pleas-ant bike trail for many, but in the nineteenth century, the calm would have been interrupted several times a day by the roar of a steam locomo-tive.

It meant the end of what was, surely, centuries of play on the fields north of St Peter's Church. But the diligence of Mason and other golfers would pay dividends for the town, as the development of the Mid Links into a series of public parks by Provost Scott in the 1890s (a Royal Albert member, incidentally) would not have been possible if the golfers had not kept development away for as long as they did.

By the end of 1849, the Royal Albert's club Council was considering, and approving, a new layout prepared by its Treasurer, John Jamie. The cost of making the changes seems to have been exactly nil. As described in the club minutes, it was mostly a matter of sticking the flags in new spots on the still abundant ground available to golf:

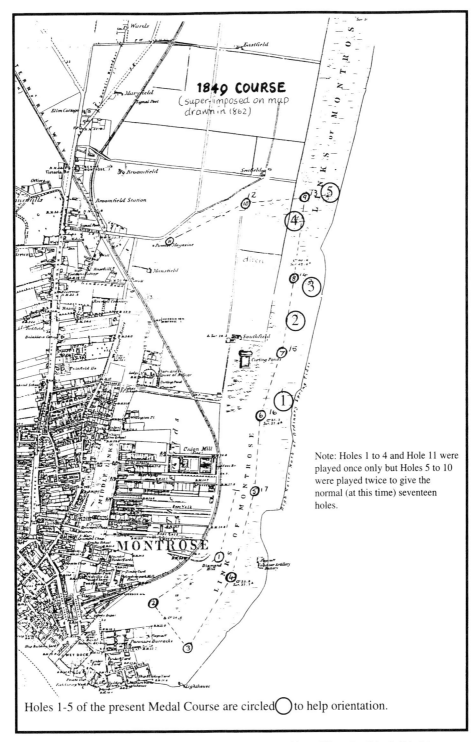

1849 COURSE
(super-imposed on map drawn in 1862)

Note: Holes 1 to 4 and Hole 11 were played once only but Holes 5 to 10 were played twice to give the normal (at this time) seventeen holes.

Holes 1-5 of the present Medal Course are circled ◯ to help orientation.

The 1849 golf course laid out by John Jamie as determined by William Coull in Golf in Montrose.

Montrose 3d October 1849

"Montrose Royal Albert Golf Club"

"Table of the Holes on the Montrose Course, with the distances."

Nᵒ		Designation of Hole	Yards
At	1	Railway Bridge Hole	360
	2	Asylum	410
	3	Light house	280
	4	Diamond Hill	410
	5	Patons	420
	6	Aberdein's	370
	7	Moore's	310
	8	Gully	360
	9	Bent	400
	10	Brandeis	270
	11	Powder House	410
	12	Brandeis	410
	13	Bent	270
	14	Gully	400
	15	Moore's	360
	16	Aberdein's	310
	17	Patons	370
3 Miles 840 Yards		Total	6120 Yards
		Average	360 Yards

Table from the minute book showing a list of holes on the 1849 course, the layout of which is shown on the previous page.

After being duly discussed and agreed to, and with a view to giving all parties an equal chance, it was considered advisable that the course be made out for the first time on the morning of the day of competition, the starting and ending points to be opposite Aberdein and Gordon's works, instead of starting as formerly at the hole South of Mr Fraser's rope works.

The Secretary included a table of the holes, which he thoughtfully inserted at the back of the minute book.

If the course could be 'made out' in a day, it could be rearranged just as quickly, and so we cannot be sure that John Jamie's work lasted any longer than Patrick Mason's. On the other hand, it may well be much the same course that so impressed H.B. Farnie, author of *A Golfer's Manual* (1857), the earliest golf guide ever published:

The Links extends between the town and the German Ocean, and is a very fine course, second only to St Andrews. The form is nearly semi circular; the play is diversified by bunkers and whins whilst the turf admits a very correct short game.

Farnie was a St Andrews man and few in Montrose would have conceded the superiority of the Fife course. For one thing, the Old Course in St Andrews was not the expansive, slick and well-groomed course it is today. When a student from Arbroath arrived in St Andrews for studies in 1855 he was struck by how rough the terrain was, and how narrow the fairways:

The greens were in the 'rough,' and the bunkers were in their natural state. If a player went off the narrow course of good

The Gully Hole in one form or another has been a part of the course since at least 1849. This picture dates from 1890.

ground he was at once landed in very 'rough Country', and the course at the ninth hole was all heathery and difficult, across its whole breadth.

The biographer of Young Tom Morris describes St Andrews of the time as 'a mangy links that wound along narrow footpaths through strands of whins, with putting greens pocked by heather crushed shells and bare dirt'.

Carnoustie seems to have been just as ragged. In 1864 a visiting golfer complained:

The putting green is in most cases very rough . . . [with] holes distended into huge triangles, and to crown it all, placed directly on the slope of a hill.

No contemporary account of the course at Montrose makes it sound anywhere as rough as these descriptions.

On the contrary, the guide that accompanied the 1822 *Woods Town Atlas* describes the Montrose links as 'this large extent of fine smooth surface' which is the 'most extensive in Scotland'. Tellingly, perhaps, the Montrose Rules of 1830 did not allow (as the St Andrews Rules did) golfers to move loose impediments before reaching the green.

The links of Montrose were, in effect, ready-made for golf, an important attraction at a time when there was no earth moving machinery and mechanical mowers had not yet come into use.

As mid-century approached, golfers in Montrose may well have enjoyed a 'golf ground unequalled'. Despite the incursion of the railway,

The rather ragged second tee at St Andrews in about 1890. In the nineteenth century, Montrose boasted a finer natural terrain than other courses.

the town had more abundant natural golfing terrain than anywhere else, and the course (in whatever configuration) was admired by all who played it. Its golfers were excelling too: Royal Albert member James Calvert Jr had just won the St Andrews Gold Medal two years running. In 1848, a member of the Royal Albert felt able to crow:

> *Our town now enjoys the reputation of having within it, as expert golf players as can be found in any part of Scotland. . . . All classes indulge in this invigorating and healthful exercise. . . . The truth must be told, though we do not wish to vaunt, we are invincible!*

The Longest Course Ever Played

This period of supreme self-confidence continued well into the 1860s, when the Royal Albert hired its first full-time professional/greenkeeper (Bob Dow) and announced one of the most extraordinary golf events of that or any other time – a lucrative Open event to be played over 25 holes. The advertisements for the tournament made a point of stating that this represented 'one round of the golf course'.

There is no evidence to suggest that members of the Royal Albert normally played 25 holes (since 1863, the annual Medal was now played over 18). So the length of the tournament course was surely meant to call attention to the scale and grandeur of the Montrose links, which boasted twice as many holes as any of the other main clubs in Scotland. It may also have been a response to the fledgling 12-hole Prestwick Golf Club on the west coast which, in 1860, had the audacity to start something they claimed was the championship of all of Scotland.

Though no layout of the 25-hole course has surfaced, the fact that none of the best professionals of the day – including Tom Morris and Willie Park – could manage it in less than 115 strokes suggests it must

The Girdle Hole (approximately today's 10th) was undoubtedly part of the 25-Hole Course of 1866. This photo is from around 1890; the buildings to the right formed Broomfield Farm, long since replaced by the airfield.

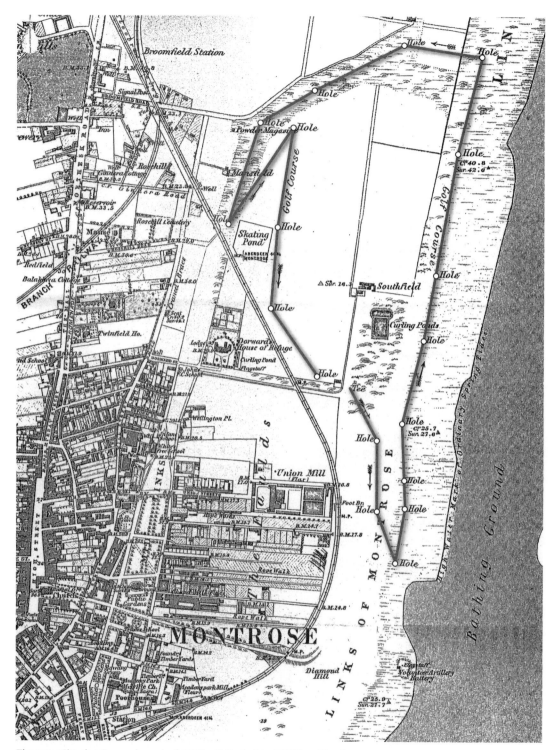

The new Circular Course layout of 1888, attributed to Old Tom Morris.

have exceeded 8000 yards in length. If so, it remains the longest course ever used in a professional tournament in this or any other country. According to a report on the match in the *Scotsman*, the players 'were unanimous in calling the course the best in Scotland'.

That there were at least 25 holes to choose from tells us that not everyone in Montrose played the same course each week. Robert Dow was also engaged by the Victoria and other clubs to insert their own holes and flags for competitions, and it is possible that each club had their favourite way of playing the links.

By the 1870s two distinct courses had emerged – a longer North course, and a South course, which utilised holes on the South Links and perhaps some of those on the North Links as well. The playing arrangements were made even more complex by increasing numbers of holiday makers, who could play for free and who might have their own ideas of which holes to play, and by the incursions of footballers, cricketers, archers and circuses.

By the 1880s things were getting out of hand. Some holes were apparently crossing each other, and at others golfers came at the same hole from different directions. Non-golfers were also under constant threat. In 1881, a boy playing cricket on the links was struck by a golf ball and died.

The Tom Morris Course

Old Tom Morris.

At the urging of the Town Council, the Royal Albert engaged in discussions with the Victoria, Star and Union Golf Clubs to consider a solution. A new circular layout was put together, combining holes from both the North and South courses, and Tom Morris was invited over from St Andrews to evaluate and improve the proposal. At a special meeting of the club in January 1886, his response to the plans in the form of a letter was read out:

> *On consideration after my arrival I can see that the intended alteration of the Montrose Golfing Course will be a great advantage (although I would have liked very much to have played over it) in so far as I consider it to be a very safe one and I hope the Town Council will be favourable to your request. Likewise I say to have the finishing hole across the road would be a great improvement and which would be similar to the St Andrews course.*

The layout for the 'Tom Morris course' – thought to be lost – was discovered in the research for this book and is shown on the opposite page. After four shortish holes on the East Links, the new layout continued onto terrain where the championship course now lies before finishing with three holes over the current-day Broomfield course. The final green was approximately on the same spot as the 18th green of the Broomfield today. As the cost of the renovations was only £100 (shared among the clubs), it is probable that many holes already existed in some way.

The new Circular Course was opened in 1888 with the Grand Tournament, organised by all three clubs and the Town Council, though the Royal Albert provided the greatest input in planning and financial terms.

The Circular Course seems to have been a popular success, as was a new way of marking the holes, as reported in the *Standard*:

> *The Royal Albert members and their energetic green keeper have evidently been taking a few hints from St Andrews recently. The placing of red and white flags at the holes to mark the outgoing and incoming course is an excellent arrangement which ought, perhaps, to have been adopted long ago, or rather not allowed to lapse. The different colours of the flags dotted over the links have a fine effect on the landscape to say nothing of regulating the play of visitors who may not be familiar with the course.*

Many members of the Royal Albert, however, continued to play golf on the South Links, which, according to a writer in the *Scotsman*, 'was held in greatest esteem, not only from the fact that it abounded in hazards'.

The Gully

No description of the golf course in the nineteenth century would be complete without special mention of this famous Gully, a hole which has been played in some fashion or another since at least 1849, and probably long before. Named after the hollow short of today's 16th green (but extending further towards the sea), it presented a much more fearsome sight in days gone by. Where now the ground consists of scraggy but by

In the nineteenth century Montrose's Gully, here depicted in an etching, was one of the most famous hazards in golf.

no means impassable terrain, in the nineteenth century it was one of golf's most famous hazards, combining a gigantic bunker, thick rough, whins and a couple of ditches.

The Gully claimed many victims over the years, including a Mr Brand of the Dalhousie Club in Carnoustie, who was a leading contender for the 1872 Carnegie Cup, played that year in Montrose. His travails were described in an account in *Bell's Life in London and Sporting Chronicle*:

> *Mr Brand played an excellent round until he came to the 'gully' hole, where he heeled his ball into the bents and lost it, and getting still further into grief he took 11 to the hole.*

Brand lost by two strokes.

In his book *Famous Golf Links* (1891), Harold Hutchinson – the most celebrated golf writer of his day – had much to say about the Gully:

> *Going to the eighth hole (360 yards), we have immediately in front the ' Big gully,' which, may be compared, without libel, to the ' Hell Bunker' of St Andrews. This is a very fearful hazard, two or three acres in extent, and in it are many lies of unredeemed malignity. A decent drive will clear it, but it must be decent in line as well as length, for on the left are two ditches, whereof one is wet and the other dry. A ball can be lifted out of the wet ditch with the penalty of a stroke, but if these things be done in the wet ditch, what shall be done in the dry? In places the lies are unplayable – consequently, however badly a ball may lie in the gully, it is never picked up until the opponent is across the dry ditch. As long as there is the dry ditch there is hope.*

The hole Hutchinson describes was played towards the north, a good drive probably landing on the current 4th fairway. After the First World War, the hole was played in the opposite direction, first as a par 4 and then as the par 3 we know today. While the 16th remains a remarkable and widely acclaimed golf hole, the gully itself is not the menace it once was.

The Town Takes Over

The affection of the Royal Albert members for the old holes on the South Links would put the club at loggerheads again with the Town Council, which took over responsibility for maintaining the golf courses for the first time in 1893. An agreement was reached whereby the clubs would split the cost of upkeep with the Town, but the clubs seem to have been shocked to find that they were to have only an advisory role in any decisions regarding the course itself. Those would be made by the Dean of Guild.

The Lighthouse hole on the South Links layout that in spite of being superceded by the new course layout to the North continued as a nine hole course up to the 1940s.

In summer months, holiday-makers thronged the links in making their way to the attractions of the beach. Courtesy of Angus Council.

The Royal Albert boycotted the whole process for a short time in protest and even withheld its annual contribution, but to no avail. The Town Council said they would only share power if the Royal Albert gave up playing on the South Links. This the club refused to do – it could do little else since its regrettable decision to relocate its clubhouse to that part of the links.

As a result, all the club could do was complain to the Town Council in 1895 when herring nets and holiday-makers interfered with play on the various holes on the South Links.

Meanwhile, the Council grew increasingly impatient to get rid of golf holes south of Dorward Road altogether. As a first step it wanted to replace Old Tom's East Links holes with ones further north.

Despite the Council's ongoing tussles with the Royal Albert, it was to one of the club's most distinguished members – William Jameson Paton – that the Dean of Guild turned in 1899 to oversee the 'general supervision' of new changes to the golf course. These appear to have been based on plans drawn up by the Mercantile Club and it is likely that the Mercantile's Sandy Keillor, an outstanding golfer and future superintendent of the golf course, was also involved.

Paton was a famously successful businessman, operating the largest textile mill in town, and he seems to have brought a no-nonsense, business-like approach to the task of extending the course northwards. There were to be five new holes 'in the bents' which would require a substantial amount of earthmoving and shaping. After a rock-bottom price had been secured from a firm in Dundee (undercutting bids from Montrose), Paton ensured the specifications on the new greens were crystal clear. The goal seems to have been the flattest greens on the planet!

> *The turf will be laid by thoroughly experienced workmen only and must be laid to an even gradient entirely free from humps, hollows or any irregularity of surface . . . and finished to a true surface with spirit level and levelling board.*

Willie Park Jr who suggested revisions to the course in 1902.

The Willie Park Jr Course

Perhaps this scientific precision did not sit well with everyone, because it was not long before two-time Open champion Willie Park Jr was engaged to suggest further refinements. He recommended significant changes to all of the new holes that Paton's team had constructed, and no doubt some of these alterations influenced future developments. But from the standpoint of today's course, the only Willie Park hole that seems to have survived more or less intact is the 4th.

Nevertheless, in its short life, the Willie Park course played host to many first class tournaments including a professional event in 1905 that attracted the Great Triumvirate – Harry Vardon, J.H. Taylor and James Braid – who would win sixteen Open Championships between them.

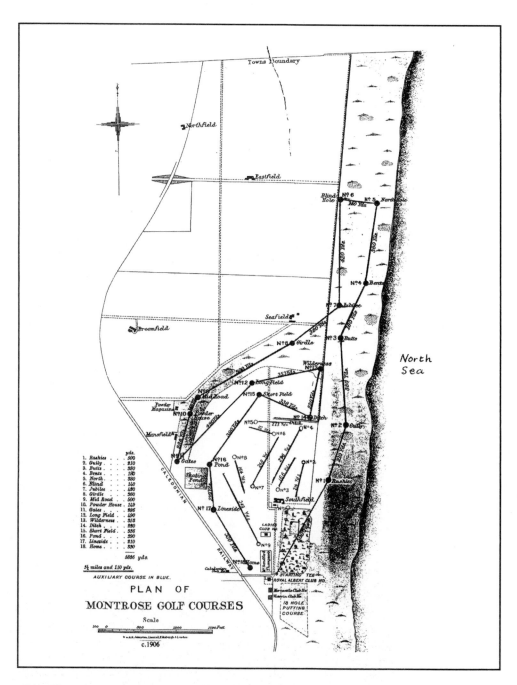

The Willie Park course in about 1906. Note the short-lived par-3 6th. Courtesy of William Coull.

Vardon came out on top, besting yet another Open champion, Sandy Herd, in the final. The Royal Albert's new professional, Charles Burgess, contended after the first of two stroke-play qualifying rounds, only to fall back.

It was a time of intense, world-class competition almost every day on the links at Montrose, with hundreds watching even preliminary matches for the Boothby Challenge Shield which determined the town's champion golfer. A good performance there could change a player's life. The winner of the 1908 event, Harry Hampton, was hired by the Brooklands Country Club in Michigan with a retainer of $8000, a mammoth sum at the time which made him, according to press reports, the second most highly paid club professional in America. Royal Albert golf professionals Charles Burgess and Fred Findlay would soon follow Hampton overseas.

For it was also a time of unprecedented explosion in the popularity of Scotland's game. Hundreds of golf clubs sprang up almost overnight in England and America, and their new courses often garnered generous amounts of publicity in the new golf magazines that also proliferated.

Short-lived fads of golf architecture began to influence even as ancient a golf town as Montrose. At a single meeting of the Dean of Guild's committee, no fewer than thirteen circular bunkers were approved ('as alike to each other as penny pies', complained one critic). Before long, most would be filled in again.

Improved maintenance meant that holes on the new golf courses could be built in places that had previously been considered off limits. Old Tom Morris at St Andrews had ushered in a revolution in greenkeeping and many courses now used (horse-drawn) mowers and complex treatments

James Braid playing off the first tee in 1905, towards what is now the 17th green. Courtesy of Lyn Coull.

for greens. For a town so proud of its golf heritage and increasingly reliant on holiday tourists, there was pressure to keep up with the times.

Another Prime Minister Lends a Hand

A successful Golf Course Improvement Bazaar in 1907, held in the town's Drill Hall, certainly helped. A joint effort of all the golf clubs and the Town Council, the bazaar included a panoply of entertainments including a magic show, concerts, plays, palm reading, a shooting gallery, hat-making competitions, skittles, a limerick contest, and the obligatory putting tournament.

The sitting Prime Minister, Sir Henry Campbell-Bannerman, agreed to come and give a speech, and the event drew national attention to the town. Honorary Royal Albert member William Gladstone may never have played the links but this Prime Minister most certainly had. As reported in the *Times* of London, Sir Henry reminisced about learning to play golf on the Montrose course as a youngster:

Prime Minister Henry Campbell-Bannerman.

> *He raised a great deal of their best turf and smashed a great deal of their best clubs, and he called that playing golf (Laughter). . . . He belonged to no club, he was a pure interloper, a poacher; and he hoped the years elapsed since then had been sufficient to constitute, under a statute of limitations, an exemption for him from any penalties he might have incurred. (Laughter).*

The bazaar raised £1500, which paid for the installation of a watering system for some of the new greens, an equipment shed and other improvements.

The golf course's finances were also improved by the introduction, for the first time, of a tariff for visitors which began at a modest 'thruppence' a round! This nevertheless produced an income of some £60 and, from then on, green fees became an important contributor to the balance sheet.

But still there was dissatisfaction. A writer in the *Montrose Standard* put the blame on the Town Council:

> *It was a bad day for the Links of Montrose, and for local golf in particular, when, by means of the Provisional Order, the Town Council obtained autocratic control of our Links and Golf Courses. . . . Since the new management took over its charge, stagnation has reigned supreme.*

As proof, the same writer noted that while Horace Hutchinson had declared in 1891 that the course at Montrose was 'undoubtedly one of the three best in Scotland', a new guide book didn't rate it in the top 20!

Others lamented the day the South Links holes had been separated from the main course. And the never-ending tussle between the Town

OPENING OF MONTROSE GOLF BAZAAR
BY SIR HENRY CAMPBELL-BANNERMAN. 26/6/07.

The Prime Minister opens the 1907 Golf Course Improvements Bazaar. Courtesy of Angus Council.

Council and the Royal Albert about the future of those holes must have been a distraction as well.

But another underlying reason for the sense of unease in the golfing fraternity may simply have been that Montrose's vast areas of ready-made linksland – such an attraction in the era of the feathery and hickory – no longer gave the town the golfing advantage it once had.

Perhaps stung by the criticism of its handling of the golf course, the Town Council decided to act. There would be one more major overhaul of the course – one that would shake the golfing fraternity in Montrose to its core.

'A Revolution on the Course' – The Harry Colt Controversy

Harry Colt is today considered one of Britain's first modern architects and among the very best of all time. He is largely responsible for the fame of Muirfied, Royal Portrush, Royal Lytham & St Anne's, Sunningdale and Wentworth. Most of those assignments were still ahead of him in 1913, but he was accomplished enough to have been asked to design the Eden course at St Andrews. The favourable publicity surrounding that project led the Town Council to ask him, in the summer of 1913, to visit Montrose and 'report on the condition of the principal course'.

After walking around the course twice, Colt instead made far-reaching recommendations that would change golf in Montrose forever. Eleven entirely new holes needed to be built, he reported, and the rest should be revised. Most controversially, the first four holes should be laid out on the 'top of the bents', the highest part of the sandy dunes next to the sea. These would offer magnificent views but had long been thought too wild to sustain golf holes.

Colt's report, which was printed in its entirety in the local press, was a bombshell.

The *Montrose Review* was having none of it. In an editorial, it said the proposals amounted to 'a revolution on the course' and would be a colossal waste of money:

> *It will come as a great surprise to most local golfers and to most of the strangers who have played on the course, that it is such a poor inferior thing, and needs as much re-modelling as Mr Colt's report implies.*

A fine amateur golfer, Harry Colt had just designed the Eden course in St Andrews when he was asked to take a look at the course at Montrose.

If Colt had struck a nerve, it was not surprising, for his report was frank about the course's shortcomings:

> *The present course contains many interesting holes, but at the same time there are several without any distinctive natural feature owing to a portion of the Links being laid out on dead flat land. I have attempted to omit such ground and have in consequence been obliged to layout several entirely new holes. The alterations may appear at first sight to be somewhat extensive, but in my opinion they are absolutely necessary if the land be used to the best advantage for the game of golf.*

An added bonus of the Colt plan was that the holes that were no longer needed could be used to extend the auxiliary course (now the Broomfield) to 18 holes.

Colt was by no means entirely critical. He praised the 'beautifully fine turf' on the putting surfaces, and said that 'where the daisies and other weeds have been exterminated, the putting greens are, I think, as good as any that I have seen'. But he also noted that 'the natural undulations have been flattened out too much' and despaired over the new bunkers that had been introduced, calling them 'intensely artificial'.

For three months the debate over Colt's proposals raged: in letters to the editor, at Town Council meetings and no doubt in the golf clubs themselves.

The Royal Albert held a special meeting to express support for the plan but that didn't carry the kind of weight it would have a generation earlier. Joseph Foreman, a former Provost still on Council, said the Royal Albert's views should be ignored 'because the members were mostly resident outside Montrose, and in any financial obligations which Montrose undertook they would have no say and no responsibility'.

Foreman said the vast majority of golfers in Montrose were against the changes and he reminded his fellow councillors that they had recently wasted another £2000 in a botched job of 'tar-macadamizing' on Murray Street. He demanded a public meeting on the golf question. The Council demurred, no doubt afraid of inflaming passions any further.

In January 1914, the Council at last voted on a proposal to implement the architect's plans. Provost Thomson said that the golf course was one of the town's greatest assets and that 'it was only by going forward that we can expect to keep Montrose in the front rank, either as a golf centre or as a place for summer visitors'.

Councillor Milne went further. Invoking Shakespeare, he declared the Colt plan was an opportunity that must be grasped: 'There was a tide in the affairs of men, which taken at the flood, leads on to fortune.'

None of this (not even a Shakespearean quote) impressed ex-Provost Foreman but the motion passed over his furious objections. The *Review* was equally livid:

> *The town council, one would almost think out of bravado, have rushed with break-neck speed into action and are leaving the thinking to be done some other day. . . . They have shown in this*

Montrose's 3rd hole designed by Harry Colt, shortly after construction in about 1919. Note the steps to aid golfers climbing up the steep bank.

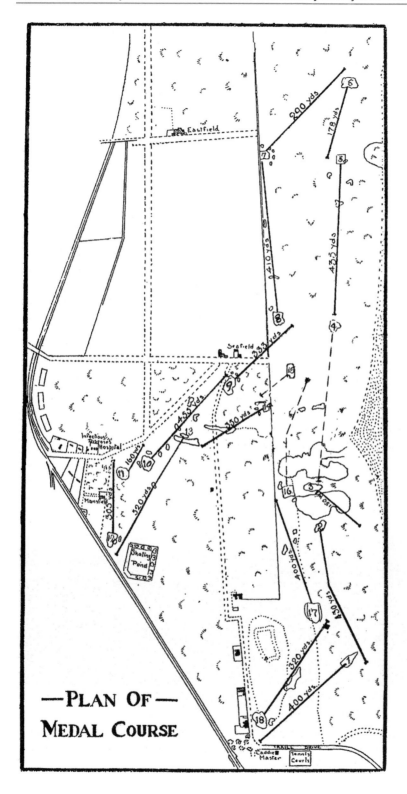

The Harry Colt course of 1921. This plan, adapted from a drawing from the early 1920s, shows the course as it was played after Harry Colt's controversial recommendations were implemented. Hole routings shown in broken lines are approximations based on newspaper accounts and Colt's own written report to the Town Council. The 4th hole was a spectacular 500-yard par 5 played over the highest dunes to the present 5th green; the 15th hole was an uphill par 3 to a now abandoned green, and the 16th hole was played as a par 4.

matter a tendency to embark on a large undertaking without thought, and in a spirit of reckless adventure which bodes no good to the town if allowed to go unchecked.

If the Council thought the affair was over, they were mistaken.

The onset of war did cause the plans to redevelop the course to be put on hold. But almost as soon as peace was declared, the wheelbarrows were rolling in earnest over the links. An exhibition match between two of the legends of the age, Harry Vardon and George Duncan, was scheduled for October 1919, and the new course needed to be ready in time.

'A howling wilderness' – The Golf Course Election of 1921

The strains of a weak post-war economy no doubt played their part but work on the new course was a struggle from the start. Montrose had never before engaged on a golf construction project of this magnitude. A letter to the editor complained that the pace of change was too slow and that, with only weeks to go, none of the bunkers Colt had specified were being built.

And the challenge of developing greens and fairways on top of the bents proved to be immense. It seemed particularly so on the 4th hole, designed to be a spectacular 500-yard par 5 running from the right of today's 3rd green across the dunes to today's 5th green. An otherwise sympathetic writer in the *Review* noted that 'it has apparently been found impossible this season to level the ground there to ensure that a well played tee shot gets a good lie'.

Brown, Montrose, Photo.   THE GATIES HOLE, MONTROSE LINKS. VARDON ON
LEFT AND HERD PUTTING.

Vardon and Herd pictured on the 13th hole in their 1905 final. Note the old spelling of the 'Gates' hole and the great concourse of spectators, not at all an unusual sight at important golf matches played in this period at Montrose. Vardon returned to open the 'Colt Course' in 1919.

The visit of Vardon and Duncan went off smoothly. As they were being paid for their appearance, it was hardly surprising that they would praise the new layout as a great course in the making once the wrinkles were ironed out. And local golfers were no doubt willing to give the new holes a year to settle in.

But as the summers of 1920 and 1921 passed with little signs of improvement, golfers grew restless. After three years, many of the new greens and fairways were obviously still in dismal condition. At the Mercantile – by now the town's largest and most active club – a rebellion was in the works. A representative of the club informed the Dean of Guild that the Mercantile was 'unanimously in favour' of abandoning the new course and reverting to the old.

The Caledonia more or less sided with the Mercantile (though they would retain two Colt holes), leaving the Victoria and Royal Albert alone to defend the new course. The two clubs conceded that the 4th hole and the 15th hole (a par 3 played from near the current 15th green to a hole somewhere on the current 5th fairway) could be sacrificed, and the 16th greatly changed, but otherwise felt that the bulk of the Colt lay-out should be retained.

A week later, in October 1921, the Dean of Guild presided over a Town meeting on the question. The event proved to be a public relations triumph for the Mercantile position. The popular Alexander Keillor, a former greenkeeper and a legendary golfer and footballer, called for a show of hands. By a margin of 70–16 those present voted to scrap the new layout entirely, even if it meant that the new Auxiliary course would need to revert to 9 holes.

The resolution was non-binding of course, but to add to the pressure on the Town Council at least two Mercantile members – A.M. Clarke and D.M. Hogg – put themselves forward for the municipal elections in November. The traditional 'Heckling Meeting', at which voters were given a chance to grill the candidates, drew a boisterous, standing-room-only crowd at the Burgh Hall. According to the *Montrose Review*, they heard Clarke give a scathing, humorous and well-received analysis of the golf course issue:

> *Mr Clarke said . . . they used to have a beautiful course in Montrose, second to none in Scotland. They had spent £2000 to £3000 on a new course and made a howling wilderness. . . . It was useless dumping down black earth (in the bents). That sand simply swallowed up hundreds of loads of it. . . . If carrots had been suggested it would be more useful. . . . If council mismanaged the golf course in that way what might they be doing in other departments. In conclusion, he hoped that as he had been the last speaker on the list he might be the first in the poll (laughter and applause).*

While Clarke didn't top the poll, he was easily elected, garnering more support than two incumbents. And Hogg, the 1914 Mercantile Club

Champion, missed being elected by only a handful of votes. It must have sent a shock through the political establishment of the town.

As far as the *Review* was concerned the Town Meeting, and Clarke's victory, had sealed the fate of the new course:

> *The Colt plan is doomed and the only good thing about it is to make it an object lesson of what to avoid in the future. . . . Mr Clarke, who was one of the two new candidates returned, probably owed in greatest measure his election following what was recognised to be a lucid and practical exposition of the views held by the bulk of the local exponents of the game.*

The survival of the course we know today hung by a very slender thread. But then, at the swearing-in of the next council, a formidable new protagonist emerged.

Thomas Lyell in his Town Provost robes. Courtesy of Angus Council.

'Out-ravelling this tangled skein'

Thomas Lyell, a 35-year old solicitor, and Secretary of the Royal Albert, was nominated to be the new Dean of Guild. In making the nomination, Baillie Jolly sounded a note of desperation as he addressed his fellow councillors:

> *They could not shut their eyes to the fact that there was dissatisfaction in connection with the golf courses. . . . He was sure that they would all hope that Captain Lyell would during what would no doubt prove a strenuous year succeed in out-ravelling this tangled skein and making things right all round.*

Lyell had certainly known 'strenuous' years before. Serving in the Black Watch, he had earned a Military Cross in the Great War and many young Montrose men who survived had been grateful to serve under him. One soldier recalled that Lyell 'could talk tactics with old Regulars, law with business men, turnips with farmers, and he always had a cheery word for his subordinate officers'. But it remained to be seen whether these skills would help in the new battle that lay before him.

The first skirmish went decisively to A.M Clarke. Within a month of being elected a town councillor, Clarke had persuaded the Dean of Guild's committee to endorse his campaign platform of abandoning virtually all the new Harry Colt holes. And it did so over the objection of the new Dean of Guild himself!

Lyell, and the new golf course, had only one more chance – overturn his own committee's motion at the Town Council meeting in three weeks' time. Normally, the Council rubber-stamped the recommendations of the Dean of Guild's committee. But this time, as the *Review* reported, when 'the great golf question came up' there was 'a very long and intricate discussion'.

Councillor A.M. Clarke, in moving that the recommendation of the Dean of Guild's Assessors be adopted, claimed that most golfers were utterly fed up:

> *They had spent all their time upon the bents to the detriment of the other parts of the Links with the result that they had not a single decent course to play on. They had made Bolsheviks of the golfers, who were . . . refusing to pay the tariff. By adopting the recommendation they would be losing nothing, but simply cutting off a diseased member which was mortifying the whole. . . . At least 80% of the golfers wished the change. . . . The golf course was driving away visitors more than a manure works or knackery would. (Laughter)*

In a highly unusual move, Dean of Guild Lyell was forced to move an opposing amendment to the motion of his own committee. His reasoning, the *Review* reported, was that:

> *The only fault generally with the present course was the fourth hole, and to remedy that all that was required was to play from the present tee down to the old third green. If they did that they would take away the cause of discontent and keep the course as a first class one. . . . If they scrapped these holes in the bents they would ultimately have to go back to them, and be faced with the same expenditure as when they adopted the scheme.*

Lyell's last-ditch appeal had its desired effect. Even ex-Provost Foreman, who had railed against the plan in 1914, grudgingly agreed to give Lyell 'another year or two', though he said he had not changed his mind about the 'stupidity of the Colt Scheme'.

The Council voted to overturn its committee's recommendation and back Lyell. The editorial writers at the *Montrose Review* were flabbergasted by this surprising turn of events and unleashed one last burst of vitriol at the Town Council:

> *It is fairly certain that the result will not remain long unchanged. . . . The holes in the bents were palpably a weird delusion. They will swallow up a mint of money, and then they can never be otherwise than a poor, sandy strip. . . . The last word in this controversy has not been said.*

The extensive Winton family club-making premises adjacent to the Royal Albert clubhouse about 1910.

The Colt course had been given a stay of execution but Lyell was under enormous pressure to improve conditions and turn the 'weird delusion' into a playable golf course. To help him in this formidable task, he turned to Robert Winton.

Winton was a member of the famous clubmaking family that still had a workshop near the first tee (Robert had by this time sold the firm to his brother William). A crack golfer, Robert had represented the Victoria Club on the golf course committee for some time when, in January 1923, Thomas Lyell proposed that he be made a part-time 'golf superintendent' at a rate of £1 per week.

For once the *Montrose Review* was pleased, calling Winton 'the right man in the right place'. Work on the course picked up noticeably after Winton's appointment, aided by a new 'triple horse mower'. There was a flurry of activity in dressing greens, rearranging bunkers, and creating multiple tee boxes on several holes (a recommendation Colt had made). New sprinklers were purchased and those daisies on the greens were finally addressed – Winton hired six women (with a man supervising) to spend a week weeding all the greens at a total cost of £80. Sheep would also no longer be allowed on the course for winter grazing.

Play and revenue on the championship course inched upwards. A ballot for tee times – begun in the busy summer months before the War – was reintroduced, with names to be submitted by 4 p.m. the previous day.

By 1924 Lyell was confident enough to suggest that Montrose should hold an annual amateur open tournament on July 28 and July 31. There would be no charge for entrants but there would be a cash prize and a cup. The Montrose Open Week was born.

From the Town Council minutes it is clear that Lyell and Winton worked closely together to gradually bring the championship course into a condition that would once again do credit to the town. They must have played a part in course design as well, creating the present 7th hole, reorienting the 8th hole, changing the 5th into a par 4, and shortening the 16th into a par 3.

MONTROSE CHAMPIONSHIP OR MEDAL GOLF COURSE.
Length of Holes (1926).

No. 1	...	391 yards	......	No. 10	...	347 yards
,, 2	...	372 ,,	......	,, 11	...	433 ,,
,, 3	...	143 ,,	......	,, 12	...	152 ,,
,, 4	...	267 ,,	......	,, 13	...	319 ,,
,, 5	...	267 ,,	......	,, 14	...	533 ,,
,, 6	...	433 ,,	......	,, 15	...	348 ,,
,, 7	...	250 ,,	......	,, 16	...	225 ,,
,, 8	...	367 ,,	......	,, 17	...	409 ,,
,, 9	...	400 ,,	......	,, 18	...	342 ,,

Total Length—5,998 yards.

A list of holes from 1926 shows the general layout was much the same as today with the exception of 14th and 15th holes.

Robert Winton died in 1926 but by then the course was very much as it is today. The notable exceptions were the Long and Wilderness holes. It was only in 1974 that Harry Colt's way of seeing those two holes would prevail, when the 15th was at last extended into a par 5 and a new double-tiered green was built on the now shorter 14th, at the instigation of greenkeeper Willie Ritchie.

Thomas Lyell would live another twelve eventful years. When he died suddenly in 1938, his funeral at St Mary's and St Peter's Church was reported to be the largest that anyone could remember in the town. Since defusing the golf course controversy, Lyell had become one of the town's most famous worthies, serving as Provost and taking on senior volunteer roles in an astonishing number of organisations, including the Boy Scouts, the British Legion, the local library and Dorward House. He was one of the leading Freemasons in Scotland and, of course, a Captain of the Royal Albert and its Secretary for several years (he was even Secretary and Treasurer of the Ladies Club!). A tribute in the *Standard* said that Lyell

> stood for all that is best in Montrose, or Angus, or indeed Scotland – the sturdy trustworthiness of the plain Scotsman, the personification of good fellowship.

Lyell's record of public service is an appropriate symbol for the immense volunteer contribution of countless Montrosians towards protecting, maintaining and enhancing the golf ground that has played such a central part in the history of the town – and of the sport itself.

A Championship Course Returns

Britain's first military airfield was set up just north of the golf course in 1913, and one can still drive on the old aircraft taxiways to reach the town's golf practice ground today. If the course escaped much damage in the first global conflict, that wasn't the case in the Second World War. The last four holes of the front nine were commandeered by the Air Ministry and fairways now featured a whole new set of hazards, including barbed wire, concrete pill boxes, tank traps and trenches. Several German bombs intended for the aerodrome dropped on the course instead, creating new bunkers and swallowing up at least one tee box.

After the war it took several years for the most northerly holes to be incorporated back into the championship course and the 4th, 5th, 14th and 15th holes of the Broomfield were used instead. The end of the war also marked the demise of the South Links course whose admirers had defied efforts to shut it down for half a century. In a cost-cutting measure, the town simply decided not to reopen the South Links holes again, reasoning that this might also make it easier to attract industry to the site. Glaxochem did in fact arrive in the early 1950s and would become the town's largest employer.

As the championship course regained its footing, Montrose once again played host to its share of significant golf events. These include the Scottish PGA championship in 1967 and 1970, and the Scottish Amateur championship in 1975. In 1991, the course played host to the British Boys championship and the British Boys International Matches, won by an English team captained by Lee Westwood.

And in 1999 and 2007, Montrose was invited by the Royal and Ancient to be one of the Final Pre-Qualifying Courses for the Open Championship at Carnoustie. Two-time Ryder Cup member Per-Ulrik Johansson shot a course record 63 in his first round to head the list of qualifiers. In qualifying for the 2007 Open, David Shacklady topped that with a 62.

A new era of links management had begun in 1981, when the golfers of the town once again took responsibility for running the course on behalf of the community, just as the Royal Albert did for much of the nineteenth century. Victoria member Bob Stirling played a leading role in setting up the Montrose Links Trust, which leased the course from the Town Council and was managed by representatives from all of the town's golf clubs.

After dealing with some severe financial challenges in the early years, every club member and golfing visitor would concur with the sentiment that local control of the courses by the Links Trust has helped to restore the links to their former glories. In 2001, a new corporate body – Montrose Golf Links Limited – took on this same role, with the club representatives being joined by two elected members and two professional staff from the Angus County Council. Chairmen of these bodies since 1981 have included club members Grigor Dunbar, Bill Tulloch, Alastair McFarlane and Alan Crow while Margaret Stewart worked as Secretary for more than two decades. Mike Fraser, who represented the Mercantile Club when he was Chairman, is now a member of Royal Montrose also.

As Royal Montrose marks its bicentennial, its members can be justly proud of the central role it and its three predecessor clubs have played in the evolution of one of golf's most historic and majestic links. Through twenty decades, these clubs have helped ward off threats to the golf ground through a combination of persuasion, influence, legal threats and sheer obstinacy. And, as other clubs have come on the scene, they have joined forces with them and the municipal and county authorities – to ensure that a precious public asset is preserved into the future.

For Montrose remains a public course that has always been open to all. It has benefited from the genius of great architects such as Harry Colt, Old Tom Morris and Willie Park Jr. But to an even greater extent, the courses that exist today reflect the inclinations, prejudices and enthusiasms of generations of players in one of the very oldest golf communities in the world.

Postscript – Coastal Erosion

While the golf course has survived many threats over the years – its greatest test may well come from the sea itself. In the last twenty years, at least one tee (at the 6th) has been abandoned due to coastal erosion, and one fairway reoriented.

The cause of the erosion is controversial. In a BBC radio documentary in 2006, leading British scientists attributed the erosion to the millions of tonnes of sand that have been dredged out of the Montrose port and deposited as far away as Aberdeen. The dredged sand, the scientists say, is replaced by sand from the beach that fronts the links. The Port Authority has cited global warming and other natural forces.

Whatever the cause, it has created a crisis for Montrose Golf Links Limited and for the town itself, parts of which are also under threat if erosion continues at the present rate (according to a study commissioned by Angus Council). Plans for a significant rearrangement of the golf course have been discussed but thus far only minor realignments have been made. In 2008, the second fairway was slightly altered, moving it away from the water's edge, following a design by well-known links designer Martin Hawtree.

As we near the 450th anniversary of James Melville's golf lessons on the links of Montrose, a resolution of the crisis is not yet in sight. It can only be hoped that Montrose's golfers – and the public bodies that can help – continue to appreciate the unique and ancient heritage that is under threat.

It is, indeed, 'a golf ground unequalled'.

CHAPTER 17

'Three into one': The Amalgamation

It was agreed that action must be taken.

Victoria Golf Club Minutes, September 1985

In November 1983, the Captain of the Victoria Golf Club reported on a meeting he had attended at the Royal Albert with representatives of the other Montrose clubs on possible amalgamation of all clubs.

A special meeting of the Victoria was consequently held on 30 November 1983 to seek authority to commence formal talks on possible amalgamation at some future date. A motion to this effect was passed on a show of hands against an alternative motion denying Council such approval.

The sequence of events leading to eventual amalgamation in 1986 as recorded in the Victoria and Royal Albert minutes is set out below.

November 1983. Informal talks are initiated by the Mercantile.

April 1984. Officials of a proposed Montrose Golf Club are appointed – Mr R. West of the Mercantile as chairman, Mr A. Crow of the Victoria as Vice Chairman and Mr J.D. Sykes of Royal Albert as Secretary – and given working funds of £10 from each club.

November 1984. A plan of a combined Royal Albert and Mercantile clubhouse was drawn up.

February 1985. Amalgamation of the three clubs was agreed to be 'not financially viable at this time', the cost of a new clubhouse being in the region of £600,000.

March 1985. At the Royal Albert AGM, the Captain was asked to open informal discussions with the Victoria to discuss an amalgamation of the two clubs. North Links Ladies were also interested in exploring amalgamation but, whilst welcoming this approach, it was decided to proceed with one possible amalgamation at a time. All the Clubs in the town were urged to hold general meetings of their members to see if they had a mandate to proceed. The Royal and Victoria clubs felt they already had such a mandate from their members. The feedback from the other clubs, other than North Links Ladies, was inconclusive.

April 1985.There was a suggestion that Royal Albert, Victoria and North Links Ladies merge, with the Victoria clubhouse retained for ladies and juniors. This was again not considered financially viable.

September 1985. It was agreed that action must be taken. The relative values of the two clubhouses were considered to be roughly equal but the majority view among Victoria members was that the loss of Royal Albert clubhouse would be detrimental to Montrose golf.

October 1985. Discussions were opened between the two clubs covering a wide range of aspects.

November 1985. Members of the Victoria voted by 55 to 16 to support a merger. Royal Montrose was proposed as the name of the new club. Royal Albert liabilities were around £12k, not including dues to the Links Trust. Four working parties were set up.

December 1985. North Links Ladies expressed their willingness to consider merger. It was agreed that this be dealt with by the new club once the amalgamation was completed.

29 January 1986. A new club constitution was approved.

12 February 1986. Election of new office bearers was held at the first AGM of the new club.

19 February 1986. The last Victoria AGM took place in their clubhouse (a suggested farewell dinner for Victoria members was not held).

After this challenging series of meetings conducted over a two-year period, perhaps there is a particular irony in the eventual outcome. Here now, in 1986, history was repeating itself.

Once again, Victoria Golf Club members – whose founders back in 1864 found an early home for their 'boxes' in a room in the then Royal Albert (Southfield) clubhouse – found themselves again moving their golfing possessions (now up to fourteen clubs contained in large bags together with assorted caddie cars) into another Royal Albert clubhouse, directly across the road from where that original Royal Albert clubhouse stood. It seemed a long way to come to cover such a short distance.

Victoria and Albert – the royal couple that is – had a very close and loving relationship and always felt they were meant to be together. The Victoria and Royal Albert Golf Club members in Montrose found, in the years that followed their particular 'union', that they were also soul mates, united in their affection and respect for the game of golf.

Their offspring was not named the Victoria and Albert Golf Club as was tentatively suggested at one meeting – a senior 'Vicky' member's retort to that idea was that 'though he might be thought an old fogey, he didn't want to belong to a golf club that reminded people of a museum full of old fossils' – but was instead given the fine name, Royal Montrose Golf Club.

CHAPTER 18

Royal Montrose Golf Club, 1986–2010

*On a motion duly proposed and seconded, it was unanimously
resolved that the name of the club be 'Royal Montrose Golf Club'.*

Minutes of the first General Meeting, 12 February 1986

The first Annual General Meeting of the new club – initially the product
of the amalgamation of the Victoria and Royal Albert clubs – took place
on the 12 February 1986 and was attended by 129 members of these former clubs. Such a healthy attendance at an AGM boded well for the
future.

Bill Richmond, the last Captain of the Victoria, opened proceedings by
welcoming those attending and then handed over to the last Captain of
the Royal Albert, James Clark, to take the chair for the first two items of
business. The name of the new club – Royal Montrose – was unanimously approved, and Alan Crow was elected as the first Captain of the
new club, also unanimously. Alan Crow then took the chair for the
remaining business of this first general meeting.

The first committee meeting of Royal Montrose Golf Club was held
a few days later, and one of the first items of business was to agree
a response to a firm expression of interest from the North Links
Ladies Club to becoming part of the amalgamation. An Extraordinary
General Meeting was held on 25 June 1986 and a motion proposing
amalgamation with the North Links Ladies was approved. By
September of that year, the details of this second phase of club amalgamation had been worked out and approved, and the ladies of the former
North Links club paid their first subscription to Royal Montrose in the
spring of 1987. Total membership of the club at this stage was an
impressive 658.

Among the first priorities of the club was the sale of the former
clubhouses of the Victoria and the North Links Ladies clubs. The
former became 'Roo's Leap' restaurant and the latter was bought and
adapted for use as 'Rompers' Nursery. The funds from these sales
allowed the new club to carry out quite an extensive programme of

refurbishment of the clubhouse and to build an extension to the ladies' locker rooms.

In the next few years membership remained at healthy levels; in 1991, it stood at 678 members. But, in common with many golf clubs in Scotland, membership slowly declined as more clubs came into being and ended up chasing fewer golfers.

In 1991, the club decided to end the practice of the Bar Steward's wife undertaking catering for club members – the departure of any Steward meant the loss to the club of both important functions at the same time – and appointed their first specific caterer. In 1992, the last resident Bar Steward to be employed gave his notice and the club decided that the next appointment would be a Bar Supervisor who would be non-resident. In 1996, the first caterer to be appointed on a franchise basis was approved. These changes set a pattern for the employment of club staff that would continue to the present time and have served the club well, ensuring some continuity of staff even when there are staff departures.

The club now had available areas upstairs that could be put to other uses, and various committees began to consider options for utilising these for the wider benefit of members and visiting golfers. Funding such further major improvements was a problem however, but a 'saviour' arrived in the unlikely form of the Inland Revenue which, in 1995, decreed that sporting clubs should not have been charging Value Added Tax on members' subscriptions as they had been doing for some years, and returned a sum of £14,000 to the club. This windfall helped to fund the conversion of the upstairs accommodation to provide extra locker room, office and lounge facilities.

What is remarkable, especially in its early years, is how rapidly and smoothly members of three former clubs were assimilated into the new club and worked together, generally harmoniously, to take the club forward. A major factor in that successful assimilation was the presence of the ladies from the North Links club who, with the small number of lady associates from the Royal Albert, proved such a positive force. Their influence was increased in 1987 when, at their own suggestion, lady members were granted full and equal voting rights and gained the right to stand for any office in the club. The club has not yet had a Lady Club Captain but it may only be a matter of time.

Since 1986, the club has largely flourished in spite of declining memberships, reduced bar and gaming machine income – similar challenges to those that face most clubs in Scotland at the present time – because it sees itself principally as a club for golfers. The joy of playing the game, be it medal-play, match-play, inter-club matches or just 'bounce games' that might have interesting side stakes, is very evident in the varied activities of the men's and ladies' golf sections.

Placing as it did the emphasis firmly on the golfing side, the new club was very pleased to continue the annual matches with the St Andrews Golf Club, first played between that club and the Victoria in the 1960s

The assembled teams for the 2008 match in Montrose with Royal Blackheath Golf Club.

and, following a discussion between Royal Montrose Captain, David Taylor, and the Captain of Royal Musselburgh Golf Club at Royal Ottawa's centenary celebrations, an agreement was made to have annual matches between our two historic clubs. These annual matches with St Andrews and Royal Musselburgh have taken place now for over twenty years, with many golfing friendships established.

In 2007, Club Captain John Anderson played a leading role in resurrecting the annual matches with Royal Blackheath Golf Club, and the third in this new sequence of annual matches took place in 2009.

In the late 1990s, the club took the decision to institute a number of seniors' matches with some other clubs in Tayside and Aberdeenshire. So enjoyable were these matches for our senior men that the club readily agreed to participate in a new venture – the Caledonian League – and many of our seniors continue today to enjoy these league matches with a slightly more competitive edge.

Royal Montrose golfers have on occasions excelled in golfing competitions both in Montrose and further afield as the selected photographs on the following pages show. County Championships have also been won by Carol Diack (nee Hay) in 1988 and Alistair Serrels in 2005.

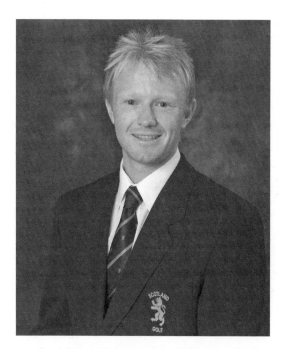

Graeme Brown was a very promising young golfer whose career took off when he took up the offer of a golfing scholarship at a college in Alabama. He was capped for Scotland in the Home Internationals in 2002 and thereafter turned professional playing mainly on the Challenge and Euro Pro tours

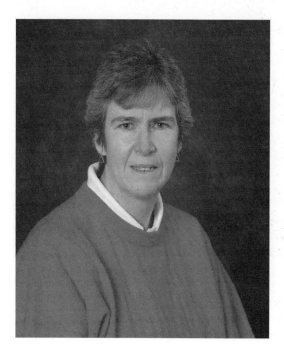

Over the years, Kathleen Sutherland – who in her younger days won the club championship of North Links Ladies twelve years in succession—has consistently played high-quality golf in various Angus and Scottish events while still representing Royal Montrose. A four-time winner of the Angus Championship and a regular member of the County team over many seasons, perhaps her most recent principal achievements have been winning the Scottish Seniors' Championship and captaining the Scottish team in the Lady Seniors' Home Internationals

Ross Coull is a member of Edzell and Royal Montrose and has won the club championships of these clubs several times as well as two Montrose Opens, and he has been a regular member of the Angus County team. Perhaps his most significant success came in 2008 when he won the Scottish Mid-Amateur title at Dundonald Links, and he is pictured playing a fairway shot in the final round of that event

In 2006 – Janet Henderson, Phyllis Sutherland, Christine Macgowan and Mary Faulkner – pictured here were the first all-ladies team to win the club's annual Am-Am tournament and end a period of domination in that event by men's teams. In 2001, Janet Henderson, Mary Faulkner and Jean Findlay with team professional Robert Arnott, were the first all-ladies team to triumph in the Montrose Pro-Am.

Man, it's a gran' game, the gowf.'

Our new club has now had twenty-three years of existence and can hopefully look forward to many more years of happy golfing and social intercourse, continuing those fine traditions established by our many predecessors.

As we come to the end of this account of two hundred years of golfing activities in Montrose, all of us involved in writing this account can but hope that the twenty-first century members, whenever they meet to play golf or to gather together afterwards in the clubhouse, may make a special connection with their golfing predecessors – be it with that small group of golfers who met at some inn in Montrose on 1 January 1810 to form the Montrose Golf Club, or with the nine gentlemen who met in the Crown Hotel on 4 October 1864 to set up the Victoria Club, or with the group of ladies who met on 16 June 1927 in a church hall to establish the North Links Ladies Club.

With this history, we seek to honour all of these club founders and, indeed, all who played a part in ensuring that these same clubs survived the passage of time, to come together in 1986 as Royal Montrose Golf Club.

We particularly honour what must now be well over a thousand men and women who, over the last two hundred years, have volunteered to serve on club councils and committees and to carry out the myriad tasks that must be done if golf clubs such as ours are to thrive. Some are singled out for special mention in these pages. The majority, however, are the unnamed heroes of our story.

The obvious pleasure that James Melville back in 1562 gained from playing golf is one that has been shared by generations of Montrose golfers ever since. If there is a particularly good insight into the special appeal of golf, this anonymous Scottish contributor (probably a Montrosian) to a South American paper, reprinted in the *Montrose Review* in 1892, seems to offer it:

> *Man, it's a gran' game, the gowf. It's a gran' game, an' ye can play till ye're an auld man, and its more excitin' than onything 'cept curling! Wi' yer clubs and yer ba' – just a wee ba', ye ken – and yer caddie, and a man that yer just itching to beat, an' the gran' air coming over the hill wi' the smell o' the gorse an' the sea, an' the green just studded wi' daisies – the modest crimson tip't floo'r – like stars, glinting at ye', an' lying dead on the green, an' yer opponent awa in a bunker wi' a broken club. Man, it's a gran' game, the gowf.*

We very much hope you have enjoyed this account of the *'gran game'* in Montrose.

List of Captains, 1817–2010

Royal Albert Captains

1817–1818	Captain James Bertram	1863–1865	Major J. Fitzmaurice Scott	1912–1914	Alexander Lyell
1818–1819	James Calvert	1865–1867	G. More-Gordon	1919–1921	David Lamb
1819–1820	Captain James Bertram	1867–1869	The Earl of Southesk K.T.	1921–1923	Colonel Blair-Imrie
1820	James Wills	1869–1870	George Keith	1923–1925	Dr R.W.T. Ewart
1820–1821	Patrick Mason	1870	W.H. Kennedy Erskine	1925–1927	Major J.J. Ronald DSO
1821	James Leighton	1870–1872	Hon. Charles Carnegie	1927–1929	Hon. H.R.G. Arbuthnott
1821–1822	Andrew Webster	1872–1874	The Master of Arbuthnott	1929–1931	Dr Mearns A. Milne
1822	Captain James Bertram	1874–1875	Colonel Arbuthnott	1931–1933	Captain T. Lyell MC
1822–1823	Robert Clark	1875–1876	Dr James C. Howden	1933–1935	J.T. Fergusson
1823	Robert Trail	1876–1877	Dr Wm M. Watson	1935–1937	Rev. Canon E.W. Millar
1823–1824	William Caird	1877–1879	George Keith	1937–1939	George Law
1824–1825	Captain James Bertram	1879–1881	Lord Carnegie	1939–1946	Dr Frank G. Milne
1825–1826	James Calvert	1881–1882	George Keith	1946–1948	Claude V. Craigie
1826–1827	Captain James Bertram	1882–1883	The Master of Arbuthnott	1948–1950	James Sinclair
1827–1828	Patrick Mason	1883–1885	Captain C. Arbuthnott	1950–1951	Brigadier W.E. Duncan CVO, DSO, MC
1828–1829	Robert Trail	1885–1888	Patrick Chalmers	1951–1952	Colonel G.E. Stranack DSO, OBE
1829–1831	Captain James Bertram	1888–1889	Lord Carnegie	1952–1954	D. Hill Batchelor MC
1831–1833	Charles Barclay	1889–1890	George Keith	1954–1957	F.A. Milne
1833–1835	Patrick Mason	1890–1891	Captain G.M. Boothby	1957–1959	Alex Colquhoun
1835–1837	Adam Burnes	1891–1892	The Master of Arbuthnott	1959–1961	Dr Herbert W. Booth
1837–1839	Captain James Bertram	1892–1893	Lord Arbuthnott	1961–1963	J. Gordon Mortimer
1839–1840	George Smart	1893–1895	W.M. Jameson Paton	1963–1965	J. Wilson Spence
1840–1843	Patrick Mason	1895–1897	A.R. Duncan	1965–1967	Thomas A. Chisholm
1843–1845	James Leighton	1897–1898	W.M. Jameson Paton	1967–1969	R.V. Stirling
1845–1849	Patrick Mason	1898–1900	Hon. C.M. Ramsay	1969–1970	G.S. Robb
1849–1850	Alexander Cowie	1900–1901	Robert Hoyer-Millar	1970–1971	T. Duncan
1850–1852	Captain Archibald McNeil	1901–1902	R.C. Hoyer-Millar	1971–1972	G. Pinkerton
1852–1854	Robert Cowie	1902–1904	Robert Hoyer-Millar	1972–1974	W.W. Pert
1854–1856	Robert Trail	1904–1906	W.M. Jameson Paton	1974–1976	S.A. Johnston
1856–1858	John Jamie	1906–1907	Patrick Chalmers	1976–1978	James Mills
1858–1860	Thomas Kerr	1907–1908	The Earl of Southesk	1978–1980	A.R.M. Imlach
1860–1862	Adam Burnes	1908–1910	Dr John G. Havelock	1980–1981	A.G. Dunbar
1862–1863	James M. Paton	1910–1912	Captain Colin G. Neish	1981–1982	David M.P. Scott
				1982–1984	A.G. Stevenson
				1984–1986	J.A.L. Clark

Victoria Captains

1864–1872	J. Watson	1908–1913	J.A. Lindsay	1958–1961	C. Graham
1872–1876	C. Irvine	1913–1920	J.T. Cuthbert	1961–1967	J. Wallace
1876–1880	F.M. Japp	1920–1921	J. Cumming	1967–1968	W.C. Thomson
1880–1882	F. Whiteman	1921–1927	J. Chisholm	1968–1971	C.S. Houston
1882–1884	J.B. Alexander	1927–1930	G. Robb	1971–1973	A. Lyon
1884–1886	J.R. Mitchell	1930–1933	C.B. Jamieson	1973–1975	D.M. Patterson
1886–1888	A. Cuthbert	1933–1935	W.M. Wood	1975–1977	G.W.J. Paton
1888–1890	J. Bowman	1935–1936	D.B. Mackay	1977–1978	H.M. Smith
1890–1891	J. Sim	1936–1943	C. Graham	1978–1980	W.J. Tulloch
1891–1893	R.R. Balfour	1943–1946	R.S. Stewart	1980–1982	G.J. Bissett
1893–1896	J.R. Pullar	1946–1949	F.A. Milne	1982–1984	A.F. Hogg
1896–1899	J. Sim	1949–1953	J. Wilson Spence	1984–1986	W.C. Richmond
1899–1905	W.F. Melvin	1953–1956	C. Cameron		
1905–1908	D. Crockhart	1956–1958	J. Smeaton		

Royal Montrose Captains

1986–1988	A.R. Crow	1996–1998	R.G. Ramsay	2006–2008	J. Anderson
1988–1990	A. Lyon	1998–2000	A.S. Jessop	2008–2010	I.A. Harley
1990–1992	D.H. Beedie	2000–2002	F.D. Cuninghame	2010–2012	B. Ritchie
1992–1994	D.A. Taylor	2002–2004	W.G. Dickson		
1994–1996	R. Murray	2004–2006	W.H. Faulkner OBE		

Royal Montrose Ladies Captains

1987	Mrs P. Nicoll	1995–1997	Miss C. Hay	2005–2007	Mrs C. MacGowan
1987–1989	Mrs A.V. Beedie	1997–1999	Miss L. Maxwell	2007–2009	Mrs P. Sutherland
1989–1991	Mrs K.M. Scott	1999–2001	Mrs M. Faulkner	2009–2011	Mrs J. Henderson
1991–1993	Mrs A.M. Anderson	2001–2003	Mrs M.E. Ramsay		
1993–1995	Mrs E. Boyd	2003–2005	Mrs E. McCaw		

North Links Ladies Captains

1927	Miss G. Adams	1951	Mrs Johnston	1970	Mrs E. Mouat
1928	Mrs Martin/Miss G. Adams	1952	Mrs J.W. Spence	1972	Mrs H. Patterson
		1955	Miss J.H. Archibald	1974	Miss C. Paton
1929	Miss G. Adams	1958	Mrs V. Dow/Mrs J.C. Cunningham	1976	Miss G. Johnstone
1930	Miss I.O. Fettes			1977	Mrs J.H. Thomson
1933	Mrs J. Soutar	1959	Mrs C. Johnston	1978	Mrs S. Gibson
1937	Mrs E.R.C. Macdonald/ Miss J.C.M. Stott	1961	Miss J.C.M. Stott	1979	Mrs M. Richmond
		1962	Mrs C. Brown	1980	Mrs M. Strachan
		1964	Mrs J.G. Duncan	1981	Mrs J. Crow
1940–1946	War Years	1966	Mrs C. Brown	1983	Mrs M. Smith
1947	Miss J.C.M. Stott	1967	Mrs I. Bruce	1985	Mrs P. Nicol
1950	Miss G. Adams	1968	Miss B. Paton		

Original Gold Medal Winners, 1818–2009

1818	J. Calvert	1853	R. Armit	1893	W.M.J. Paton
1819	Capt. J. Bertram	1854	R. Cowie	1894	R. Soutar
1820	J. Wills	1855	R. Cowie	1895	Rch. Millar
1820	P. Mason	1856	Capt. Boothby	1896	James Duncan
1821	J. Leighton	1857	S.C. Thomson	1897	Rev. T. Cameron
1821	A. Webster	1858	S.C. Thomson	1898	P. Chalmers
1822	Capt. J. Bertram	1859	T. Kerr	1899	Norman Boase
1822	R. Clark	1860	S.C. Thomson	1900	P. Chalmers
1823	R. Trail	1861	J. Hastie	1901	R.C.H. Millar
1823	W. Caird	1862	J. Hastie	1902	R.C.H. Millar
1824	Capt. Bertram	1863	Capt. Dempster	1903	R.C.H. Millar
1824	P. Mason	1864	W. Nairn	1904	A.B. Pearson
1825	J. Calvert	1865	J. Lindsay Carnegie	1905	R.C.H. Millar
1826	Capt. J. Bertram	1866	J. Allardice	1906	R.C.H. Millar
1827	P. Mason	1867	Capt. Young	1907	A.C. Deuchar
1828	R. Trail	1868	Not Recorded	1908	R.B. Pearson
1829	Capt. J. Bertram	1869	Not Recorded	1909	R.C.H. Millar
1830	J. Scott	1870	G. Keith	1910	D. Lamb
1831	J. Keillor	1871	G. Keith	1911	E.C. Millar
1832	Capt. J. Bertram	1872	H. Cook	1912	Lord Dalhousie
1833	P. Mason	1873	G. Keith	1913	Dr R.W. Ewart
1834	J. Calvert Jnr	1874	Lord Carnegie	1914	R.M. Balfour
1835	R. Mason	1875	Capt. Young	1914–1919	War Years
1836	R. Mason	1876	Dr Watson	1920	R.C.H. Millar
1837	J. Calvert Jnr	1877	G. Keith	1921	R.C.H. Millar
1838	J. Calvert Jnr	1878	J. Corsar	1922	Dr R.W. Ewart
1839	J. Calvert Jnr	1879	D. Lindsay Carnegie	1923	Rev. R.C. Blair
1840	Capt. J. Bertram	1880	Lord Carnegie	1924	Not Recorded
1841	J. Calvert Jnr	1881	P. Chalmers	1925	Not Recorded
1842	Capt. McNeil	1882	D. Lindsay Carnegie	1926	C.V. Craigie
1843	J. Calvert Jnr	1883	W.M.J. Paton	1927	C.V. Craigie
1844	Capt. McNeil	1884	Lord Carnegie	1928	M.P. Tennant
1845	J. Jamie	1885	W.M.J. Paton	1929	C.V. Craigie
1846	J. Calvert Jnr	1886	P. Chalmers	1930	C.V. Craigie
1847	P. O'Brien	1887	P. Chalmers	1931	J. Mcintyre
1848	A. Cowie	1888	Rev. R. Forgan	1932	C.V. Craigie
1849	J. Calvert Jnr	1889	Lord Carnegie	1933	C.V. Craigie
1850	R. Trail	1890	Rev R. Forgan	1934	M.P. Tennant
1851	J.C. Lindsay	1991	Rev. R. Forgan	1935	C.V. Craigie
1852	D. Hunter	1892	W.M.J. Paton	1936	Not Recorded

1937	Not Recorded	1964	R. Stirling	1987	W.B. Strachan
1938	C.V. Craigie	1965	D. Cuninghame	1988	A.G. Dunbar
1939	C.V. Craigie	1966	W.W. Pert	1989	A.D. Mclean
1940	Not Recorded	1967	N. Mclean	1990	C. Welsh
1941–1946	War Years	1968	D. Mowat	1991	G. Hemsley
1947	Dr Ewart	1969	D. Mowat	1992	D. Macnaught
1948	Not Recorded	1970	A.D. Stalker	1993	W. Bremner
1949	Not Recorded	1971	A.D. Dunbar	1994	S. Lyon
1950	Not Recorded	1972	A.G. Dunbar	1995	J.M. Pert
1951	F.A. Milne/H.W. Booth	1973	T. Duncan	1996	D. Watson
		1974	G. Pinkerton	1997	A.R. Crow
1952	A. Colquhoun	1975	A. Anderson	1998	F.D. Cuninghame
1953	H.T. Martin/ D.M. Ferguson	1976	P. Wilson	1999	S. Paton
		1977	R.A. Lumsden	2000	W. Bremner
1954	D.M. Ferguson	1978	J.S. Richardson	2001	D. Saunders
1955	A. Colquhoun	1979	G.D. Mitchell	2002	G. Milne
1956	A. Colquhoun	1980	G. Pinkerton	2003	J.M. Pert
1957	A. Colquhoun	1981	J. Leslie	2004	J. Sharp
1958	A. Peggie	1982	D.J. Hawkins	2005	C. Traill
1960	M. Booth	1983	D.J. Hawkins	2006	R. Coull
1961	A. Peggie	1984	W. Irvine	2007	B. Reid
1962	I. Thom	1985	J. Murray	2008	I. Harley
1963	B. Colquhoun	1986	S. Gauld	2009	J. Strachan

Club Members in 2010

Honorary Members
Alan Crow
Lyn Nicoll
Davie Stott
Ian Sykes
Bill Tulloch

Ordinary Members
Fraser Auld
David P. Barbour
Robert Bardner
Andrew Baxter
Morag Boyd
William D. Bremner
William M. Bremner
David Bridges
Barbara Brown
Rick Brown
Craig Bruce
Derek Bruce
Peter Buchan
Steve Butler
Mae Cairnie
James Calder
Lorna Calder
Louise Cameron
Rob Carnegie
Christopher Chapman
Robert Cheyne
Ian Christie
Brian Church
Martin Clark
Betty Cole
Dave Coull
George Coull
James Coull
Lynn Coull
Ross Coull
Elizabeth Cowie
Daryl Craig
Michael Craig
John Crawford
Tricia Cresdee

Janice Crow
Michael Cummins
Shona Cummins
Frank Cuninghame
Christopher Curnin
Claire Curnin
Lindsey Dalgarno
David Darnell
Gordon Davidson
Patricia Davis
Carol Diack
John Dorward
Margaret Dorward
Stuart Duff
John Dunbar
Sinclair Dundas
Derek Duthie
Barry Edwards
Anthony Faccenda
Kenneth Fairweather
Harry Faulkner
Mary Faulkner
Alex Ferguson
Arthur Forsyth
Peter Forsyth
Michael Fraser
Colin Frew
Thomas Frost
Brian Gall
Ian Gall
Mark Garnes
Ian Gibney
Sheila Gillespie
John Graham
Michael Graham
James Grant
Stephen Grant
Pat Grove-White
John Hall
Jeannie Hannah
Ian Harley
Siggy Harley
Norman Haygreen

Graham Hemsley
David Henderson
Janet Henderson
Ron Henderson
Irene Heron
Colin Herron
John Hillyear
Hazel Howatson
Michael Hutchison
Stephen Hutchison
Mark Jamieson
Scott Jappy
Sandy Jessop
Harry Johansen
Graham Johnston
Ian Johnston
Ken Johnston
Lynn Kearney
Charles Kelly
A.S. Kydd
John Laing
Ed Lamb
Steve Lewis
John K. Lloyd
John Logue
John Logue Jnr
John Lownie
Steve Lyon
Jim MacDonald
Christine MacGowan
Kenneth MacGowan
Duncan MacGregor
Judy MacKay
Julian MacLean
Mike Maguire
Gordon Maiden
Ann May
David May
Ann McCarthy
Elizabeth McCaw
Ian McCaw
Kevin McGeachy
Hamish McGhie

Peter McGuone
Brian McGurk
Edna McGurk
Shaun McGurk
Eric McIntosh
Brian McKay
Malcolm McKenzie
Angus McLean
Derek McLean
Alasdair McNab
Bob McNaught
Duncan McNaught
Lynn McNaught
Michael Miller
Gordon Milne
George Mitchell
Helen Mitchell
Ian Mitchell
Jim Moir
Maureen Moir
Russell Moir
David Moss
Donald Munro
Neil Munro
Gordon A. Murray
Jamie Murray
Ron Murray
Calum Neill
Gordon Nicoll
John Ogilvie
Gordon Paterson
Azzie Paton
John Paton
Neil Paton
Scott Paton
James Patterson
Gail Penman
Jamie Pert
Soren Petersen
Andy Petrie
Stuart Philip
Richard Phinney
Alan Pocock
Marian Pyper
Alasdair Ramsay
Graeme Ramsay
Mary Ramsay
Ron Ramsay
Tony Rance
Andrew Reid
Barry Reid
Denis Rice
Lyn Richardson
John Richardson Jr
Alison Ritchie
Brian Ritchie
George Ritchie

Doug Robb
Sandra Robb
George Robertson
Gordon Robertson
Ian Robertson
Adrian Robinson
John Rome
Sheila Russell
Frank Samson
David Saunders
John Scott
Robert Scott
Alistair Serrels
Charlie Sey
James Sharp
Graeme Shepherd
Wendy Shepherd
Charles Simpson
Gary Simpson
John Simson
Derek Smart
John Smith
Murray Smith
Steve Smith
Tony Smith
Colin Soutar
Margaret Stewart
Michael Stewart
Jane Stock
Jason Stone
Grant Strachan
Jeffrey Strachan
John Strachan
Pam Strachan
Rae Strachan
William Strachan
Cathy Stuart
Ian Stuart
Peter Stuart
Donald Sutherland
Kathleen Sutherland
Phyllis Sutherland
Tony Sutton
Alan Sykes
Jonathon Taylor
Lynda Taylor
Mark Toshney
Craig Traill
Stephen Valentine
Douglas Walker
Jan Walker
Angus Watson
Barbara Watson
Donald Watson
Hamish Watt
Sheena Watt
Malcolm Watters

Michael Webb
Campbell Welsh
Rob Whelan
Brett Williams
Sarah Williams
Tony Williams
Alison Williamson
Bob Williamson
Janine Wilson
Bob Yacamini
John Young
Sharon Young

Country Members
David Crouch
Neil Cuninghame
Nathan Imlach
Clive Reid
Dennis Robertson
Gordon Shepherd
Murray Sykes

Lady Associates
Audrey Mill
Patricia Cummins

Life Members
John Anderson
Christopher Batchelor
Colin Baxter
Aileen Beedie
Dougal Beedie
William Beedie
George Bissett
Sheila Brown
Jean Cuthbert
James Davidson
Chris Dealtry
Pam Dealtry
Christine Don
Gregor Dunbar
Kenneth Easson
Jean Findlay
John Forsyth
Alistair Hogg
Betty Hope
Margaret Hugh
Sandy Imlach
Celia M Jenkins
Syd Johnston
Jack Kearney
S. Kennedy
Donald Kirkwood
Derek Lakie
Alec Lang
Elizabeth Leslie
William Lorimer

Alan Lumsden
Isabelle Lyon
Alistair Macfarlane
Nancy Macfarlane
John W. McDougall
Niall McNab
Moyra Mills
David Milne
John Morris
Alec Mouat
Jack Murray
Pam Nicoll
William Nicoll
John Page
Bill Pert
Alistair Reid
Una Reith
John Richardson Sr
William Richmond
Mina Robb
Alistair Russell

Moira Smith
Peter Stevens
Anne Stewart
Iain I. Stewart
Elizabeth Strachan
Sandy Strachan
Elizabeth Stuart
Pat Sykes
Bill Taylor
David Taylor
Sheila Taylor
Jean Thomson
John Thomson
Jean M. Watson
William Wilson

Junior Members
Jonathon Aitken
Ashley Alston
David Raitt Alston
Robert D. Cheyne

Alyson Crowley
Amber Kennedy
Liam Kennedy
Katie-Louise McIntosh
Rory McIntosh
Ross Pert
Jack Richardson
Susan Richardson
Sarah Richardson
Jack Rodger
Andrew Simpson
Fern Sykes
Ronan Valentine

Student Members
Jonathan Atkinson
Joss Beharrell
Josh Clarke
Lucy Hutchison
Graeme Lamb
Andrew Weir

RIG-SOL LTD

**PROCUREMENT & LOGISTICS SOLUTIONS
TO THE WORLDWIDE OIL & GAS INDUSTRY**

CONGRATULATES

ROYAL MONTROSE GOLF CLUB
ON ITS BICENTENARY

AND

IS DELIGHTED
TO OFFER SUPPORT

TO THE

CLUB HISTORY PUBLICATION

sales@rigsol.com

www.rigsol.com

SCOTTISH MIDLAND CO-OPERATIVE SOCIETY LIMITED

150

1859   2009

SCOTMID
at the heart of
Scottish communities

"Of capital they had little or none, and their business experience was extremely limited; still their hopes were high and their courage inexhaustible. It was in this atmosphere that Co-operation began; but honest men and sound principles triumphed over all difficulties. We, today, reap the reward: we reap where the pioneers had sown."